# The Promise and Limits of Computer Modeling

T0338644

# The **Promise**
# and **Limits** of
# Computer
# Modeling

## **Charles Blilie**
Trissential Consulting, USA

NEW JERSEY · LONDON · SINGAPORE · BEIJING · SHANGHAI · HONG KONG · TAIPEI · CHENNAI

*Published by*

World Scientific Publishing Co. Pte. Ltd.

5 Toh Tuck Link, Singapore 596224

*USA office:* 27 Warren Street, Suite 401-402, Hackensack, NJ 07601

*UK office:* 57 Shelton Street, Covent Garden, London WC2H 9HE

**British Library Cataloguing-in-Publication Data**
A catalogue record for this book is available from the British Library.

**THE PROMISE AND LIMITS OF COMPUTER MODELING**

ISBN-13 978-981-270-795-6
ISBN-10 981-270-795-6

Printed in Singapore.

# Contents

# Chapter 1

# The Jade Mountain

Perhaps my favorite object in our local art museum is a Chinese jade sculpture of a mountain. Although a massive piece of stone, it is truly miniature compared to what it represents: tiny jade trees cling to its diminutive cliffs; a procession of poets and scholars ascends its paths; its rocks mimic the condensed shape of alpine crags. It is obviously a lofty mountain; perhaps it is the distillation of a sacred place. The artist surely intended it so. He created a microcosm that perfectly abstracts the macrocosm.

To capture the world in miniature has long been a human dream. Or, more accurately, to capture just that part of the world that is really meaningful, to distill its essence, has driven both science and art forward from the beginning. Such a blueprint or model of reality would grant both the knowledge of its vast structure and the primary means to manipulate it by, recalling Francis Bacon's remark that "knowledge is power." It would provide the aesthetic and even spiritual satisfaction of beholding reality in a single view. And this is, more or less, the aim of every model ever built: to reduce reality to a smaller, yet more concentrated form.

To jump in scale from the jade mountain to the world — to the whole of reality — seems an impossible leap. Yet the advent of computer modeling and simulation opens up this tantalizing possibility. Computer scientist David Gelernter calls such comprehensive models *mirror worlds*[1]:

"A Mirror World is some huge institution's moving, true-to-life mirror image trapped inside a computer -- where you can see and grasp it whole. The thick, dense, busy  sub-world that encompasses you is also, now, an object in your hands ... Oceans of information pour endlessly into the model (through a vast maze of software pipes and hoses): so much information that *the model* can mimic *the reality's* every move moment-by-moment... Mirror Worlds are devices for showing you the big picture, *the whole*."

The computer simulation, the "mirror world," is nothing less than an attempt to construct a digital microcosm. It places a model of the universe — or that fraction of the universe you're most interested in — on your desktop. The model provides a unified view of systems and organizations extending far beyond our own limited perspectives.

This is heady stuff. But is it really possible? Certainly computer modeling, simulation, and design are finding ever-wider applications, to an extent most people are unaware of. They are essential to many of the products we encounter every day. Chances are the car you drive was designed and tested through computer simulation. Modern aircraft are entirely prototyped in the virtual space of computer software, tested and "flown" on the computer long before the first "real" new plane rolls out onto the tarmac. Even advances in computers themselves have become dependent on computer simulation. Modern CPU chips contain millions of integrated transistors and circuits; a computer itself is needed to keep track of such complexity and numbers -- and to verify a new design works.

Such examples show us the main reason for the success of computer modeling. Building models can be dramatically less expensive than building a real system. Simulation -- the exercising of a model through its possible states and behaviors -- provides a means of exploring the system's advantages and pitfalls in a rapid, easily repeatable fashion. Computer models have taken hold precisely in those areas where the actual system of interest, whether a microcircuit or a spacecraft, is difficult and expensive to build in reality. There is a premium on getting it right the first time. More subtle modeling advantages arise from the complexity of systems. Consider a modern commercial airplane. It contains millions of parts, and the parts are very different depending on what subsystem of the plane you look at: engine turbine blades made of advanced alloys, the cockpit avionics suite and control system, the shape and structure of the wings, the most comfortable and safe design for passenger seating, and so on down a list of thousands of subsystems. Integrating these complex subsystems into a single harmonious design is beyond the grasp of a single unaided human mind or any group of human minds equipped only with pencil and paper – hence the long program of mockups, aerodynamic wind tunnel testing, and sometimes dangerous experimental flight testing that had traditionally gone into aircraft engineering. The computer model provides entirely new means for managing that complexity and integrating the design into whole. Aerodynamics can now be tested using computer models of fluids; important subsystems like the engines can be designed with the aid of combustion dynamics models. In other words, computer model grants a unified view of the aircraft that would otherwise be hidden; it lifts the designer up to see the entire "forest," a perch above those blocked by the "trees."

A simulated world takes form gradually, crystallizing one small piece after another into a moveable computer image. The piece might be a railway system, a business organization, or a hospital instead of a complex machine, but the principles are the same and the benefits similar. Economic gains from computer technology in recent years have largely resulted from managing companies along lines of greater, fine-tuned efficiency through software. Financial/accounting database software is now absolutely essential to the smooth running of large corporations. We see again the indispensability of computers in dealing with complexity and numbers, but there is more to it than that. The implementation of accounting software for a major company means replicating its business structure and practices within the software itself -- in other words, building a computer model of the company. Information flow within the software's virtual business governs the flow of actual goods, services, and money within the real business. By refining the model, one refines the company. And the contents of the model are continually updated from any number of sources, which need not deal with the entirety of the model or even be aware of it. When an order is shipped out of a certain warehouse, this fact is immediately reflected in the inventory system and corresponding account changes. The database system provides the means by which to view and analyze as an integrated whole the thousands or millions of such events that take place in the company.

The computer model's ability to handle complexity not only makes it an ideal design tool, but a powerful instrument for exploring nature. Models are essential for understanding complex systems where direct calculation is impossible.   One example is weather and climate prediction, which Chapter Seven discusses at length.  The question of global warming, for example, has catapulted climate modeling from the research lab into the headlines. Comprehensive understanding or prediction of global climate would be utterly impossible without computer models.  The atmosphere is a fluid extended not just as a spherical shell, but also vertically.  The forces and influences acting on it are so various that predicting the properties at a given point mean a consideration of the whole.  Tomorrow's weather in my city depends not only on the solar influx at this place; it depends still more on the properties of large air masses and earth-circling jet streams.  In other words, local weather is determined by a host of remote factors, all interconnected, the most important of which might be something on the other side of the world. Heating of the southern Pacific Ocean, the El Niño effect, leads to a stormy and rainy winter in North America. Global circulation of the atmosphere clearly is not something one can calculate by hand like a simple mechanics problem. Even if the calculations were finished, their predictions would be long obsolete.  Instead, one builds a computer model by taking the known physical properties of air, setting up a grid of points representing the atmosphere, and then applying the energy inputs and losses to it. The model replicates atmospheric behavior and thus can make predictions: whether this summer is likely to be rainier than normal or whether industrial inputs of carbon dioxide into the atmosphere will cause it to warm significantly over the next century.

The connection of complexity and computer models applies to many other areas of scientific research, for systems as small as molecular chemical reactions or as large as coalescing galaxies.  Without computer models, understanding such systems would be reduced largely to qualitative description or guesswork.

Computer modeling and simulation are increasingly important scientific tools.  Indeed, as Chapter Five explains, they are where theory and experiment come together. Since the interaction of theory and experiment is science's dynamic force, modeling and simulation are closely connected to the heart of the scientific method. Like theory and experiment, they are complementary. The model is like a theoretical construct in that it attempts to replicate reality; simulation is like experiment in that provides a means to test the model. Computer models are like microscopes or telescopes, except that peering into the very small or the very far, they grasp the incredibly complex.

Modern physics has striven mightily to develop a unified field theory that would be a "theory of everything," explaining all natural forces by a single set of equations. The direction of computer simulation is to develop of a *model of everything*, unifying the models of all parts of the world in a single system, replicating everything about everything. Models of individual phenomena would eventually interlock, like the formation of a crystal, and the world model will emerge. Not only would this model provide a virtual copy of the world — both human and physical — but would also provide a means of controlling and understanding complex systems up to the whole[2]. The microcosm would perfectly copy the macrocosm. Being a digital copy of the world, continually updated with the latest information, the world model will be able to answer *any* question, predict *any* future. It would be a crystal ball that realizes the dream of the 18th Century Encyclopedists — the containment of all knowledge.

But doubts interrupt this reverie. And these doubts take us directly to this book's central questions. What do computer models really tell us? Is it possible to build a perfect model of the world — a true microcosm — or are there inherent limits that prevent such comprehensive models? And what is the true status of a computer model: is it an image of the world? A theory? An experiment? An equivalent in its realm to the jade mountain, capturing the essential and blocking out the meaningless? Or is it a glorified fiction, like a motion picture or video game? Can computer simulations of the world extend our knowledge of the world? These questions admit no simple answers. Since there is an increasing tendency to treat computer models as if they *are* reality, these questions must be answered without glib overoptimism.

Indeed, the very terms "model," "simulation," imply some separation from or fragmentation of the world. They mean a copy or partial outline rather than the original or the whole. Computer models are, after all, constructs. Programmers devise models on the basis of present data and known laws, type in the computer program, compile it, and run it. It is not the reality. And how does one *know* if the model has really captured the reality? Physical scientists often feel this doubt most acutely, even though fields like chemistry or physics, because of their obvious mathematical character, are a computer model's most natural home. The scientist knows how difficult it is to get computer models to match data and to give unequivocal answers regarding the causes of what is observed. The astronomer Clifford Stoll expressed such misgivings in his book *Silicon Snake Oil*. His description of his model of Jupiter's atmosphere illustrates well both the possibilities and limits of computer simulation[3]:

"So simulate Jupiter's atmosphere in a computer program. Mix in some clouds and clear gas. Calculate how much polarization you ought to see. Compare it to the spacecraft data and see if your program got it right. If not, tweak the computer program and try again. It's computer modeling, the same method used by population planners, geographers, and sociologists. Measure, model, and compare. ... Slowly, my computer models made sense. According to them, Jupiter doesn't have a solid surface — just layer after layer of clouds. Near the top, there's a thick cloud bank made of ice crystals. As gases rise from below, ammonia freezes, forming crystals. That's what I'd been watching. From their scattering properties, they're probably about two microns across. Above these clouds, clear gas. ... Yes, but do I believe it today? That question makes me squirm ... After years of modeling Jupiter's atmosphere and exploring parameter space, I'm not certain. ... Probably the only way to clinch the issue is a visit to the planet with a microscope and tweezers."

And the same physical assumptions and data can give rise to quite different models and predictions[4]:

"Plenty of computer models are just plain wrong or conflict with one another. Suppose the amount of carbon dioxide in the atmosphere doubles. What'll happen to the climate? The global climate model developed by the Geophysical Fluid Dynamics Lab predicts Chicago summers could be seven degrees warmer and 30 percent drier. In comparison, the Goddard Institute model expects only a three-degree warming, and 5 percent wetter. Much of the difference depends on programmers' assumptions about the complexity of the global-circulation patterns or the reflectance of the ground. But you won't know which programmer was right unless you wait a hundred years. Often, computer models can't be tested."

Can't be tested? This is a damning criticism. And, to the extent such criticism is valid, what distinguishes computer models from computer games?

So the computer model inspires not complete confidence, but an equivocation, a murkiness about what the model really means. It is a problem, in a way, roughly analogous to what Galileo faced when he made the first astronomical observations with a telescope and published his remarkable discoveries (lunar mountains, Jupiter's moons, Saturn's rings) in the *Starry Messenger*[5]. His critics claimed his observations were impossible; they violated the dictum of Aristotelian cosmology that the celestial realm of the planets was perfect and could not be flawed by mountains, craters, or orbiting moons. Galileo, with the guileless empiricism of the natural scientist, replied: if you don't believe me, then come have a look for yourself. Yet most of his opponents refused to look through his newfangled telescope, and those that did look claimed to see nothing real. They asserted the lunar craters or Jovian moons were an illusion created by the telescope itself, like the images in a kaleidoscope. The recourse was, of course, to independently verify the observations, which left Galileo's opponents looking pretty silly in the eyes of history. So where is the analogy with models? A computer model is like a telescope that peers not into the depths of the sky, but into the complexity of a system. Suppose the same criticisms were leveled at model predictions as were hurled at Galileo's telescope: its novel results were artifacts of the model itself. Unlike the telescope-builder, the model-builder could not simply say "run the model yourself" or "construct your own model, then." The controversy could be answered ultimately only by reference to hard data and scientific laws. In comparison to the telescope, the computer model is crucially limited, for the model on its own brings us itself and not other worlds.

Is the computer model a telescope or a kaleidoscope?  Actually, we will see it is a little of both:

(1) Computer modeling and simulation, while hardly omniscient, can reliably reflect reality. We *can* make valid inferences from them. At the same time, however, there are limits to those inferences and that knowledge. The model's crystal ball will always be a little clouded. Indeed, in some scenarios we will have to admit defeat and see that our entire view is fogged in.

(2) Modeling and simulation can even extend our knowledge of the world; they can be instruments of scientific research. They can do so in two ways. Computer models and simulations can implement scientific theories and yield predictions of new phenomena. In this, they are no different from any other predictive technique of theory. Computer models can also extend our knowledge through computer-aided design. The model provides the ability to exhaustively test all the aspects of a design virtually, and thus select the best possible design to actually construct. Once more, however, there are strict limits to where computer-aided predictions and designs can take us — they go only as far as the theories on which they are based.

(3) The problem of the validity of computer models and simulation is closely connected to the problem of *induction* — how we draw scientific laws out of observations. In many ways, computer modeling and simulation attempt to achieve the ultimate goals of science, and thus represent the ultimate extension of natural science.

Computer models and simulations can also be understood in terms of the ultimate destination they attempt to reach. Actually, there are three distinct destinations they can aim at:

The first is to build *a unified model of physical phenomena*. And this goal is the most obvious. Computer models originated in engineering and the hard sciences, and it is there they have met with their greatest successes. Already, large swatches of phenomena can be adequately modeled. In future years, not only will models of particular phenomena and regions of study grow more numerous, they will also become more closely knit together. For example, geological models can be integrated with models of the oceans and climate to form a single earth model, which in turn can be extended with other planets and integrated with still-larger models of the cosmos. In other words, the ultimate goal of this branch of computer modeling is nothing less than a complete model of the universe and everything in it. It would be based entirely on the laws of physics and chemistry. Given the initial conditions, one could sit back in one's chair and watch galaxies, stars, and planets condense out of fiery beginnings. Turning down the time rate, then presumably the earth transforms into a reasonably comfortable nest and life blossoms forth. And one would always be able to "rewind" the show and start it all over again. Such a world model would realize the dream of the 18th Century mathematician Laplace, a dream important enough to be the subject of Chapter Six.

A second ultimate aim of computer modeling would apply the approach used for the cosmos to the human realm: *a unified model of human society and its history*. It could not be exactly the same, for we would all agree that the "objects" being simulated are far more complex than natural phenomena. Nonetheless, computer models of various human phenomena, such as population growth or economic systems, are built and find increasing application. And as in the natural realm, the tendency is to form models that are both more comprehensive and more unified. The culmination of such a model would not be limited to present human society, but would delineate the whole of historical development and provide a theory of history. It would explain not only the significance of past events, but would also claim to predict future ones. It would explore different ways things might have happened — alternative presents — that could radiate from the same past event (assuming that chance and/or freedom break the mold of a single deterministic future). Now, such models are sure to stir more general interest than scientific models of nature. At the same time, it is easy to see the much more difficult problems that any model of human phenomena must face. Suppose, for example, I have developed a stock market model with the uncanny ability to predict tomorrow's closing prices. The moment such predictions are generally known and given credence, the prices will be different from what the model predicted. Even this simple example points out the inherent difficulties — and indeterminacies – that await any simplistic computer model in human affairs.

The third destination toward which computer modeling heads is the construction and presentation of any number of different, seemingly realistic, alternate worlds. This is the problem of *virtual reality*. Virtual reality is a computer-aided extension of human imagination. The programmer fabricates a world and then presents it to the viewer; unlike a movie, however, the viewer can interact with the picture. Virtual reality raises interesting problems regarding reality itself: if we can both see something and act on it, is it not real in a way? Virtual realities themselves tend to divide into two distinct areas, depending on their aim. The first are *simulated realities*, where the aim is to reproduce, as accurately as possible, a given situation and display it to the participants. The best example of a simulated reality is a flight simulator, which present the would-be pilot with a real cockpit, but simulated images and motion, such as landing at a particular airport. The main purpose of the simulated reality, not surprisingly, is training. The second type of virtual reality is the *fictional reality*. The fictional reality attempts to fabricate a new world from the imagination of the programmer and makes it seem as realistic as possible. The natural realm of the fictional reality is that of entertainment; it already exists in the increasingly sophisticated form of video games. The question of model versus reality in fact leads us to the question, what is reality? Virtual reality's simulated worlds shed interesting light on this. The virtual reality is meant to substitute for reality and replace it. Can a virtual reality be "real enough" to be real?

Computer modeling and simulation are only a small fraction of the way down the road to their ultimate destinations. Can they reach them at all? And, if so, in what form? To answer those questions, we must first explore exactly what models are and how they work. Next, we will look at their limitations, capabilities, and applications, both to the physical and human worlds. Last of all, we will see how simulated worlds and virtual realities might act substitutes for reality itself.

# Chapter 2

# What are Models?

Chapter One presented some glinting facets of what computer models could do, but it did not give us an adequate understanding of what a model is, and much less of what a simulation is.

Webster's *New World Dictionary* defines *model* as "a small copy or imitation of an existing object, as a ship, building, etc., made to scale" or "a preliminary representation of something, serving as a plan from which the final, usually larger, object is to be constructed" or "a hypothetical or stylized representation, as of an atom."[1] It further defines *simulation* as "pretense, feigning" or "a simulated resemblance" or "an imitation or counterfeit." These definitions imply that models and simulations are essentially derivative, a miniature copy of something, rather like a picture of it. A model is a stylization of the real thing and less than it.

Chapter One did give a provisional definition of modeling and simulation as the point where theory and experiment come together. It is not obvious how such a definition can be squared with the notion of an imitation. We have also seen that the status of computer models as a source of knowledge is controversial. They are not exactly theory *or* observation. They seem to be a little of both and yet neither. It is important to keep in mind that the term model is broader in scope than just computer models. Models can take a number of forms: physical replicas (either full size or miniature), images, schematics, systems of concepts, as well as software. Drawing from many different fields of study, they are still as much art as science[2].

So let us build a definition of models piece by piece. It is clear at least that all models are *representations*. The whole notion of a replica as well as that of data means the model represents some original object or system. Others define models similarly. To quote a systems engineering text[3], a model is:

"a representation of a system or part of a system in mathematical or physical form suitable for demonstrating the way the system or operation behaves or may be considered to behave. ... a model is a qualitative or quantitative representation of a process or endeavor that shows the effects of those factors which are significant for the purposes being considered. ... A model may be pictorial, descriptive, qualitative, or generally approximate in nature, or it may be mathematical and quantitative in nature and reasonably precise."

A physicist whose specialty is computational study of molecules defined model a little differently[4]:

"A model is an attempt to decouple and remove interactions that have little or no influence on the observables being studied. Thus, a model is simpler than the system it mimics: it has access to fewer states .. the model is a subsystem of the original"

This notion of model as a decoupling -- or isolation -- of a system from its surroundings is important. And, lastly, from a text on computer simulation[5]:

"A model is a simplified representation of a system (or process or theory) intended to enhance our ability to understand, predict, and possibly control the behaviour of the system. ... The term model means different things to different people. The clay models for children, fashion models for an advertising agency, mathematical models for control engineers, and physical models for architects are some examples."

The above definitions outline several important points. The model represents some original. But it also isolates one phenomenon of interest or importance and excludes others, based on a purpose or perspective. Like a picture, the model delineates something to us. Yet, also like the image, it does not bring the thing to us as a whole. There are also many different things that can act as models; they seem heterogeneous.

## Kinds of Models

Other than the sheer fact of representation, we need to plumb deeper as to what ties the different kinds of models together. A preliminary step is to enumerate the possible kinds of models, and the most important way of categorizing models is by *medium*. Every model must have a medium, whether it be earthenware clay, colored ink on paper, a set of gears and springs, a computer program, or a mental image. There are three basic categories of modeling media, and they parallel the possible ways we can approach the world through representations: *things*, *images*, and *concepts*. Models can assume any of these three forms, and the same subject can be represented by models in different media.

*Physical models* represent things by other things. Such models are as old as civilization. Physical models are constructed of physical materials (clay, plastic, metal, wood) or parts (machinery, electronic components), and reflect both the capabilities and limitations of the materials chosen. A simple example of a physical model is a globe as a model of the earth. More modern examples are wind tunnel models of aircraft -- a small model of an aircraft is used to study the aerodynamic properties of its full-sized subject. Similar modeling approaches are used to study the behavior of ships (tow basin models) or the appearance and setting of proposed buildings (architectural models). Physical models can be scale models, as in the above examples, or simplified full-size figures, like crash test dummies or store mannequins.

Physical models usually replicate one or a few desired features of the original and ignore the rest – the size, shape, and dynamics of the human body for crash test dummies, for example. Physical models can thus be much simpler than the original. A wind tunnel model is a solid representing the shape of the aircraft, scaled down, without any of the complexities of the real aircraft. It represents aerodynamic and mass features only. A crash test dummy represents human bodies as a collection of solid plastic sections connected by elastic joints. That is all that is required for its purpose. A mannequin is an even simpler representation of the human body, reflecting its purpose of displaying clothing.

A special subtype of physical model is the *analog model*. Analog models are mechanical or electrical systems that replicate the behavior of original subject. They require both model and modeled to be reduced to the same system of mathematical relations. For example, we can build electronic analogs of complex mechanical systems and vice-versa, as shown in Figure 2-1. A number of such devices can be combined to form an *analog computer*. Before they were eclipsed by digital computers, analog computers were built to solve practical problems in ballistics, aerodynamics, and power network analysis, as well as purely scientific problems[6]. Most analog computers were electronic, composed of circuits that added, multiplied, time-integrated, and time-differentiated voltages. There were also mechanical analog computers[7] — with masses, springs, dampers, torsional flywheels, etc. — that could be used to model similar mechanical systems.

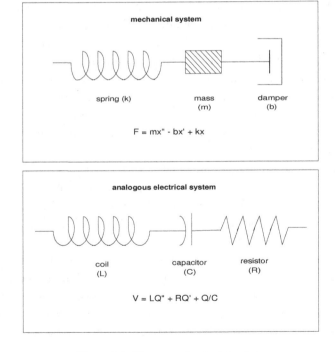

Figure 2-1. Electromechanical Analogs.

There are three basic uses of physical models. The first, and most important, are models that *behave like* the subject, usually in some very narrowly defined area of interest. The second are models that *look like* their subject. Architectural models, for example, fall in this category. Sculpture could even be seen in this light as a special kind of physical model with an aesthetic purpose. The third use is for the physical model to act as a *prototype* many other instances. Engineering mockups are an example, but so are fashion models: the fashion model represents an idealized version or template of human form. It is this aspect of models we allude to when we say "the model of perfection" or "role model."

The second kind of modeling medium is the image, and correspondingly there are *imaginary models*. Since the term "imaginary" in English has the implication of "not real" or "false," perhaps a better label is *schematic model*. Such models include blueprints, plans, maps, circuit diagrams, as well as actual pictures. Imaginary or schematic models are typically static, reproducing only one state of the system. Not surprisingly, such models are used where the original is effectively fixed. Landscapes may be considered static for the purposes of mapping; buildings are unchanging for blueprints or architectural plans. In theory, imaginary models could be built for dynamic systems (e.g., using motion pictures), but in actuality such dynamic modeling is done using computer models (e.g., CAD/CAM systems and flight simulators).

A schematic model's purpose is normally quite different from that of a physical model. If physical models represent a particular kind of behavior of the original, schematic models try instead to represent the *structure* (usually spatial structure). Indeed, schematic models are intended as a shorthand or summary of the structure, and that is what makes them useful for design. Blueprints convey structure from the architect to the builder for actual construction. A map shows us the network of roads so we may reliably find our destination. Electronic schematics tell what parts should be connected to what others.

Schematic models have something new, not found in physical models: they invariably use symbols and idealizations. Lines represent walls or roads, political boundaries or geographic contours, pipes or wires. Each kind of schematic will have its specialized set of signs: map symbols, electronic component symbols, and so on. These are collections of conventional ideograms, with each sign standing for an instance of a concept or class.

Symbolization leads to the next class of models: *conceptual models*. As the name implies, conceptual models are composed entirely of symbols or concepts. Conceptual models are often mathematical equations, especially when modeling physical phenomena. But conceptual models also include written descriptions of a system (which may be a preliminary for a more sophisticated model) or purely mental conceptions. Computer models are nothing more than conceptual models translated into computer software.

Conceptual models concentrate on the logical features of a system independent of any particular implementation[8]. They try to capture the essence of the original in symbolic form alone. This what makes mathematical relations the typical (and preferred) expression of conceptual models. For example, suppose we wish to model the output of an electronic component, such as a diode or transistor, as a function of input voltage. We measure the response for specified input voltages, obtaining a set of data points of outputs versus inputs. But the *model* of the response will not be any particular data point, but the best mathematical curve that joins them. This curve is represented conceptually by an equation, such as an exponential, power law, or polynomial expansion. The equation captures that aspect of the component (i.e., voltage response) needed for our model in a simple, straightforward fashion.

Conceptual models can have corresponding imaginary models, as when we make a graph of an equation. Indeed, most conceptual models have idealized images of systems as counterparts. Classical mechanics has an abstract model of a point particle with location, velocity, and mass. The abstract nature of the conceptual model allows its transference to new, analogous problems[9]. The harmonic oscillator, as shown in the examples of Figure 2-1, is used as a basic conceptual model of a wide range of different physical processes.

Conceptual models are often (and preferably) expressed mathematically. Mathematical models themselves can take two different forms[10]. The first is an *analytic model*, where we have a function, define the arguments of the function, and obtain a result. The second is a *numerical model,* where the model equations are known, but cannot be solved directly. The latter are very common in models of physical phenomena, where the laws governing model transformations take the form of differential equations. Many different techniques have been developed to solve numerical model equations, most famous among them Runge-Kutta integration of differential equations, Newton-Raphson iteration to find roots, and Monte Carlo numerical integration to find areas and volumes. Such techniques are a branch of applied mathematics and are important tools in scientific and engineering models.

Conceptual models, like imaginary models, replicate the structure of the original system. And like physical models, they also replicate the dynamics of the system, which imaginary models generally cannot do. They allow for the use of well-established, quantitative physical laws and properties in the model. But conceptual models do all this at the price of a more generalized, abstract view of the system. This is particularly true of purely analytic mathematical models, which can be used on their own to understand complex systems only with difficultly. To develop a mathematical model of a single electronic component may be relatively straightforward, but combine several together into a circuit and the problem may become practically insoluble for any direct calculation.

This is where computer models come in. The computer model is, to repeat, nothing more than a conceptual model translated into a computer program. Computers can easily capture a complex system in mathematical form (due to their higher capacity to store large multiplicities) and thus make them capable of being modeled. There is also the practical consideration that computers can calculate much more quickly and accurately than human beings.

Computer modeling grew out of mathematical modeling of physical phenomena for these reasons. Computer modeling and simulation emerged during the Manhattan Project out of a need to determine how neutrons diffused in matter[11]. The first of all digital computers, ENIAC I, was employed. A battery of scientists armed with calculators could have solved the problem, but in practical terms, that would have taken far too long and had too many possibilities for error. Nearly all early computing was related in some way to scientific and engineering models, and these models were almost entirely devoted to solving mathematical equations. (So deep is this connection that even today scientific computing is seen as little more than a translation of mathematics into software.)  As computer technology has progressed, the advantages of computer models have steadily grown – so much so that computer models are now the modeling medium of choice in nearly all fields of study.

In addition to medium, we can also classify models by their level of detail or complexity.  One can have a single monolithic model or a model with many components and hierarchical levels, each of which may be a distinct submodel.  The simple monolithic model may be little more than a "black box" model, mapping inputs to outputs.  Such models are typically used when the causes of system behavior are unknown, so the model is purely empirical.  They yield prediction without explanation[12]. At the other extreme, and certainly to be preferred, are models where the causes of the phenomena are explicitly modeled, and any predicted phenomena can also be explained on the basis of these laws.  In scientific computing, these are sometimes referred to as "physics-based" models, indicating that the physical laws governing the phenomena are included and govern the model.

We may term "black box" models as "endodatic," as the model results apply strictly only to the range of data they are based on. Predictions beyond that range may not be reliable or even meaningful. Detailed models, on the other hand, are "exodatic."  Being based on general laws, their extrapolation into new states beyond existing data constitute meaningful predictions, likely to be confirmed in future data. This has important implications for the validity of models.

Often the behavior of the system being modeled is so complex that a single model does not suffice and several partial models must be used, each with a different area of validity.  Despite decades of research, this is case in nuclear physics, for example.  The atomic nucleus can be modeled as a liquid drop, as quantized states of individual particles in a central field (the shell model), or as a collectively moving whole. Due to its complexity as a quantum many-body system, the nucleus cannot be effectively represented by a single model, either theoretically or practically.

A third division of models is between those that are static and those that are dynamic. We have already seen that schematic models are static, physical models are capable of dynamism for some restricted classes of phenomena, while computer models can model dynamic systems including many different kinds of behavior and interactions simultaneously.

*Static* models replicate only one state of the system, although that state can be very complex in the number of components and details it includes. A blueprint or circuit diagram can represent a large structure, but at the same time, the structure does not change. Certain engineering models, as of structural loads or object shapes, can be effectively static as well.

*Dynamic* models, in contrast, represent the multiple states that the original system can potentially assume. They also model the connections of the possible states to one another. These are the *transformation rules* of the system. All simulations, as discussed below, involve dynamic models, and most dynamic models are built to be used in simulations. Most mathematical models, since they are functions mapping input quantities to output quantities, can be used as dynamic models. This is even true when the aim is a singular result, such as the solution of an equation or an optimization problem.

Dynamic models can further be subdivided by how many states there are and how they are related[13]. *Continuous* models have large numbers (or an infinite number) of available states connected together. Their state variables undergo smooth changes. Mathematical functions are an example and so are physical forces. *Discrete* models, on the other hand, have only a limited number of states available. Such are atomic states (at a microscopic level), but also digital circuitry and many queuing problems, such as the number of customers waiting for service at a bank or the number of vehicles waiting at a stoplight. Nothing prevents a model from including both discrete and continuous state variables. The state structure also affects how the time element is handled in the dynamic model. Discrete states lend themselves to corresponding discrete events in time, while continuous states often mean that the system dynamics must be handled as continuous process.

A closely related division is between *deterministic* and *stochastic* state variables. Deterministic system models will always produce the same result for the same inputs. Stochastic variables, on the other hand, have a random element, which means that the same input can produce different outputs. Stochastic variables are introduced in models precisely to handle unknown or random phenomena in the real system.

## Models as Abstract Images

The preceding survey of model types showed that all models are representations, assuming either a physical, imaginary, or conceptual form. Models are usually partial: they do not have all the states or attributes of the subject being modeled. Any model seeks to replicate its object accurately. Yet, at the same time, the model does not build an exact and complete replica of the object — for a physical model, this would mean making an identical copy of the object, which would no longer be a model. The model reduces a system to some idealized or abstract form. Although the model can and will represent details, it usually does not (or cannot) model things in their complete particularity. Indeed, the main point of modeling is often to represent only a single interesting aspect of the object. In scientific research, the aim often is to represent as much of the system being studied as possible (an *isomorphic* model), while in an engineering design model, it may be enough to represent overall effects leaving out details irrelevant to the model's purpose (a *homomorphic* model)[14].

Abstraction means separation: the model separates, extracts, or disengages certain features of the system from others. Those left behind are either not of interest or are minor disturbances which do not affect the outcome. Perhaps most important along these lines is the effective decoupling of the modeled system from its enclosing supersystem or environment. What is excluded depends on the scale and type of system modeled. When modeling the reentry of a satellite into the earth's atmosphere, for example, the influences of the gravitational pull of the sun and moon can be excluded, because, while present, they are so tiny compared to other forces (the earth's gravity, air resistance, etc.) that it is less than random fluctuations that may be encountered in an actual reentry. If, on the other hand, we are modeling ocean tides, the gravitational forces of the sun and moon are key and essential parts of the model.

Models are like experimental data in that they represent actual things to the best degree possible. They may involve theoretical laws, but they are inherently pointed towards the world, like data or an image, and not towards systems of concepts, like pure theory. This is even true of conceptual models: a mathematical model, to be a model at all, must represent some phenomenon or measurement in the real world. The whole notion of representing requires the model to "stand for" the original.

This guides us to a number of analogies between models and images. Images, like models, are partial, from some specific perspective. They are projections of the original. The whole of the original can be taken in only by integrating many different perspectives. Images, again like models, can be detailed or vague, taking in a large view or a small one. Images may be used to elucidate different aspects of the original. Aerial photographs give us a very different view of a landscape from those taken for purely aesthetic purposes.

Analogies between model and image are obvious in the case of a schematic model: they take the form of images. But the analogy holds for physical and conceptual models, too. Physical models are like images in that they involve projection and partiality: a wind tunnel model is the surface shape of an airplane regarded alone and transferred to another material. In this, the model is no different from a shadow of the original – it is a sort of three-dimensional shadow. Conceptual models are like images, too, in that they possess a schematic structural representation of the system, which is capable of being represented as a visual plan. A computer model could almost be viewed as a "structural x-ray" of the original system.

It is apparent, however, that models are not *concrete* images of the subject. There is something else present. In physical models, it is the replication of a certain behavior of the system. In schematic models, the structure of the system is presented almost pictorially (as in a blueprint), but includes also idealizations and symbols. The conceptual model is entirely composed of symbols, and any visualization is secondary. So models, as representations, appear to be a special kind of image, or something very like an image, but not simply a picture of something.

Compare, for example, a map with an image. A map describes geographic and human features – the lay of the land, roads, settlements, and sites of interest. It almost always views the region mapped from above, and because of the curvature of the earth, must have some projection. So far it is like an image. In this era of satellite photography we might ask ourselves: why use maps at all? We could instead just use a picture from space. It is an image of the land and contains all the specificity and details of the land. And sometimes aerial photos are used in place of maps.

So why do we reach for the state highway map when driving instead of a photographic plate? The reason is that the photograph alone is not very useful. Looking at the image, could I identify the road I wished to take? Could I identify roads at all? On a statewide satellite photograph, could I tell a highway from a railroad or a hiking path or a stream? What towns are those? Is that oblong shape a lake or a forest? The information I want – what highway to take from A to B – is somewhere in that spider's web of fine lines, but I don't know how to extract it. So the aerial photograph has failed me as a highway map. It lacks the information I need, whether it be highway numbers, street names, city or state boundaries, or elevation contours. At the same time, it is cluttered with a lot of information I *don't* need for driving purposes, and this extra information just gets in the way of the information I *do* need.

Now I unfold the official state highway map on the table. It is very different in detail from an aerial photograph of the state: it is a useful summary about the state for drivers. First of all, one notices that features such as cities and highways are represented by symbols and labeled. They are also classified or conceptualized: many different towns are represented by the same map symbol or different highways by the same kind of colored double line. Purely conceptual features, like boundaries of states, counties, and parks, have been introduced as yet other lines. So the map involves a symbolization, conceptualization, and idealization that are not present in the concrete image.

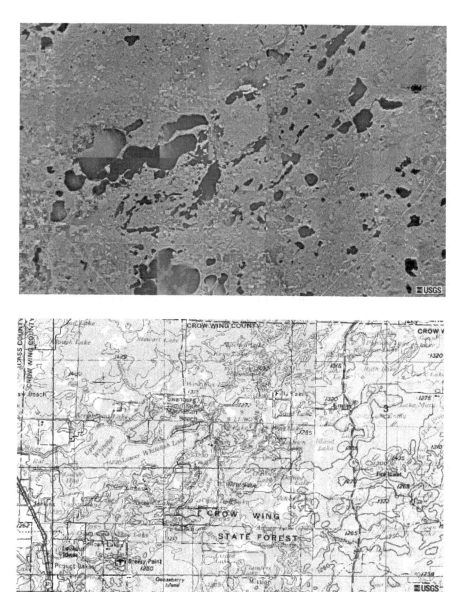

Figure 2-2. Comparison of Aerial Photo and Map.

Only the information we really need is included in the map. Details of the color and shading of the land, of the exact shape of settlements, and so on, are excluded. Extended features have been "regularized," in that lakes are represented as solid blue and forests as solid green. The map *summarizes* the information we need and ignores the information we don't need – from a driver's point of view. (Many maps of the same region are possible, based on how the map will be used: a vegetation map or population density map will be different from a highway map.)

Finally, we notice one major similarity that remains between the map and the photograph: the spatial arrangement of the features. The map is just like the image in that it maintains the particular spatial relations of the objects in the map. In this regard, the map is as if we have taken our state and given it a conceptual CAT scan. The features are laid out as we would expect in an image, but some features are suppressed and those that remain are represented by symbols or idealized lines.

The map, in sum, is not just an image of the land. It is a schematized image or schematic. It is both an "image minus," in that background features are excluded, and an "image plus," in that symbols and names have been added. The schematization is pragmatic in nature, since the information included or excluded depends on the map's purpose. The map, like any schematic, not only uses symbols, but also attempts to reduce the number of kinds of symbols to a minimum. This implies a large number of like features are being grouped under a single kind of symbol, like using an open circle to represent towns of a certain population range. A map is, of course, a purely static model. But by extension, we can see that any model is like the map. It just deals with multiple states with transformation rules connecting the states of the system. It is a representation that is actually a collection of other representations. We have already seen the ways in which both physical models and conceptual models are like schematic models.

The map, and by extension any model, is both abstract and an image: it is an *abstract image*. Models are abstract in two different senses. First, and more superficially, they involve disengaging the original system from its environment. This is actually the essential first step of the modeling process, as the next chapter explores in depth. Along related lines, as we have seen, the model ignores or summarizes features that are not necessary for its purpose. Second, the model involves conceptualization and symbolization of common features within the model. We analyze the original system into objects, classify the objects, and represent them in some way. Models also simplify features by replacing them with an idealization, as when a map represents a road as a thin line or a blueprint represents a wall as a thick line. Despite the abstractions involved, the model still represents the specific structure of the original: the model attempts to extricate the essence of the system under study from its inessential surroundings. Even in the case of a physical model, we transfer a conceptualized understanding of some behavior of the original to a new material.

The model as abstract image leads to a close analogy between models and mathematical figures. At one level, a mathematical object is represented conceptually, as when we represent a circle of radius 1 by the equation $1 = x^2 + y^2$. Corresponding to this equation there is an ideal image of a circle. This ideal and abstract circle in turn can be used to stand for any number of imperfectly actualized circular objects in the real world. If we try to draw a circle on paper, it is the ideal circle that is the prototype for the less than ideal circle that actually results. This analogy also holds if we consider how models are used for design. The blueprint is an ideal design for a house, from which any number of houses can be constructed. Each actual house will vary to some degree from the house plan in the blueprint. So in one sense, the model is a simplification of the original (or of desired features of the original) and in quite another it forms an ideal prototype that can describe a large number of similar systems.

## Why Build Models?

There is one question that has been lurking behind the scenes during our discussion of representations and abstract images, and it now insists to be dealt with. And we are now ready and willing to tackle it when it jumps onto the stage. It is: why build a model at all? *Why not use the original instead?* This is a good, solid pragmatic question. The model replicates the states, structure, and behavior of the original, but the original of course replicates them best of all.

The most straightforward answer is the practical one of cost or scale[15]. Building a full size prototype of a new design of jet airliner is much more expensive and likely to fail than first building a wind tunnel or computer model of it. The model allows one to quickly and cheaply test various designs. Scale matters, too. We can't conduct experiments on the solar system or with galactic dynamics, but it is easy to do so with a computer model. There may also be cases where changes to the original would cause major disruptions: suppose one wished to discover what effect closing two lanes of a freeway for construction would have on traffic patterns. Investigating this in a traffic simulation costs less and causes no problems for real drivers.

There *are* times when using the original really is better than building a model. Models as actually implemented will always have limitations and take time to build. If we need to know specific information about an original where cost or hazards are not a concern, then it usually is better to use the original. For example, in automotive crash safety tests, crash test dummies replace fragile and indispensable humans, but real cars are used. So the practical arguments for modeling are often a tradeoff.

There are more compelling reasons, however, why a model can be preferable to the original. We often are interested in studying only a few features of the system and want to ignore the rest. This is similar to the desire to isolate certain features of things for study in scientific experiments. A crash test dummy isolates the physical shape and dynamics of human subjects, and ignores other features that are not only irrelevant for our purpose, but could obscure the information we want. It stands for any number of actual human bodies; it is an idealization based on a certain need. We want an average or idealized form for a crash test dummy. A randomly selected human subject would not provide information as widely applicable (as well as being unpleasant for the subject involved).

Models can predict new states of a system or how a system that does not yet exist (a new design) will behave in actuality. This is a very powerful reason for using models, and is really the key to their usefulness. Not only does this make models a useful tool for design, it also provides a means for their validation and even the discovery of new phenomena: computer models can act as numerical experiments that point to future observations in the real world. They can also, as previously alluded to, isolate features of systems for modification, which might be impossible for the real system (e.g., if the solar intensity at the earth decreased by 2%, what would the effects on world climate be?). Models can have hundreds of controllable factors, which would be impossible in a real experiment[16]. Because they contain information about systems, models can also serve to store and organize that information: they can act as databases.

Models can allow one to see and deal with a system that ordinarily would be invisible, like a telecommunications network, a four dimensional space-time, or a complex molecule. This capability for visualization is an increasingly important feature of scientific models: once the system is seen, the human researcher can draw conclusions that would be impossible with tabular data, just as it is easier to recognize someone from a picture than from a verbal description.

Models provide a means of training personnel, as the usefulness of flight simulators shows. Once again, the matters of cost and safety recommend the model: it costs nothing to lose a simulated fighter plane, either in human or monetary terms. Indeed, it could be an educational experience.

Models, then, are not just abstractions, but *useful abstractions*. They aim to capture the essence of the original system. But they need not capture the entirety of that essence to be useful – what we model may be some useful subset of attributes, perhaps only a single feature. The wind tunnel model shares only shape with the actual aircraft: it is much smaller, made of a different material; it is solid and unpowered. None of that matters since the aerodynamics depend on the shape of the exterior, and that the model can represent well.

The abstraction of features inherent in modeling is actually a blessing. It limits the scope of problems and allows calculation of a solution for our problem space. Without such separability, we would be forced to model every aspect of a system and its interaction with other systems. And in many cases, that would negate the feasibility of using a model.

We can make a model as general or particular as we like. A generalized model will represent only average or overall features of things, but the particularized model can represent an object to the limits of the detail given in data: the more data, the more particular. A model representing all the features of the original we may term a *total* or *complete model.* Computer models open up the possibility of the complete representation of the original, capturing its every feature and attribute, to whatever level of detail one desires. But such a model would be practically useful only if its purpose called for it.

Modeling involves the ability to separate "important" features of the subject from "unimportant" ones that can safely be ignored. And this in turn depends on the specific problem and its underlying assumptions. The wind tunnel model does not consider the possibility of a bomb exploding in the airplane or the airplane flying through a tornado (even though such conditions would radically change its aerodynamics!); the crash test dummy does not allow the driver to avoid the crash altogether. Even when we model something purely mechanical in nature, we must consider its purpose. At first glance, modeling an ice skater seems to be basically no different from the crash test dummy; what matters are the mechanical properties. In that respect, the leaps and twirls of the skater are governed by the same laws as the launching of a cannonball. But for the ice skater, what really matters is far more difficult for the modeler to get a grasp on: the strength and training of the skater, experience, the effects of recent injuries, or the mental state and attitude on the day of competition. Suddenly the simple mechanical problem is not so simple. Such assumptions are very important limiting criteria for models. If there is intervention from outside its "problem space" — and such intervention is usually human — then the entire model may collapse.

Any number of valid models can be built of the same original system, each for a different purpose and/or in a different medium. The jade mountain can be represented by a sculpture, but for the purposes of a weekend hike, it would be represented on a topographical map of Jade Mountain National Monument, and in the computers of the local university's geology department, there is a detailed stratigraphic model of the area (Figure 2-3). Different uses mean different models. A furniture showroom may model a personal computer as a plastic shape for display purposes, while the same original computer could be represented as a block diagram of components, a circuit diagram, a 3-D image in an on-line catalog, or a computer model of its functionality (in which case, the computer would contain another computer).

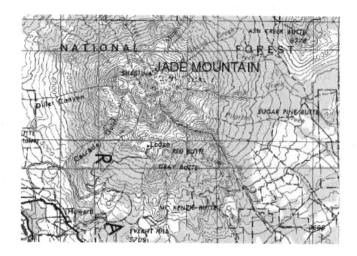

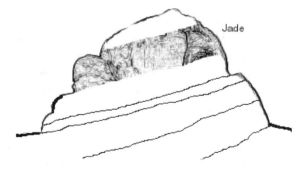

Figure 2-3. Three Different Models of Jade Mountain.

## Simulations as Models in Motion

We now have a pretty good grasp on what models are, but not simulations. Up to this point, models and simulations have been treated as if they were synonymous. But it is important to examine in more depth how the two differ. The first chapter claimed that a simulation is a model set in motion. And, in actuality, there is probably not a better definition. The model, in isolation, is static. Yet, because any good model is not just a snapshot of the thing modeled, but based on laws, we can use it to examine other states of the system, perhaps states that have never before been observed in the real world. It has an inherent *possibility* of dynamism, and simulation is nothing more than the examination of the possibilities of the model. A model is a series of representations of states interconnected by theoretical rules. The simulation traverses those interconnections, like walking through all the rooms of a house.

The primary goal of most computer modeling is often just that: to gain a greater understanding of the dynamic behavior of a system, whether it be weather systems or aircraft. The contrast of simulation to model is thus one of dynamism and the exploration of different states[17]:

"[Simulation] involves subjecting models to various inputs or environmental situations in such a way as to explore the nature of the results which might be obtained by the real system."

"a simulation is more complicated than the system it simulates: a simulation can generally reach many more states than can the original system."

The simulation can make predictions; it is an extrapolation of the model into new areas. This is seen every day in the computer models used to make weather predictions. The current state of the atmosphere (to the degree it is known) is put into the model. The model projects these initial conditions into the future using the well-known laws of fluid dynamics and thermodynamics. It is in essence a simulation of future weather.

Simulations are how most models are both used and tested. Simulation predictions can be compared with data and then the model can be corrected. This is the theoretical-predictive role of the model.

The simulation also allows comparison with the outputs of other models or testing the behavior of the model under extreme conditions to see if its results are reasonable (e.g., in the case of a computer model, that the results don't "blow up.") In general, predictions of simulations can be tested against data according to the statistical measures of any theoretical prediction.

Models and simulations are essentially complementary. There is a reciprocity of the two. The model is like an observation and in many ways the best end result of data reduction and visualization. The model, like the data itself, also represents the particularities of the object modeled. Simulation is like theory in that it makes predictions that can be tested. The iterative, self-correcting relation of model and simulation is exactly the relation of theory and experiment — the model leading from data to theory, and the simulation from theory to data. Chapter Five discusses this point in depth.

Every simulation is also a numerical experiment. Simulations provide a way of solving problems intractable to direct calculation. Such problems commonly involve integrating nonlinear systems of equations or stepping a complex system with many kinds of interactions forward in time. One commonly used simulation technique is the famous and venerable Monte Carlo method.

Monte Carlo methods integrate equations by "brute force" in taking randomly selected points and comparing which outcomes succeed or fail. For example, consider the area of a very complicated closed curve. Direct integration of the curve to obtain the area might be all but impossible. However, as long as we can determine whether a point is inside or outside the curve, it is very simple to find the area using the Monte Carlo method (Figure 2-4). The curve is enclosed in a rectangle of known area A, randomly selected points are thrown at the area like so many darts, and then the ratio of the number of points inside the curve to the total number of points gives the area of the curve as a fraction of A. Unlike an analytic solution for the area, the simulation approach does have an error, which decreases with the number of points used. This is why simulations are often called numerical experiments, and the results of simulation are termed data. Indeed, like experiments, simulations must be designed and performed systematically to ensure both the reliability of results and economy of effort[18].

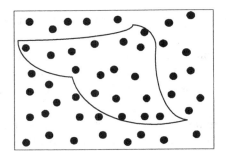

**Area of curve**
= ( points inside / total points ) X area of rectangle
= (17/48) X 7.72 square inches
= 2.73 square inches

Figure 2-4. Finding the Area of a Closed Curve using Monte Carlo.


The simulation and the model as a collection of states also opens up a new possibility. What if I am not interested in matching any "real world" data with my model? Instead, suppose I am more interested in producing an entirely imaginary world that pleases me, and that I can interact with? There is nothing that prevents this, and it is particularly easy to do with computer models. The computer simulation becomes a way of creating, experiencing, and exploring entirely different kinds of worlds. The simulation becomes virtual reality. Here is another similarity between the computer model and theory. History is full of theoretical systems that gave into the temptation of envisioning conceptual cities that later proved to be little more than mirages. Indeed, the same concepts we use to describe the world can also be used, and often used better, to entertain and engage us through fiction. The problem of virtual reality is of a similar nature. It is an important enough problem that the last chapter is devoted to it.

The simulation means, once more, setting the model in motion. This implies simulations have new elements that were not present in the model: time, events, and simulation management. Each possible event governs a transition of model state variables. Any model capable of dynamism (and hence simulation) is from the simulation point of view a collection of states with certain rules for transitions from one state to another. The density of events in time defines the basic time scale of the simulation: a rapidly changing system will have a high event rate, and a slowly changing system a proportionally lower rate. In a discrete simulation, there will be a finite number of possible states and events. For continuous simulations, there can be an infinite number of possible states in a model and an infinite number of possible transitions. There is nothing to surprise here. If I am modeling the acceleration of a possible car design, there is a continuum of speeds the car can assume, and Newton's laws govern the transition from one speed to another.

Also, just as models can be recursive — a model containing submodels that represents systems containing subsystems — so also each submodel in a simulation will have its own events, its own order of interrelations of states, and its own time scale.

The new additions represent quite obviously the time element of the model, both the continuity and the change of the system in time. The structure of the interrelations of the possible states of the system is a central feature of the order of the system. We are not just attempting to model one particular state of a system; the model must embrace the entire spectrum of possible states. A model is not complete until it describes the network of possible interrelations and the conditions and likelihoods for moving along each of those interrelations.

Models can treat time as a discrete or continuous variable. Continuous time implies the model can assume a continuum of states, while discrete time implies that there are a finite number of states with discontinuous transitions between them – hence, discrete events. Time in discrete models is generally handled by an event list, where each event has a specific time (and sometimes a priority, for resolving overlaps of events). The simulation is then performed by stepping through the event list until done – new events may appear on the list as the simulation executes, so the stopping time of the simulation can be indeterminate. In a continuous time simulation, in contrast, time is handled as a finite time step, although ideally it should be infinitesimally small. Because the time step must be finite, an error is introduced. But also the starting and stopping times of the simulation are given and known ahead of time.

The distinction between discrete and continuous models can be overworked, as can that between event-list driven and time-stepping approaches to simulation. Due to errors in model data, the accuracy of any continuous model is finite, so the additional error introduced by finite time steps may be unimportant. Analog computers were once employed in continuous system simulations, but the errors inherent in analog computing made them less accurate than digital computer simulations, even with the discrete time steps inherent in digital simulation. Also, time-stepping approaches often allow the simulation manager to vary the size of the time step, which makes it effectively the same as an event list. The event list and time step approaches can in fact be combined: the simulation can step forward a fixed time step, and see if any relevant events have occurred during that time.

A number of related events scheduled together in an ordered sequence is a *process*[19]. For example, the process "change oil in car" can be broken down into distinct steps to be carried out one after the other: raise car on ramp, remove oil pan plug, drain old oil, replace oil filter, and so on. The process, as a collection of events, will function in the simulation as an event with a finite duration, unlike an isolated event, which is treated as instantaneous. Simulations can be built around the paradigm of processes and their possible interactions[20].

In general, while models abstract entities and their properties, simulations in addition abstract events and processes. Events become point-like, instantaneous actions on the state variables of the model. Processes are collections of such point-like events, with distinct starting and ending points in time. Just as system properties will be selectively used or ignored by the model, depending on purpose, so also with events: a simulation of traffic on the Golden Gate Bridge models only traffic events, not the flexing of the bridge under its weight or the flow of water from San Francisco Bay into the Pacific Ocean.

Model state variables can be either fixed or stochastic, and this means model processes can be either deterministic or random to a greater or lesser degree. The deterministic simulation, given the same input conditions, will always have the same result. In simulations of natural phenomena, a singular result is usually the goal of the simulation.

Stochastic variables are introduced into models and simulations precisely to deal with unknown or random factors in the real system. In a stochastic simulation, the same inputs will not always result in the same outputs, any more than the real system would. Rather, in stochastic simulations one makes several runs of the simulation and averages the results, in a similar fashion to how experimental data is statistically averaged.

Stochastic models are often used in the study of human systems as well as in searching for an optimal system design (the "random walk" approach to optimization). The previously mentioned Monte Carlo technique plays an important role here. Consider, for example, a classic queuing problem: customers being served by bank tellers (Figure 2-5). We want to know the number of tellers required so that, on average, a customer has to wait two minutes for service. Too few tellers, and we get a "traffic jam" of angry customers building up in line; too many tellers, and we waste effort. We cannot solve the problem directly; it must be simulated. We know on average the rate that customers use the bank throughout the day, but any particular customer will arrive randomly (from the bank's point of view). We also know the average amount of time required to serve a customer, but the actual time in a particular case will vary randomly from the average. Given this information, we abstract the customers as discrete units that arrive randomly at some rate in our system, are placed in a queue (i.e., wait in line), are served by tellers (modeled as a station with a time delay), and then depart. The states of the system and transitions are discrete, so time is dealt with by a list of discrete events. We can then vary the number of tellers for different runs of the simulation until the desired waiting time is obtained. A simulation of this nature is prototypical for many practical problems and for stochastic simulations in general.

Models and simulations are thus *synergetic* in nature. Models are abstract images of things and systems of things in the real world, implemented in a particular medium. They can attempt to represent the original in all its features (a complete model) or just those aspects of interest for a particular purpose. The simulation sets the model in motion for purposes of prediction or optimization.

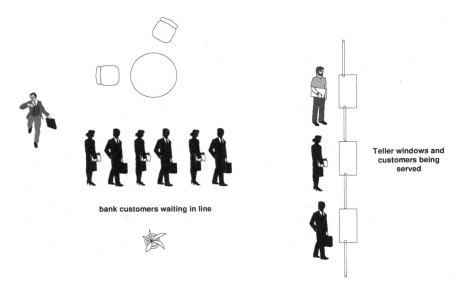

Figure 2-5. A Classic Queuing Problem: Customers in a Bank.

The foregoing raises a number of questions. Given that models are abstract images, how are such images constructed – on both the conceptual and practical levels? And perhaps most importantly of all: how do we know models are true? Indeed, can they be used as a source of knowledge? The next four chapters attempt to answer this set of questions.

# Chapter 3

# The Modeling Process

Our discussion now moves from the question of what models are to how they are constructed. This means not so much a shift from theory to practice as definition of a reliable modeling method. There are, as we will see, more than a few parallels between the modeling process and scientific method. And, as there are no models without the method, the two are really inseparable.

There have been several attempts to construct an adequate definition of model, but fewer to define the modeling process. W. R. Franta, in *The Process View of Simulation*, defines modeling thus[1]:

"the process of developing an internal representation and set of transformation rules which can be used to predict the behavior and relationships between the set of entities composing the system."

This is to say that the modeling process develops models, which is tautological. In fact, we cannot encompass a modeling method in one sentence.

What most authors (including Franta) present is a series of well-defined steps that constitute the modeling process. Table 3-1 lays out the author's understanding of the modeling method[2]. This modeling method does not necessarily mean "software modeling." It applies equally well to any modeling medium. Regardless, the method moves from abstraction to analysis to verification to prediction. But the method is not necessarily linear: it can, and usually will be, iterative. (In software design terms, it is not a "waterfall" method, where design tasks cascade from one step to the next, but a spiral pattern of development, revisiting tasks and refining them.) The final result will be a model that captures the essence of the system being represented, and summarizes that information necessary for its purpose.

The definition of the model's purpose is the starting point and often forgotten step of the process – forgotten either because it seems obvious or too far removed from the technical scope of model building. Yet it is crucial for deciding what sort of model actually results. A limited and specialized model will be much smaller and simpler than a complete model of the same phenomenon. The same is true of a vague or generalized model in comparison to a detailed model. As the previous chapter showed, we can build many different models to represent the same subject, perhaps even in different media, based on different purposes.

Table 3-1. Steps in the Modeling Process.

| Step | Name | Description |
|---|---|---|
| 1 | state purpose | Clear statement of use, goals, and purpose of the model. This will determine what is to be modeled and the level of detail. |
| 2 | system identification | Identify and abstract (decouple) the system to be modeled from its background. This step assumes the system can be treated in isolation (internal relation strength >> external relation strength). |
| 3 | find boundary conditions | Characterize boundary conditions of system (i.e., the relations of the system to the outside) and identify any distinct events and corresponding system responses. |
| 4 | system analysis I | (1) analyze system into relevant subsystems (objects) and their relations (interactions) <br> (2) identify like subsystems (classes) |
| 5 | system analysis II | (1) identify and characterize relevant attributes (state variables). <br> (2) find possible state transformations (behaviors) <br> (3) characterize time scale of system from (2) and internal events |
| 6 | subsystem analysis (complex systems only) | Apply steps 2 through 5 recursively until all relevant subsystems have been analyzed into effectively simple entities. |
| 7 | system implementation | (1) choose appropriate model medium or representation method <br> (2) construct model from models of subsystems (system synthesis) |
| 8 | verification | verify that implementation is correct |
| 9 | validation | validate model against data from actual system |
| 10 | inference and prediction | use model as a tool for prediction |

## Identification of Systems

The previous chapter showed that models are abstract images, representing some system in the real world. What do we mean by "system"? Both Franta and Neelamkavil define a system as "a collection of interacting elements that act together to achieve some common goal"[3]. But while what the model represents is some *thing* in the world, what gets abstracted is a *system*. The modeling process is largely one of identifying, abstracting, characterizing, and representing systems. So modeling – which depends on the notion of abstractable system – has a close connection with systems theory. This is of definite advantage, since systems theory has built up a large set of analytic tools.

Given this dependence on system, the modeling process rests on two basic assumptions. The first is that *there are systems* capable of being modeled in the real world. In other words, the entities in the real world we try to model can be cast, in whole or in part, in the form of systems. This seems obvious, but it is (as we will see later in the book) by no means a given. It is entirely possible the original is not a system or cannot easily be represented adequately as a system. In such cases, modeling stops at the very first step.

The second assumption is that we can reliably *identify* these systems and isolate (i.e., abstract) them from their surroundings. In other words, modeling depends on the ability to draw a line between "inside" and "outside" the system – a basic requirement of systems theory. If we cannot do this, we will not have a valid model. Nor is this requirement trivial. In some cases, it is easy to identify the system to model. The solar system can be considered independently of external galactic influences for the purposes of planetary motion. But whether "America" can be considered a system depends on the purpose of the model. It would be a valid assumption for a political or a socioeconomic model, but a poor one for global weather modeling. Every model is an abstract system that effectively represents some real system relative to the model's purpose.

The marks of a system are *coherence* and *structure*. However spread out over a set of entities, this is what the system analyst must look for.

By coherence is meant that the components of the system are correlated in time; they "stick together" as the system interacts with its environment. It is coherence that allows one to draw the boundary line of the system. System coherence need not be absolute; indeed, it generally is not. Only a perfectly closed system would have absolute coherence. Actual systems only have relative coherence – relative implying that the forces holding the system together are stronger than any external interactions. A hydrogen atom is a system of an electron orbiting a nucleus with a single positive charge; it coheres due to their electrical attraction. A computer model of an atom would consider these entities and forces. It would also consider interactions with external radiation that could push the hydrogen into an excited state. But a strong enough external stimulus – a quantum of ultraviolet light, for example – can overwhelm this coherence and break the atom apart, destroying the system. This applies to any physical entity. Systems are "knots" of more dense interactions as compared to a much looser connection the outside. The greater the relative difference between the strength of the internal binding forces of the system and its interactions with the outside world, the greater time span we may consider the system to be effectively isolated. The abstraction of systems depends on this. Such isolation is in directions of both smaller and larger. In a model of the solar system, we ignore not only the interaction of the sun and planets with the other stars in the galaxy, but also with their smaller components. Lunar gravity causes tides on earth, but we can exclude a consideration of the earth's oceans when understanding lunar motions.

Sometimes identifying the system is obvious: if I am modeling an aircraft, it is crisply distinguished from its surroundings. But at the other extreme, in a study of economies or societies, identifying the boundaries of the system may be difficult. It may even be impossible. There may be times when the distinction of a distinct system is not meaningful – we have already seen that America is not a system for weather purposes. Simply because we can distinguish an entity from its surroundings in some way – which is to say identify it – does not mean it should be treated as a system. Conversely, one of the most serious systems analysis mistakes is improperly drawing the system's boundaries.

For biological or social systems, definition of "system" has within it the notion of purpose. It is such a purpose or essence that ultimately defines the scope and boundaries of the system, regardless of the seeming unity or disunity of its physical structure. In other words, even in cases where it structurally divisible, the system is *functionally indivisible*. This implies that some essential characteristics of the system will be lost if it is not considered as a whole. Such functional unity manifests itself even at the purely physical level: hydrogen and oxygen molecules do not display the same properties as water molecules, even though water is composed of hydrogen and oxygen[4]. A pile of sawdust or a stack of boards are not the same as the system we call "tree," even though they are *materially* exactly the same. Conversely, the system "automobile company" is defined by its purpose of producing automobiles, and does not depend on whether the company produces cars one at a time by hand or in many different factories around the world.

The essential connection of systems and purpose applies to general categories as well: the generalized system "predator" depends on its function of catching and eating prey animals, regardless of whether the particular implementation of the predator happens to be a bear, a tiger, an eagle, a snake, or a dragonfly. Each of these predators would, of course, be modeled differently in detail. But we could logically arrange them into a set of models coordinated by the general concept of a predator.

This provides us with clues as to how to disengage the system – which for modeling purposes is an abstraction – from the matrix of its surroundings. The essence of every system is ultimately its purpose, and the purpose is carried out by a set of fundamental activities[5]. For a predator, such fundamental activities include sensing the presence of the prey animal and capturing the prey. Without these capabilities, no animal could play the predator's role. We have seen already that a particular systemic purpose can be implemented in any number of ways, depending on circumstances. (The systems theorist Stephen McMenamin calls these the *incarnations* of the system purpose.[6]) This means that a generalized model could represent very different actualizations of the system. This is one advantage of models, but it also means that abstracting the system from any particular instance of the system is correspondingly difficult[7]:

"the essence of a system is an intangible set of ideas ... Since you can't perceive the system's essence, you must make deductions from observing the system and talking to others who know the system. In effect, you a playing a game of charades with the object to deduce the essence of the system from the clues provided."

Because the model is essentially abstract, it can stand for any number of actual implementations, and the more generalized the model, the broader the range of implementations it can stand for. This complicates abstracting the model of any particular original system or implementation, because the natural tendency of mind is to treat the particular system under study as the prototype of all systems of its class. However, in the predator example, this is not the case: the model predator is not an eagle or a snake, but abstract properties that both of them actualize. This means also that the abstraction process invariably involves conceptualization; the import of this will be discussed further below. To identify the system "predator" means at the same time having some concept of the same.

## Boundary Conditions and Interfaces

The assumption of "inside" and "outside" does not imply a completely closed system, hermetically sealed against external influence. A model may indeed treat the real system as if it were closed: a solar system model, for instance, would behave as a closed system if we were interested only in celestial mechanics. It would also be effectively closed in the case of a passive system, such as a bridge, which is static. On the other hand, the dividing line between "inside" and "outside" is central to systems theory since it allows us to characterize precisely the interactions of the system with its environment[8]. Such a characterization defines the *interface* of the system – how it appears to, acts on, and is acted on by exterior objects. Figure 3-1 illustrates this division.

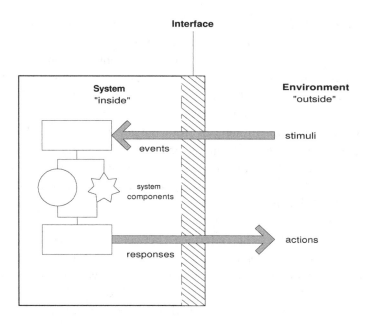

Figure 3-1. The Division of a System and its Environment.

The keyboard, mouse, and monitor of a personal computer constitute its interface to the user. Computer users do not have access (unless they open the case) to the other components of the system, nor would they want to. They care only that the interface accepts their commands and produces the desired results. The details of how this happens "behind the scenes" are only a secondary consideration. Not only is this of benefit to the computer user, it is essential to the designer of the computer system: to limit how the computer interacts with its environment and characterize it precisely.

In systems terminology, these transactions between the system and its environs are *events* and *responses*[9]. The system receives stimuli from the outside world. Some stimuli are relevant to the system, and trigger events that the system must deal with. Others stimuli are unimportant from the system's point of view, and it ignores them (i.e., it is effectively shielded from them or apathetic). In a perfectly closed system, there are no events or responses. For each event, the open system may have a response. Responses can be planned, such as taking money from a customer and returning any change, or spontaneous and essentially random. (Such spontaneous responses are modeled by stochastic variables.) Events and responses are the systems theory equivalent of sensation and action.

Thus, while models assume isolated systems, systems theory provides a way of dealing with influences from outside the system. Indeed, in complex systems, it is such characterization that permits modeling of such systems at all. Each object in a complex system is itself a subsystem, with its own properties and interactions with other objects in the system. If we could not characterize the interface, we could not model the relations of objects in the system to each other.

The dividing line or interface between the system and its surroundings, with its corresponding events and responses, can also be viewed as the *boundary conditions* of the model. We model the system inside the boundary; we ignore the world outside the boundary except insofar it can be reduced to events and responses relevant for the model. There is a boundary not only in space (i.e., some objects and relations are modeled and not others), but also in time: we do not simulate all times, but have starting and ending times. Ideally, one would like to ignore everything outside the boundary. Yet there is often a need to account in some way for interactions between the model and its "outside." In many cases, the model cannot be treated as an isolated box. This is particularly true of cases when the model is itself a component of another larger model. The boundary condition is, in essence, a way of reducing the "outside" to another object contained by the model itself. It becomes a source or sink of energies, material flows, or messages. The boundary condition in time requires defining the initial conditions, and also assuming that potential model states before the start time and initial conditions are irrelevant. Clearly, the boundary condition approach is possible only when model interactions with surroundings are weak and have a very simple nature. If such interactions are significant or complex, then one must build a bigger model.

It is the system structure that makes the interrelations of the system components, as well as it interactions with the outside world, possible. System structure also expresses the purpose of the system. In the case of an atom, the structure is provided by the electrical attraction of the electrons and nucleus as balanced by centrifugal repulsion. For an eagle, on the other hand, its structure represents a more or less optimal implementation of a hunting bird.

From the view of the "outside world," the system *is* its interface. Internal structure is inferred from the connections of responses to various events given to the system. This means at some level, all systems are (or are composed of a collection of) "black boxes," from which we draw some empirical correlations of inputs and outputs (or action and reaction, to use physical terminology). This fact has great implications for the ultimate validity of models and simulations as a source of knowledge, and will be discussed further in Chapter Five. As Figure 3-2 illustrates, the interface screens an observer from certain unobserved or hidden variables of the system[10].

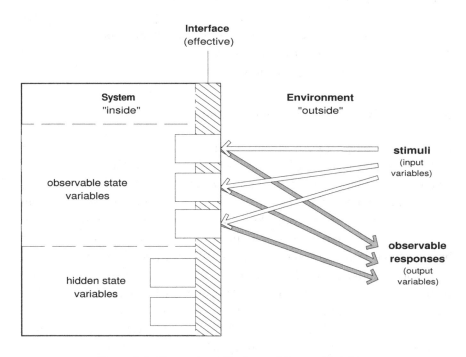

Figure 3-2. Observed and Unobserved System Variables.

Often, the screening of certain state variables by the interface is intentional and is governed by the model purpose. The hidden variables are irrelevant to model purposes. This fact is true not only of model system interfaces, but also of real systems – the interactions between the external users and the system itself should be carefully controlled. It is a very different matter in the case of scientific models, where one would like to know everything about the system. Here, the hidden variables are unknown properties of the system. Whether these become relevant may depend on circumstance, such as the energy of interaction between the system and an external stimulus.

For example, chemical valence is a property of atoms that characterizes the "interface" of one atom to another. Valence is a collective property of the atom that is due ultimately to its internal state: the quantum states of its outer electrons. At typical energies of interest to chemistry, however, this internal state is screened and manifests itself as valence.    Recurrence of valence and chemical properties, which allows construction of the periodic table of the elements, is due to certain recurrences of patterns in the electron states. The chemist does not need to know this detailed structure, however, to make use of these properties.

## System Analysis I: Find System Components

Drawing the line between the inside and outside of a system does not preclude further analysis of the system into parts. To the contrary, such an analysis is founded on the ability to abstract: each part is potentially a subsystem, whose relations to other subsystems or entities in the system are its interface to the outside.    The analysis into entities can be recursive: the system is analyzed into components, which in turn are broken down into their components, and so on, until effectively simple and atomic subsystems are reached.    (Such simple systems generally correspond to the "black box" models previously discussed.)    Such a recursive analysis of the overall system produces a hierarchical structure for the system – its "part of" hierarchy[11].    Such a view of the world is common both to science and the everyday way of describing reality. The watch on my wrist is composed of various gears and springs, which in turn may have smaller parts, that are made of metal atoms, and so on. In other words, we automatically analyze the system into a set of objects. And it is the same for any simulation — it represents either one object or a related collection of objects. What the subject gets analyzed into depends, of course, on its nature. An atom would be represented as a nucleus with orbiting electrons, a molecule as a collection of various atoms, a galaxy as a collection of stars, the human body as a system of organs, and so on.

As we identify distinct components in the larger system, we push part of the system into the background – and this background constitutes the relations between the components. In other words, we analyze complex systems into *objects* and their *relations*. The system is the sum of both. The object - relation distinction is crucial to the entire systems view of the world, and as such will be a recurring theme throughout the balance of the book.

Analysis of a system into components or subsystems often means the *spatial* analysis of the system into distinct parts. This need not be the case however: the important thing is that subsystems are *functionally* distinct from one another. The cardiovascular and nervous systems of the body overlap in space, but they remain functionally different and would be modeled separately.

Aiding both analysis and modeling is the fact there are usually only a few types of components of complex, hierarchical systems. In other words, there typically is not a complete organic division of labor between parts, except at the highest levels. Any number of circuits can be composed of a few basic kinds of electronic components, such as capacitors, resistors, inductors, transistors, and so on. The most complex of computer software is written in a language with a finite number of basic commands and other lexical units. The complex organs of the human body are ultimately composed of vast numbers of similar cells. The physicist divides mechanics into three broad areas based on how the system and its components are abstracted: bodies considered as mass points (i.e., particles), leading to point mechanics; bodies as extended and impenetrable, which gives us rigid body mechanics, and lastly bodies treated as elastic or fluid, which yields the mechanics of continual[12].

From these three types of idealized body and their equations of motion, it is possible to solve any problem in classical mechanics.

The preference of both nature and man is to construct systems from a small number of basic building blocks, which are in turn subsumed into larger systems. This is one reason why modeling the world as a system can produce meaningful results. It also points to a second systemic hierarchy the next chapter discusses at more length: the "is a kind of" hierarchy. Large numbers of similar components of a few basic kinds naturally lead us to group the components into classes and represent them as instances of the class. For example, each cell in the body is different, but we comprehend them under the general term "cell," which may be further specified as a "muscle cell," "nerve cell," "skin cell," and so on. We group larger entities of the body under the term "organ" – the heart *is a kind of* organ. The ability to identify and construct such classes of components leads to a drastic simplification of the modeler's task. They also point to the conceptualization – previously discussed with regard to models as abstract images – that naturally takes place in the modeling process. Constructing the "part of" hierarchy leads us also to construct the "kind of" hierarchy of concepts representing the parts.

There is another set of boundary conditions at work, then. The "part of" hierarchy arise from defining crisply defined boundaries between what is inside and outside a system – and imposing such a boundary as a working assumption of the model even when it is imperfectly defined and fuzzy in reality. The "kind of" hierarchy defines analogous boundaries between classes of objects that occur in a system[13]. The model assumes that components can be pigeonholed into a basic set of types, even if in reality they do not fit so nicely into the categories we have set up. The key question here is whether the components can be treated as functionally belonging to distinct classes, allowing the modeler to ignore the possible uniqueness of the components in all other respects. In the case of a completely organic system, where each component performs a unique function, a "lumping" of components into one or a few models would not be possible. On the other hand, there are a large number of physical problems where systems can be represented completely adequately by treating all the system components as the same: we can model the dynamics of galaxies, for example, very nicely as a collection of particles with different masses representing stars.

The choice of the system's basic components may be arbitrary and derive from the purpose of model of the system. The primitive components of an economic model of a country are quite different that those that would be used in a political model or an ecological model. That is because the widely differing purposes of those models bring out different kinds of interrelations and entities as the most important, while sending the rest to the background to be ignored.

The foregoing assumes that a clean distinction between objects and their relations is possible. However, this is not always the case for continuous subjects, such as fluids. At the microscopic level, of course, the fluid is composed of molecules that interact through forces that are ultimately of an electromagnetic nature. But to build a practical model of (say) aerodynamic flows on that basis would be impossible. So the fluid is treated as a continuum with properties like density, pressure, temperature, and velocity fields. All is not lost, however. Modeling a continuous subject is typically done using a special sort of software system known as a *grid*. To make the problem tractable to modeling at all, the programmer divides the space filled by the fluid into a grid of cells. The grid is essentially a set of *virtual* objects with *virtual* relations. Each grid cell acts as a discrete object; it is a container whose properties are the pressure, density, and velocity of the fluid at that point. The relations between the objects are the rules that define how material flows from one grid cell to another. Analogous problems are faced when trying to model anything continuous, or any system in which the distinction of object and relation begins to break down. Grids are used not only in fluid mechanics, but also in the modeling of electromagnetic fields, combustion (and other chemical reactions), wave phenomena, and stresses in extended structures. The whole grid approach assumes we are dealing with a subject extended in space, with definable boundaries (because the grid cannot be infinite in extent), and homogeneous enough in properties that we can subdivide it into similar cells. The cells need not be of the same size. In an atmospheric model, for example, the cell sizes typically increase in the upper atmosphere where densities are much lower. It should also be fairly obvious that the quality of the model will increase the number or density of cells. The homogeneity requirement is important. In an earth model, the same grid would not represent the oceans and the atmosphere, because their properties are so different. A model would use two separate grids instead, even if the two interacted.

## System Analysis II: State Variables and Transformations

After we have isolated the system to be modeled and analyzed the system into any component entities and subsystems, the next step is to characterize the properties or attributes of the objects -- in other words, the *state variables*. As we have seen, we don't necessarily care about *all* the attributes of what is modeled. The model separates "relevant" properties to be included from "irrelevant" properties, which are ignored. In a solar system model, for example, suppose the aim is to determine the motions of the planet and their location at any time. The relevant properties are the masses, locations, and velocities of the planets, moons, and sun — a very basic set of physical attributes. The other details of the planets — their sizes, compositions, atmospheres, continents and craters, icecaps and seas — are irrelevant because the problem is defined as mechanical, and their influence on celestial mechanics is negligible. A different subject or different goal of the model means also different relevant properties. If our aim is to model where and how the planets will appear in the sky through a telescope, then the sizes and colors of the planets do matter. In a model of an atom or molecule, the most important attributes may have little meaning or equivalent on the scale of human experience, such as quantized electric charges, inherent angular momenta ("spin"), magnetic moments, or energy state probabilities.

The preferred way of dealing with object properties in any computer model is to reduce them to mathematical form. This is straightforward with physical properties, since such properties generally are available in the form of measurements already; they conveyed as mathematical relations. A problem arises with qualitative information. If the modeler reduces qualities to mathematical relations, meaning gets lost — there is a translation into symbolic form. Suppose, for example, we are modeling a system where the color is an important attribute (a flight simulator's visual model of landscape, for example). To describe color in a mathematical fashion, there are several different systems, such as quantifying the red, green, and blue levels at a given point, or defining the hue, saturation, and brightness. However, a set of three numbers is not the same thing as a color; it is the symbol of a color. To reconstitute the meaning of the color, it would have to be displayed and viewed by a human observer in the simulation.

As with the entities in the system, what properties are considered will depend greatly on the model's purpose. Two criteria enter here: we want the model to reproduce all the states and state variables necessary, and we also want to use the simplest possible model to attain this. Simplicity is an essential criterion of a good model[14]. From potentially a large number of system properties, we abstract only those that are needed to describe the system states that are integral to the model. It is also often possible to collapse several properties of the real system into one property in the model; this is the method of lumped parameters, which often means reducing some subsystem to a "black box" model.

Properties of any system that occur together in a *coherent* fashion are a *state* – hence the term "state variables" for the properties. Just as we decompose a system into a set of objects in space, we also analyze it into a set of states in time. The states need not be all actualized, but need only be potential. Radioactive nuclei have a certain probability (high or low) of decaying at any given moment, which must be included in a nuclear model. A model may contain any number of states, from one up to infinity. The states can be interrelated in any way, from all being collinear like beads on a string up to a vast intricate network of interconnections.

A state, then, is characterized by a set of quantitative state variables, which may also be termed a *state vector*. The set of all possible state vectors in the system defines the *state space*[15]. Actually, there are four distinct kinds of state variables to consider:

(1) Properties of the system as a whole, such as energy.
(2) Relational state variables, that define the (external) relations between components in the system, such as position, velocity, or material flows.

(3) Properties intrinsic to the components, such as mass, electric charge, or valence.

(4) Internal state vectors of components.

We can rule out dealing with (4) at the outset, unless it impacts (3). The internal state vectors of components are important at a higher level only as exposed in the form of properties, such as chemical valence.

System properties can be constant (e.g., total mass), assume a finite number of discrete values, or assume an infinite number of continuous values. A constant property of a complex system we may also term a *conserved property*[16]. This means that it is a constant for the entire system, while for each entity, it may vary. In a closed plumbing system, such as an air conditioner, the total amount of fluid remains the same. The conservation laws of classical physics, such as conservation of energy and momentum, are of this nature.

The assumption of an isolated system is essentially the assumption of conservation laws for the system. The isolated system is closed, if not in space, then at least in time. In a physical system, this assumption takes the form of the laws of the conservation of energy and momentum. Even when inflows or outflows of energy are allowed (e.g., heat flow or radiative losses), the sources and sinks of that energy are in a sense part of the system, too, through the characterization of the system interface. In the model of a social or economic system, the conservation law may be that there nothing appears in the model that was not programmed into the model. At any rate, the whole notion of model involves a separation or isolation from its surroundings, and this in turn implies some rule of closure; the model is a sort of bubble from which nothing essential appears or disappears.

Often, the state vectors of most interest in a system define the relations between components. The counterpoint to the object is the *relation*. Relations knit a collection of objects together to form a system. We naturally analyze any system as a set of objects and their relations. Without relations, there would be no system; each object would be isolated and no state of the system could connect to another.

The simplest relations are spatial, such as position and velocity in mechanics. At very minimum, analysis of a complex system into parts gives us a set of their spatial relations. It is always possible to cast relations in a spatial (hence mathematical) form, at least on a superficial level. The set of relations in a system will always define a space of some sort. The geometry of the connections of the subsystems need not be a three-dimensional Euclidean space. It can be any sort of topology, including a spaghetti of network cables. Such relations might be only instantaneous snapshots of a system. In any model of a physical system, the positions and velocities of objects are of this nature. They may always be changing, but at any instant they assume a configuration. Another commonly occurring kind of relation of components takes the form of a flow, such as electric current, optical rays, or fluid advection. The queuing problem is another flow-like model. In flow models, the components shape and/or store flow material. If the "shaping" components (e.g., electronic components, lenses, etc.) are affected by the state of the flow itself, the result is feedback − on which there will be more to say below.

Needless to say, important model relations are those that affect dynamics. In the solar system model, the velocity of each planet is important because it relates the location at one time to the location at the next time, while the locations of the planets determines the gravitational forces. Likewise, important component properties are those that enter into the dynamics of the system, such as mass. Other planetary properties (e.g., what the planet looks like from earth at a given time) may be of interest to the model user, but have no relevance to the relations in the model itself.

This leads to the entire area of system dynamics, the transitions between system state vectors in time. Indeed, the existence of multiple possible states implies dynamics and transition rules between states. Multiple states would be meaningless without dynamics, since only one state could be actualized in a static model. In fact, even a static model may be conditioned by possible dynamics: in the calculation of forces within a structure, the actual solution is conditioned by the other possible outcomes, not only stable ones, but the unstable also, such as the collapse of the structure.

System dynamics requires a function, or set of functions, that governs the transition from one set of state vector values to another over some time interval.  We may call this function the *state transition function* or the *time development operator*.  In mechanics (both classical and quantum), the time development operator is called the Hamiltonian.  It expresses both the forces and conservation laws of a mechanical system, and maps one set of energy states in the system to another at a later time. The physical Hamiltonian takes the external relation state vectors (position and momentum) of a mechanical system's components and combines them with relevant component properties (e.g., electric charge) to determine the new state vectors.  System-wide conserved properties, such as total energy, are also expressed by the Hamiltonian.  The time development function of any dynamic system will bear similarities to the Hamiltonian functions of physics.

The state transition function and relations in the system are often so closely joined that we can speak of them together as *interactions*. Consider once more the solar system model.  At each instant, each planet has a certain location and a certain velocity.  Observations of the planets tell us what these are.  Knowing that planets, moons, and the sun are all related through gravitational forces, however, allows us to understand why they move as they do, and, perhaps more importantly, provides a system that relates one state of the system to another.  Chapter 6 considers this problem at length. To a first approximation, the planets move about the sun in nice, elliptical, Keplerian orbits — in which case, we need no computer models, because we can calculate the position of any planet exactly with pencil and paper.  But in more detail, the gravity from each planet influences all the others, and the solar system becomes a complex many-body problem soluble only through simulation. Gravitational relations allow the model to determine the future state of the system from its present state.  And so with the real relations in any system and hence any model. They govern not just the possibility, but also the probability, of moving from one particular state to any other.  It should also be obvious that relations need not be mutual; the influence of object A on object B need not equal to B's influence on A.  The gravitational influence of the sun on the earth is far greater than the reverse, even though the mutual forces are equal, since the sun vastly outweighs the earth.

The distinction of external versus internal interactions is itself relative to the perspective we take. The gravitational relations of the planets, which constitute external relations for the planets, are internal to the solar system as whole. External relations can trigger transformations of internal relations, and vice-versa. To return to the solar system example, the external relation of the sun's gravity caused tidal forces in the innermost planets of Mercury and Venus that eventually stopped them from rotating on their own: they are now in rotational lock with the Sun. A similar thing happened to the moon with regard to the Earth.

In cases where system properties are conserved, one can often model transition rules as flows, as previously discussed. The system can be viewed as consisting of a set of storage tanks with connecting pipes as relations; the state of each system component is determined by its level of "fluid," and the changes of state are represented as fluid flows from one component to another[17]. As simplistic as this seems, it is an analogy with wide applicability in modeling. Electronic circuits are modeled in this fashion (since electronics ultimately is dealing with the flow of electrical current), and most continuous system simulations, including analog computers, were based upon the notion of flow.

Interactive flow relations can give rise to *feedback* phenomena, where a current flow level helps determine future flows[18]. If the feedback tends to reduce the flow value, it is termed negative feedback; if it amplifies the flow, then it is positive feedback. A combination of negative and positive feedbacks around some equilibrium state will result in a self-regulating system or a stable bound state. In contrast, an unregulated system typically results in exponential growth or an unstable system. The phenomenon of self-regulation and equilibrium states can be taken advantage of by the modeler, since the identification of a stable system implies an equilibrium. After characterizing the stable state (or set of states), one can expand beyond it using such techniques as the Liapunov methods[19].

Transition rules between states can be deterministic or admit a random element. In the former case, the model is deterministic, with fixed rules for transitions between states: when state A is in situation X, state B always follows. In the second case, the model is stochastic. In a stochastic model, state A will be followed by some range of possible states; the actual state that follows in any situation will be random.

The isolated system is also closely related to the notion of the deterministic behavior of the system. In other words, models presuppose a deterministic world and can only deal with deterministic relations — preferably expressed in mathematical equations. Intervention from without the system is essentially an unknown, something outside the cognizance of the model, and hence an indeterminate factor *from the point of view of the model*. It is something the model doesn't control, so it will throw the model's predictions off. Another possible indeterministic factor is random variation. In contrast to outside intervention, random variation is often used in models, usually to simulate different outcomes from different initial conditions, as in Monte Carlo simulations. Random variations can be used in model because it can be a controlled part of the model. It also does not violate the notion of determinism in the other model components -- they calculate answers according the same formulas as before, only their inputs have changed. Random variation may be only apparent, in that the process is assumed to still be deterministic on the microscopic level, as in the case of phenomena like the motions of air molecules, the diffusion of photons in clouds, or Brownian motion[20]. The degree of randomness and what it affects can be defined. So the general effect of a random factor (e.g., a random number generator) in a model is to selectively blur out the model's results or to investigate a spectrum of different model outcomes.

Introducing human participants in a model or simulation can be thought of as effectively stochastic. To any model, a free agent represents intervention from outside the model and is an unknown for the model. Any truly indeterminate factor breaks down the modeling assumption of systemic isolation. To restore the modeling paradigm means expanding the model to envelop the outside influence, but in the case of something *essentially* indeterministic (or at least beyond what the model can characterize), the model can never "absorb" and account for the exterior factor. So indeterminism of its nature violates the modeling paradigm. Chapter 7 will deal with the implications of this fact at more length. Indeterminism means that model results will have no general implications -- they only tell us what happened in that particular instance.

The only time such an outcome is meaningful is if the model or simulation is being used to train the human participants. Not surprisingly, this is the typical use of models using human participation, like aircraft simulators.

## Simulation Management: A Digression

As a preliminary to the implementation step, we must consider that, in any computational model, there must be a software container for the objects and relations. This container is the simulation manager mentioned in the previous chapter. The simulation manager controls the model in time. It defines the time step that advances the model from one instant to another; a sophisticated simulation manager will have an event list. The event list contains the operations or commands that will be carried out in the system in temporal order. The objects in the system can enter events on the list, and these events will express the relations of the various objects. In other words, the simulation manager and its event list provide a communications system between the objects, and the relations of objects are seen ultimately to be interactions through a set of messages. It is assumed each object knows what to do when it receives a message of particular type (which might be sent to one particular object or broadcast to any number of objects). Events need not involve relations of the objects, however. They can include output requests, starting a simulation, and ending a simulation.

As alluded to in the previous chapter, there are two basic ways of handling time steps[21]. The first is event-oriented simulation, where updates to the system occur at specific event times. In any event-oriented simulation, the time increments are variable, since they depend on the events going on within the system. The second is interval-oriented simulation, where there are evenly spaced time steps.

The approach chosen depends entirely on the kind of system being modeled. If the system has discrete events (or its state transitions can effectively be treated as discrete events), then the event-oriented method should be used. The modeler analyzes the system behavior into distinct events and selects those that are relevant to the model purpose. Such an analysis is very similar in general approach to locating attributes and subsystems within a larger system; it is the same principle applied to time instead of space. As the previous chapter discussed, the events can be isolated, occurring at specific times, and inserted on a system event list. The system is then updated by moving through the list and executing each event in its turn. Alternatively, a series of related events that must occur in the same sequence is a process – in which case we have a process view of simulation. Individual entities will proceed through their processes and interact with other entities. A third, less used possibility is activity scanning. The simulation manager polls entities within the system, and when certain conditions are met, schedules a system update.

All event-oriented approaches depend on identifying discrete and effectively instantaneous events within the system. In contrast, in interval-oriented simulation, there is usually a continuum (or at least a very large number) of possible events, so that the notion of discrete events at specific times becomes meaningless. In such cases, we impose a set of virtual events in the form of evenly-spaced time steps in order to update the simulation. Evenly spaced time steps are the temporal analog of what the grid is for space: both are dealing with effectively continuum situations. And in both cases a set of virtual objects and relations are imposed on the system. In space, we can usually analyze the subject into a system of objects and their relations. If we are dealing with a continuous subject, we can break it up into a grid. In time, the object/relation will apply only when there is a set of discrete states. Otherwise — and this is the normal case — one must use the grid approach, breaking up time into a series of steps. A particular event on the event list represents a time the model must consider, because something important, and perhaps discontinuous, happens at that time. The smaller the time step, the higher the quality of the simulation, but the longer the run time. Hence, there is always a tradeoff between modeling quality and quantity of time steps in a simulation.

Nothing prevents the model from being a series of nested models or layers, each with its own simulation manager, events, and event list, paralleling the nesting of subsystems in systems. An object that belongs to a model may itself be a system with its own internal (or private) objects and relations. Such a subsystem may have a dynamic scale entirely different from that of the larger system that contains it. For example, suppose we wanted to use the solar system model to determine ocean tides on the earth. In such a scenario, the model can no longer represent the earth as a simple discrete object. It has to be a complete submodel, containing as its objects representations of the continents, a grid for the oceans, etc. It would have its own simulation manager, with its own events (e.g., updates to the hydrodynamic grid) that have no relevance to the larger solar system model. It would have its own time scale or clock that is much faster than the one in the solar system model, since tidal behavior changes on a scale of minutes or hours rather than days, weeks, or months. Nonetheless, we see that the basic paradigm of systems composed of objects and relations holds at whatever granularity we wish to look at a particular modeling problem.

## Model Synthesis: Implementing, Verifying, Validating

We can summarize the modeling process up to this point as one of repeated analysis. We abstract the system from its surroundings, and then analyze the system into relevant attributes, subsystems, behaviors, and events. The system is analyzed in both space and time. We recursively apply this analysis to all levels of the system until effectively simple and elementary entities are reached. At the end of these steps, we have all the information needed to construct the model. Having chosen an appropriate modeling medium, we now build a model prototype. We might now suppose that our task is done; the model is ready to use. But we have forgotten one crucial thing: how do we know the model really is an adequate representation of the original? If we cannot be sure of this, then our model is of very little use. Anyone with a modicum of programming ability can construct a computer model; constructing a computer model that is true is another matter.

This brings us to the next step in the modeling process: *verification* and *validation*. These are two terms used loosely by modelers as if they were one and the same thing, but there are important distinctions between the two.

*Verification* proves or disproves that the model's *implementation* is correct – meaning that it properly represents the model specifications previously discovered in analysis. In computer models, this is the debugging and quality assurance phase of software development. Verification may also involve consulting with experts in the field (walkthroughs), checks for consistency and accuracy of results, and testing the robustness of the model[22]. A failure in verification leads back to the correction of the implementation (e.g., removal of program errors), but no further than that. It merely assures the model has been properly built, and thus represents the abstract system the model defines. Verification is often an iterative process: known errors in the model implementation are corrected, then a new verification discovers new problems to be fixed, and so on, until we are satisfied.

It is important to keep in mind that verification alone says nothing about the ultimate truth of the model. Just as we can build a model of planetary motions, we could also build an astrological model of the effects of planetary motions on human lives. Such a model could easily pass the verification step. But in verifying it, we are only saying that it correctly implements the assumptions of astrology, not that astrology is true. Like strictures apply to the construction of models of imaginary worlds, virtual realities, and in computer games.

Determining the truth of models is where *validation* comes in. Verification is a necessary preliminary to validation, because it would make little sense to verify an improperly constructed model. Validation then goes beyond verification to find if the model adequately represents the real system. This is a topic that Chapter 7 will take up in more detail; here we only sketch out the general scope of the problem. Unquestionably, an unvalidated model is of little value. However, validation is only not often difficult, it is also one of the least developed areas of modeling and simulation studies[23]. There are several points, however, that any validation must deal with.

Validation involves comparison of model outputs to real data. This can be done in two different ways. The first – and most important – validation criterion is to match existing data (*replicative validation*[24]). It should also match (or implement) any empirical laws derived from existing data. Really, this is a test that the model analysis has been properly performed. Given a set of initial conditions for which data for the subject system exists, model results are obtained and compared with the data. Although simple agreement with real world data does not imply the model is necessarily valid, it is a requirement that any model must meet. The second possible validation is to compare against future data – that is, to make *predictions*. This is a very powerful means of validating models, and an area of similarity between models and theoretical predictions. If a model (like a theory) consistently predicts new phenomena that are later discovered in observations, then we can have great confidence in the model. A third means of validation is *structural*[25]. Structural validation assures the model correctly mimics the internal behavior the system. In other words, not only are the overall observables of the system correctly replicated, but also the details of the parts.

The greater the range of the data matched adequately (by some statistical measure), the more valid the model may be assumed to be. Conversely, the more complex the model, the more data is required to validate it. In general, a model that represents existing data and the system structure can be considered provisionally valid – with the understanding that any model may be invalidated (that is, its results or predictions falsified) by future data. Absolute validation would mean we are sure the original system is completely represented in the model. This, again, is a question for future chapters. The model will not, in general, match all existing data exactly; then again, all empirical data has some error associated with it. Once the model results fall within data's error bars, we may consider the model valid. There is also the test suggested by Schruben and Turing: if experts in the area under study cannot tell the difference between model results and real data, the model is valid[26].

A model that fails verification, as was shown, needs merely a correction to its implementation. Validation failure, on the other hand, leads farther afield, since it means there is something wrong with the model itself, not just its realization in software or some other medium. It can lead all the way back to an improper abstraction of the system from its background (this would be a serious to require building an entirely new model). More normally, however, it means tuning properties of the system, or obtaining better data about system properties, or devising a better representation of property data. Validation, like verification, is an iterative process. The modeler validates, corrects problems and improves the model, and then revalidates, and so on. It can be a never-ending process, with models making gradually better and better representations.

**Summary: The Modeling Paradigm**

To sum up, we discern two basic assumptions behind any model or simulation. These assumptions together can be called the *modeling paradigm*. Figure 3-3 summarizes this paradigm in flowchart form: it reiterates the information in Table 3-1, but with an emphasis on the process itself. The first is the *analysis* of the subject of the model into objects and relations. The model may consist of one large object or have any number of objects as subsystems. The relations may be between different objects or between different states of the same object. In any case, we naturally view -- and analyze -- anything in this manner, and it is how the computer model must proceed. The second assumption is that the model is an *isolated system*, a system moreover that changes deterministically in time. The future state of the system can be found from its present state, preferably according to mathematical relations or physical laws. In other words, the modeling process leads to some definite structural characteristics that all models have in common – and that the systems they represent must also have for the model to be valid. This modeling paradigm or "metamodel" is essentially that the system is either an isolated "black box" with state variables or an isolated set of interacting components with deterministic transition rules.

Computer models and simulations are meaningful to the degree their subject fits the paradigm of an isolated system with well-defined properties, clean separation of objects from relations, and deterministic behavior. The solar system, as discussed in earlier examples, fits this paradigm very well, and can be modeled as a set of mass points interacting through gravitational relations. Given any instantaneous state of the solar system, the model can in theory calculate any other.

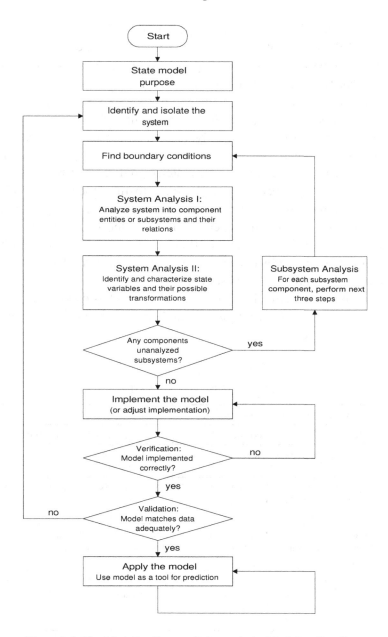

Figure 3-3. The Modeling Process Reiterated: the Modeling Paradigm.

Conversely, the less a subject fits the modeling paradigm, the less meaningful the results of any model for that subject, and the predictions of that model, will be. It is very important to grasp this, for it is the key to much that follows in this book. The model is one way of looking at reality, one that happens to be congenial to the coworking of the human mind and computing machines. It does *not* follow that the model's take on reality, its perspective, is the only valid one. Models and simulations are inherently limited by their assumptions of objects, deterministic relations, and isolated systems. Computer models cannot be considered universal tools if subjects do not conform to the modeling paradigm. Obvious examples that jump to mind here are human beings, cultures, and societies (as will be discussed in later chapters). But we need not stretch that far for an example. In fluid mechanics, we have seen how the neat dichotomy of objects and relations has vanished. A grid, a set of virtual objects and relations, must be used.

The dynamic systems theorist Foster Morrison has classified systems with regard to their conformity to the modeling paradigm[27]. His scheme is summarized in Table 3-2.

Table 3-2. Dynamic System Types.

| Type | Constraints | Description | Examples |
|------|-------------|-------------|----------|
| Zero | absolute | constant state | images, gravity models, structures |
| I | analytic integrals | solvable dynamic system | gear trains, two-body problem, physical pendulum |
| II | approximate analytic integrals | amenable to perturbation theory | satellite orbits, lunar and planetary theories |
| III | quasi-deterministic; smooth but erratic trajectory | chaotic dynamic system | climatology, Lorenz equations, discrete logistic equation |
| IV | rigorously defined only by averages over time or state space | turbulent or stochastic | quantum mechanics, turbulent flow, statistical mechanics |

The higher the number, the more difficult the system is to model. For types Zero and I, models are easily built, since conformity to the model paradigm is complete, but for such systems direct solution is often also possible, and no explicit model is required. Models are definitely required for Type II systems, such as realistic celestial mechanics problems, and here the conformity to the paradigm still holds. Thus, Type II systems are in many ways the home ground of modeling and simulation. Problems begin to arise with Type III (chaotic) systems, since exact solution over a long period time becomes impossible. Finally, with Type IV (stochastic) systems, the modeler is confronted with a situation where exact modeling and simulation are impossible, and only the statistical properties can be dealt with.

# Chapter 4

# An Object-Oriented Universe

Every model must have a medium, a means for its expression. The second chapter discussed types of models: physical models versus software models, for example. Tangentially, it also implied that computer models have emerged as superior to all others.

In other words, some modeling media are better than others. For physical models, clay or plastic, which can be molded to assume a shape and then hardened, will typically be preferred to media that are hard to work (e.g., steel) or incapable of preserving a shape (e.g., any fluid). The ideal modeling medium is one that is capable of flexibility, precision, control, and detail. The versatility of the computer model is such that it has become the modeling technique of choice in the vast majority of cases. If the measures of a modeling approach are flexibility, depth, completeness, dynamism, and precision, then the triumph of computer software becomes obvious.

Computer models are easily constructed, and computers are now readily available, fast, and inexpensive. But these are basically superficial reasons. A computer model's real advantage is its greater depth and breadth than other modeling techniques: it can treat more aspects of a system than physical, analog, or conceptual models. It can represent an "x-ray view" of the system. This is usually impossible in physical models if only because of scaling laws. The parameters of computer models are easily changed (and precisely changed) to explore different possibilities or regions of the model. A computer model and its results can easily be distributed to others. All these advantages add up to a clear decision in favor computer models in scientific research and engineering design.

Thus, any examination of modeling and simulation must give computer models special attention and examine what their essential elements are. Computer simulation has been around, in one form or another, since the 1940s. Only in the past decade or two, however, have programming languages and techniques become entirely adequate to deal with the simulation of reality — or, more to the point, with the representation of reality. This chapter looks at two different, yet related, approaches to representing the world. The first is *object oriented programming*, which models entities and systems as collections of attributes and possible operations on those attributes. Object-oriented languages such as C++ and Java are widely used and familiar to software developers. The second approach is the less well-known *cellular automaton*, which reduces objects to their simplest possible form.

Physical models do retain an advantage over the computer models in one area at least. There is an aesthetic, or at least psychological, satisfaction in models totally apart from their utility. Such is the attraction of toys to children, which carries over in adulthood in the impulse to build model railroads or fly radio-controlled airplanes or collect china figurines. Here the desire is to have a miniature replica of the object for its own sake, and that desire is, at least at present, better met by a physical model than a computer model, which do not yet have the sort of sensory realism that is wanted.

Perhaps, however, even that is changing. The attraction of the physical miniature is that it grants us a single view of a much larger system: the architectural model let us look at a huge building in one glance. This is once again the "topsight" that Gelernter alludes to – obtaining a unified view of a complex system that would ordinarily be invisible or glimpsed from some limited perspective. But this is precisely the benefit a computer model gives that a physical model cannot. The computer model can show, as a unified whole, systems that are in real life spread out over a vast space in disconnected units: a communications network, for example. It can be viewed from any perspective, in way that no other modeling medium can match. It is little wonder that computer software models have triumphed over all other forms.

But software is not generic either. Just as all modeling media are not equal, so also are some computer languages superior to others in modeling and simulation. This is no surprise, since the various computer languages arose to solve specific problems. This fact can be seen in the names of the two earliest true programming languages, COBOL and FORTRAN. COBOL (COmputer Business-Oriented Language) was designed to meet the needs of data processing in businesses, which mostly involves structured files, databases, display, and data entry. FORTRAN (FORmula TRANslation) was developed to meet the very different needs of scientific and engineering programming, which concentrates on complex mathematical calculations. It is supremely good at this, while deficient in its capabilities for input/output, display of results, and database interaction. It is, of course, possible to write business software in FORTRAN or perform higher mathematical calculations in COBOL. The point is that neither is as efficient at doing so as other languages would be.

## Modeling Through Object-Oriented Languages

Computer models and simulations date from the dawn of electronic computing in the 1940s. Since much of this modeling was done to solve scientific or engineering problems, a great deal of modeling software was written in FORTRAN. (Even in the 1990s, vast new computer simulations were still being coded entirely in FORTRAN.) Most of the literature in computer modeling and simulation, especially in scientific and engineering computing, focuses on the implementation of efficient numerical algorithms, such as methods of solving systems of differential equations. Sophisticated and powerful symbolic mathematical software applications like Mathematica, Maple, and Matlab not only solve equations but also present the results visually. All of these numerical computing approaches are useful and in some respects necessary to the modeling task. But they really pertain to how particular processes in a model are calculated, rather that the model itself. They are techniques of how to realize a model – in other words, of applied mathematics translated to the computer.

Modeling goes well beyond the boundaries of just calculation. Computer modeling and simulation awaited their own language, a more generalized language capable of capturing the paradigm of systems containing objects, properties, and relations. One would also like to have a language that would embrace the general needs of a simulation system use, such as a system clock, event scheduling and handling, a random number generator for stochastic variables, a wide array of output formats (text, histograms, line plots, contour plots, etc.), error handling, statistical analysis support, and a tool, preferably graphical, for user definition of simulation scenarios[1]. Also desirable is an ability to define and run the model without a great deal of technical expertise. If possible, the simulation system should handle both discrete and continuous models.

Toward these ends, several different computer simulation languages were invented. One of the earliest and most widely used is GPSS (General-Purpose Simulation System), first developed by IBM in 1962[2]. GPSS is particularly well adapted to discrete event simulations such as queuing models, since it models systems as a set of processes similar to flow charts. Another simulation language, almost as venerable, is SIMSCRIPT, originally developed by the RAND Corporation. SIMSCRIPT models systems on the basis of objects (e.g., customers) and the sequence of actions they undergo during their duration in the simulation (e.g., entering, shopping, buying something, and leaving a store)[3]. These modeling languages are not exactly household words, not even among software engineers. The reason is their lack of power, flexibility, and generality. Each tends to represent an abstraction of one kind of modeling situation (e.g., queuing problems) and be much less applicable to other areas. Despite attempts at being comprehensive, they were inherently limited, just as general-purpose programming languages were.

Something else was needed, a language that encompassed systems, objects, and relations in general. This need was met by what computer science calls *object-oriented languages,* which are built around the object/property paradigm. The fact that most software, regardless of application, is now written in object-oriented languages like C++, C#, or Java, should not obscure this basic fact. Object-oriented languages were developed to represent objects as such, just as previous languages had arisen to represent numbers or data operations.

In fact, object-oriented (OO) languages originated to deal with computer modeling and simulation. The very first object-oriented language, Simula, was developed in the 1960s by a group of Norwegian scientists attempting to simulate nuclear reactor operations[4]. Simula is an extension of Algol. (Though little used today, Algol has a large progeny: Pascal, Modula, C/C++, Ada, C#, and Java all owe a good deal to it). Simula's innovation was to extend Algol's data blocks to become programming objects. Each object represents a component of the system being modeled, with both the attributes and operations typical of that object[5]. Moreover, each Simula object could run as an independent process (coroutine) and interact with other objects. This permitted the simulation of an entire system as a set of parallel processes.

Simula's objects were a very different way of looking at programming when compared with procedural languages like FORTRAN. Instead of writing a series of operations on memory locations, object-oriented software shifted attention to a higher and more abstract view of what the software system represents. In this, it united aspects of the structured programming approach, which splits programs into distinct modules based on functionality, and the data domains typical of relational databases. Objects organized into neat packages both the data and the possible data operations need to describe systems. In essence, each object can function like a tiny, independent machine[6].

Object–oriented software had an importance that went well beyond the needs of scientific modeling. Indeed, the next major OO language, Smalltalk, had nothing to do with it. It was developed by Xerox PARC as the programming language for its Dynabook computers, which in turn became the parent of modern personal computer graphical user interfaces, such as those of Apple Macintoshes and Microsoft Windows. Smalltalk is a pure and consistent object language (everything is an object, even numbers used in arithmetic calculations) that demonstrated the wide-ranging utility of the OO paradigm.

For various practical and marketing reasons, Smalltalk never became widely adopted. Instead, object-oriented software as a ubiquitous tool grew out of the widely available, compact, and relatively cheap C language – namely, C++. Now the most extensively used OO language, C++ not only came about as a way of dealing with modeling, it was in fact a direct descendant of Simula. Bjarne Stroustrup, a computer scientist at AT&T, grafted Simula-like classes and objects onto the existing (procedural) C language, in order to deal with network simulations[7]. The result was what he called "C with Classes," which was later contracted to C++. (C++ is a pun, incidentally, meaning C Plus One. Presumably, the next generation of C++ will be called C+=2.) A more recent OO development is Java. While Java did not have a modeling origin — its most common use is for Internet programming — it nonetheless owes much to C++, Objective C, and Smalltalk. Most other new languages that have been developed since the 1970s have adopted the object-oriented approach in greater or lesser degree, among them C#, Ada, Eiffel, the Common Lisp Object System (CLOS), and the OO scripting language Python.

Even more recently, an OO design language, really a meta-language for objects, called the Unified Modeling Language (UML) has been developed[8]. UML represents objects and their relations at an abstract level, independently of any actual programming language. A UML class diagram, containing the attributes and operations of that class, can be used as a template to generate actual classes and objects in some particular programming language. UML is not a programming language, but an architectural language for designing systems of objects.

We are wandering off into a meadow of wildflowers or weeds here, depending on your attitude toward computer languages. The important question is: what does "object-oriented" really mean? What makes object-oriented languages like C++, C#, and Java superior to (supposedly) outmoded procedural languages like COBOL, FORTRAN, and C? One must keep in mind that modeling is only one small part of computer programming; at least as big a motivation for OO languages is found in the possibility of code reuse and data organization. Once an object is defined, it becomes a component that can be shared between programs and programmers. Entire libraries of objects are built and exchanged. In other words, when one builds an object that represents something in the real world, whether it is an atom or a bank account, that object (being a model of the real thing) is a "software thing" which can be used elsewhere, transferred from one location to another, etc. In other words, the same features that make OO useful for the computer modeler also make it useful in more traditional areas of computer programming, like business transaction processing or graphical user interfaces.

It is also important to remember that an object-oriented language, all by itself, does not constitute a simulation system, such as are provided in specialized simulation languages. Rather, it provides a convenient conceptual framework for computer models, just as grammatical rules provide the framework for speech and writing.

All object-oriented computer languages share several essential features — classes, encapsulation, and inheritance — which are only summarized here. For the interested reader whose wishes to explore the topic in more depth, there are several excellent works available[9].

Central to any OO language, as the name implies, are objects. An *object* contains both data and the procedures that operate on that data: its properties and possible relations. The data items belonging to the object are generally referred to as *attributes* and the procedures are called *methods, functions*, or *operators*. The definition of an object, which amounts to a definition of its attributes and methods, is a *class*. The class is essentially a template from which any number of instances, the actual objects, can be generated. Think of the class as a cookie cutter and the objects as cookies.

The only way to access or change the data belonging to an object is through its methods or functions. This important aspect of OO programming is known as *encapsulation*. Each object is a self-contained entity with an interface defined by its methods. Put differently, the program using the object doesn't "see" the object's data directly, but only what the interface allows it to see. Any other data is hidden. The interface acts as the control panel of the object – it is the aperture that allows us to both view and act on the object's data, and only that data it permits us to.

As an example of classes and objects, consider how we would render the solar system model in software objects. Chapter Six will examine the problem of modeling the solar system from a conceptual angle; here we look at it from a computer software point of view.

The solar system model is a collection of objects and their relations. There is one object for the sun, for each planet, and for each moon. Yet it is quickly apparent that all these objects can be brought under the same class, since they have similar properties for the purposes of the model. Let's call this general class SolarSystemObject. What are its attributes? First of all, the spatial state of each object is described by its location and velocity (in three dimensions) — for our model, each planet can be treated as a point. Second, since the objects interact through gravity, we must include each object's mass. Finally, we include a name for each object to identify it. (Time is not included as an attribute because it belongs to the entire system and hence the simulation manager.) Figure 4-1 shows a UML-like diagram of our SolarSystemObject class.

SolarSystemObject is a cookie cutter for planet-sized cookies. When we initialize an object as the instance of this class, we give it a name, such as "Sun," "Earth," or "Moon"; and a corresponding mass, position, and velocity. For convenience, we would initially place the sun at the center of the system at position zero and velocity zero. The other objects would be placed at their appropriate distances from the sun, with their orbital velocities, etc. In other words, as we instantiate each object, we define its initial conditions in the model.

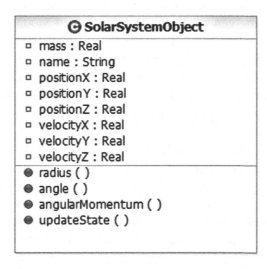

Figure 4-1. Diagram of the SolarSystemObject Class.

Likewise, we would define whatever functions/methods are needed for an SolarSystemObject, such as an angularMomentum() function that would calculate the angular momentum for each object at a given distance or updateState() which uses an input gravitational acceleration from other objects, and a time interval, to update the position and velocity of the object. Notice that the attributes of mass and velocity are "invisible" to the outside. The velocity is not relevant to the relations of the objects, while we have decided to represent mass through acceleration instead.

*Inheritance* is another central feature of OO languages. Having built a simple computer model, suppose we extend it. We want to represent the objects in our model in more detail —for example, we want to know how a given object would appear from another object. We would end up with some of the attributes being different for different objects — like luminosity for the sun, or surface reflectivity, color, and pattern for planets. We could, of course, simply add all these new attributes to the SolarSystemObject class, turning it into a catchall for properties, then define a switch or flag to distinguish between object types. But it would be much more elegant and satisfying to have the SolarSystemObject class be a general class, with subclasses to treat special cases — let's call the subclasses Sun, Planet, and Moon — as subclasses. Subclassing means that at some general level Sun, Planet, and Moon share the same attributes and functions (those encompassed by the SolarSystemObject class), while having specific attributes and functions all their own. In other words, each subclass *inherits* the attributes of its more general base class. This inheritance relationship is represented in Figure 4-2. Inheritance allows the programmer to establish class hierarchies, from specific to most general, and provides a powerful means of organizing objects and their relations. Indeed, in the Java language, all classes are derived from a single general object class.

In the solar system model, we instantiate one Sun object, nine Planet objects starting with "Mercury" and ending with "Pluto," and many Moon objects with names like "Moon," "Phobos," "Ganymede," "Titan," etc. The more generalized model is also more flexible: we could use it to represent the Alpha Centauri system with its three suns (and whatever

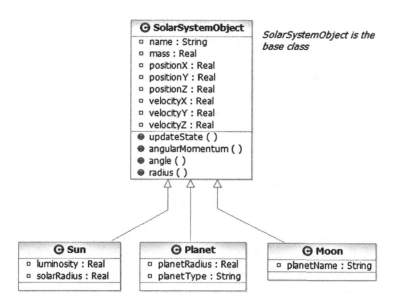

Figure 4-2. Relation Between SolarSystemObject and Derived Classes.

number of planets it turns out to have). The same classes could actually be used to model the galaxy (which would presumably have only star objects and ignore planets altogether.) Even in this simple example, it is easy to see the great power that OO programming provides the modeler.

The power of inheritance in object-oriented software can be abused by the unwary. For example, the Australian armed forces recently built a terrain simulator for helicopters that was so realistic that it included wildlife in addition to plants and rocks. One feature the programmers wanted to include was how kangaroos behave in the presence of helicopters[10]:

"Being efficient programmers, they just re-appropriated some code originally used to model infantry detachment reactions under the same stimuli, changed the mapped icon from a soldier to a kangaroo, and increased the figures' speed of movement."

"Eager to demonstrate their flying skills for some visiting American pilots, the hotshot Aussies "buzzed" the virtual kangaroos in low flight during a simulation. The kangaroos scattered, as predicted, and the visiting Americans nodded appreciatively... then did a double-take as the kangaroos reappeared from behind a hill and launched a barrage of Stinger missiles at the hapless helicopter." (Apparently the programmers had forgotten to remove that part of the infantry coding.)

"The lesson? Objects are defined with certain attributes, and any new object defined in terms of an old one inherits all the attributes. The embarrassed programmers had learned to be careful when reusing object-oriented code, and the Yanks left with a newfound respect for Australian wildlife."

Let us now step back from the solar system model and try to understand it in terms of the steps of the modeling process. First of all, we state its purpose: to model the dynamics of the solar system. The fact we are interested only in dynamics – the celestial mechanics – of the solar system is a vast simplification. Next, we identify the system and separate it from its background. For the solar system, this is easy and obvious: it is the sun, the nine planets and their moons, and any asteroids and comets we care to include, all coordinated by the dominating factor of the sun's gravitational field. It's a long way to the next star, so the solar system is effectively a dynamically closed system. (This need not be the case with stellar systems, however. Consider the dynamics of a planetary system in the heart of a globular cluster, where stars are packed together far more densely than in our own solar neighborhood. Such a system could no longer be so easily separated from its surroundings – or could be so separated only on a short time scale. In fact, models of just the sort as SolarSystemObject have been used to study why globular star clusters do not collapse in on themselves[11].) Since the solar system is effectively closed on time scales of interest, the boundary conditions are also very simple: they are an impenetrable barrier, with no events or responses.

Next, we analyze the system into components. This is equally easy and natural: sun and the planets. We can choose an arbitrary cutoff size for other bodies, so we can include as many or few asteroids as we like. We continue to analyze the system recursively. Most of the planets are actually planetary systems, with moons. But no moons that we know of have moons themselves, so there the recursive analysis stops, and we are left with a set of roughly spherical massive bodies, similar enough that we can organize them into just a few classes, as Figure 4-2 outlined above. So we have completed the subsystem analysis, and have built "part of" and "kind of" hierarchies representing the system. The Earth, for example, is a part of the earth-moon system, which in turn is part of the solar system as a whole. Likewise, the Earth is a kind of planet, and planet is a kind of astronomical object.

Consider now the attributes and behaviors of the system. Since the model is interested in dynamics, it can ignore all attributes of the bodies except mass, position, and velocity. Our initial intentions make the model very simple. Likewise, the only force in the model is gravitation, determined by the masses and relative distances of the objects involved. So the model's attributes are complete and straightforward. The behaviors of the system depend only on these factors.

We implement the model in computer software, due to the complex calculations involved. For, although the equations involved are simple, there are a large number of bodies in the problem, so it cannot be calculated directly. Ever so little do the various planets perturb each other's courses, but over a long period of time, it is significant. Perhaps we are building the model precisely to study such little disturbances. And since we are dealing with objects, we will program it in an object-oriented language, probably C++, but perhaps Java, Python, or C#. We will thoroughly debug our program until it is error-free and thus is verified accurate. Our program of validation will take longer, and may mean comparing the results of many millions of simulated years against known facts. Next we make predictions about the future, and can predict solar and lunar eclipses and the nightly positions of Jupiter's moons to our hearts' content.

We see then how natural the object-oriented method of representation is, how useful it is, and how closely parallel it runs to the ordinary functioning of human thought. This fact is in many ways ironic. For the algorithmic way of thinking required by traditional, procedural computer programming is in many ways unnatural, and is difficult for novices to learn and apply. There is a good reason for the difficulty: algorithms are the way that machines work, not necessarily the most convenient way for us to think. To program in FORTRAN or C is to press one's mind into the mold of machine instructions. Yet even this can become a habit of thought, so when OO languages like Smalltalk or C++ first appeared, programmers trained in older languages had trouble dealing with the new way of looking at software. In essence, they had to unlearn machine thinking to return to the natural tendencies of human thinking. Younger generations trained from the start in OO languages will not be so encumbered. Although it often takes time for programmers trained in older, procedural languages to get used to the nuances of the object-oriented way of approaching a problem, once it is grasped, it is a much more natural way of representing the world, whether that "world" is a solar system model or a database application. The programmer builds a set of objects, logically related in various ways, and then puts them together to solve the problem. The work of software development is divided into two distinct stages: analysis and design, where a system of objects is defined, and implementation, where the basic OO blueprint is turned into actual code in a particular language. Such a division of labor is like that between the architect and the builders, except that the OO program designer is a really an architect of objects. Most of the effort in design is directed at finding the most efficient set of objects to solve the problem.

## Class Patterns

Software *patterns* are an extension of object-oriented methods of analysis and design. Just as object-oriented programming built upon earlier software ideas by unifying data structures and functions, so patterns expand the scope further by seeking out sets of interrelated classes and objects. Patterns are object systems that recur again and again in software architecture and implementation. They were introduced to the computer software world by the book *Design Patterns: Elements of Reusable Object-Oriented Software and Design* by Erich Gamma and others[12]. Patterns are standard models of a structure or process that can be applied to specific cases in a consistent way. Patterns thus enable the reuse not only of code, but also of the results of one object analysis or design in other contexts. Many of Gamma's design patterns, for example, arose from solutions in building graphical user interfaces.

In a dynamic systems simulation, such as the solar system model, the most important distinction here for patterns is between discrete and continuum systems. Discrete systems will have a conceptual model of discrete objects with some set of relations that provides an equation of state or motion. Celestial mechanics simulations are the most obvious example, but many of the same approaches used to model the dynamics of interacting planets or stars can be applied to molecular dynamics and the many-body problem in general. Essentially, all these reduce to a conceptual model of mass points with locations and velocities, whose dynamics are governed by some combination of force fields (electromagnetic, gravitational, Van der Waals forces, etc.) – in other words, particle mechanics. Our simple solar system simulation thus leads to a more general class pattern that is applicable to many physical systems[13].

Continuum systems, such as fluids and fields, as well as quantum wave packets and extended elastic objects, can be modeled (other than in very simple cases) only by approximation on a lattice of points or grid of cells. In other words, to model the continuum, we are forced to reduce it to a discrete form through a virtual set of objects and relations. Grids, lattices, and closely related finite-element approaches, are thus another set of common object patterns for physical models.

An enumeration of all class patterns that occur in modeling and simulation would be a book in itself, and that is not the intent of this section. Rather, one should see that patterns represent a powerful extension of the object-oriented approach to represent different types of systems – a pattern is itself a kind of conceptual model.

## The Categories of Object-Oriented Reason

The OO way of looking at the world, just like the modeling paradigm, reflects our ordinary way of thinking. This is both the *advantage* and (ultimately) the *limitation* of the OO paradigm. It follows that the limits of computer software are the same as the limits of the human mind that originated it. We naturally think of the world in terms of concepts. The concepts represent things, actions, or abstract ideas. They do so by, in essence, acting as *containers* for attributes and operations. We use the attributes to characterize the something represented by the concept. Now this is exactly how classes and objects in an OO language work, as we have seen.

As one of my coworkers put it on first being exposed to object-oriented analysis and design, "Ah, this is just Aristotelian logic with computers." Indeed, it is. Or classes are like Platonic forms or Kantian categories, depending on your philosophical preferences. Object-oriented programming attempts to crystallize not just *logic* (which computer languages have done since the beginning) but *concepts* into software form. Put differently, if the object-oriented representation of the world is ever completed, we will not only have a model of the world, but will have realized the dream of Leibniz of a new ideography, along the lines of mathematical symbols, for all concepts known — an object encyclopedia. Objects and classes capture what was meant when concepts were referred to as "mental words," of which the spoken or written word is merely a sign.

Actually, we can discern several different "categories" in object representations. Following the modeling paradigm, the first is the mental separation between the system and its environment – the *system/background distinction*. OO analysis likewise assumes there are entities and systems with well-defined boundaries, either spatially, temporally, or functionally. It presupposes we can consider the modeled system apart from the whole, at least on time frames of model interest.

A closely related "category" is the analysis of the system into entities and subsystems. There is a clean and absolute distinction in models between the *objects*, on the one hand, and their *relations*, on the other. The objects are the "foreground" and the relations are the "background." Put differently, the objects exist in the model, while the relations merely subsist; we suppose them to have no reality apart from the objects they relate. This is once more a natural inclination of mind: in approaching any whole, we divide into various discrete things, at various locations in space, which are assumed by be interrelated somehow. At the same time, we have already seen cases where this assumption of a clean distinction between object and relation breaks down, as in dealing with fluids: to model them at all, a grid of virtual objects and virtual relations must be defined. Any similar sort of "forest and trees" question posed for human understanding leads to similar problems. We have trouble beholding unified multiplicities as just that. We tend to think of them as unities *or* as multiplicities, but not as both at the same time. Object-oriented analysis has the same tendency, except that it can at least represent the whole and parts together. It is from this analytic category, recursively applied to the system, that we arrive at the "part of" hierarchy for the system and its subsystems.

System analysis applies not only to parts, but also to attributes. This yields the previously mentioned notion of an object as a *container for attributes*. In object-oriented analysis and design (e.g., a use-case analysis), one assumes that any noun in the problem -- whether that noun is a planet or a bank customer — is a potential object, while any verb is a potential operation. The object is described by a set of attributes, which may themselves be other objects (composition). This dichotomy of object/attribute is identical to the logical distinction of substance/quality — which is to say once more that we view the world in terms of things that have attributes. Probing deeper into what the substance of each thing is (as we understand it conceptually), it dwindles to a mere container for the attributes – "substance" simply binds together the attributes into that single package we call a "thing."

The same analysis applied to interactions between objects provides the temporal distinction between *cause and effect.* In computer modeling and simulation, all "action" is controlled by discrete, instantaneous events that occur at various times. The continuity of time is broken up into finite time steps or events, with definite rules of change at each event. In the interval between events, "nothing" happens. Now, when we approach any temporal continuity, we do exactly the same thing: we break it up into a series of discrete instants at which we act or perceive. We introduce a division of causes discontinuously followed by effects into the temporal continuity. We cannot think about processes in any other way, and this limitation reflected by the software we write.

Finally, whenever there are a large number of similar components in a system, we arrange them into a few classes based on like attributes and behaviors.  Then, we try to organize the classes themselves into a set of a few broader classes, and these in turn into fewer classes, until we have a single supreme class or genus, embracing all concepts and objects in our system.  These facts lead to a twofold dichotomy.  The first is the distinction between the object and the class to which it belongs – the "is a" or "instance of" relation.  The Earth (a real thing) *is a* planet (a conceptual thing).  The second is the distinction between a class and some broader superclass – the "is a kind of" relation.  Together, these allow us to organize the "kind of" conceptual hierarchy describing the system.  This is, of course, how inheritance works in OO programming. The most generic class is also our base class.  Abstract classes tend to act as containers for more concrete classes, and as classes become more abstract, they also tend to have fewer and fewer attributes.  Presumably, the most generic of all classes would simply be a container with no other attributes.   In other words, in OO programming, abstraction and generalization are one and the same thing; the most abstract is also the most general.

Just as with the object/relation and object/attribute dichotomies, the organization into classes presents its own problems, which formalisms like UML tend to mask.  One problem is how do we know our classes are right?  This in turn will depend on what attributes we consider important. If we follow classical categorization by common attributes, then different choices of attributes will produce different class hierarchies.  There seem to be any number of different ways of organizing our objects, in other words, and which one to use is a pragmatic choice.  We see also there are many cases where we have multiple superclasses of a class: is a seaplane an aircraft or a boat?  This points out one typical limitation of class designs – the pyramidal hierarchy of classes, culminating in one supreme class.  The supreme class has the fewest attributes of all (since it unifies all its subordinate classes), but the attributes it does have seem to be uniquely chosen as "most important."   Along the same lines is the "metaclass" – a "class about classes," whose instances are other classes. Smalltalk, Clos, and Java all have metaclasses (and they are actually surprisingly useful), but exactly what they mean is not clear – simply to say the Earth *is a* planet, while a planet *is a* class (which is very different from saying a planet *is a kind of* astronomical object), tells us little.

All the above "categories" are rooted in the inability of the human mind (and hence software) to entirely comprehend the infinite and the infinitesimal. We can't grasp unified multiplicities as such conceptually, and this leads to the distinction between objects and their attributes, as well as the analysis of systems into objects and their relations. We *must* introduce such divisions or dichotomies to conceptualize at all. Since objects represent concepts, this limitation applies them, too. Likewise (and closely related) is the inability to grasp continuities, especially continuous processes in time, as such. We can only comprehend continuities when broken up into a series of points, a conceptual picture that leads to Zeno's paradoxes of Achilles never catching the tortoise or the moving arrow that is standing still. This limitation, as we will see in Chapter Seven, is a crucially important one for computer models and simulations. Dealing with unified multiplicities and with continuities is thus a conceptual barrier for software ultimately rooted in the human mind.

## Cellular Automata as Micro-Objects

It is possible to view object and computer models from an entirely different angle. Instead of pragmatically representing things by objects and systems of objects, with all their panoply of attributes, consider instead the simplest possible object. What would the simplest object be? First of all, it would have a single attribute. This single attribute would be binary (a Boolean variable); it could assume only the values of 1 and 0 (or "yes" and "no," "true" and "false"). Second, the only class functions would be the four elementary logical operations of equivalence, inversion ("not"), "and", "or". In other words, the simplest software object would be a logical or Boolean variable. It does not appear to be very useful for modeling (it is a primitive data type), but suppose we build systems of these objects. Simple logical cells can be arranged into larger arrays or grids, with rules governing their interactions and interrelations. Each logical cell will assume two (or through combination, a small finite number) of states, and the change of state will be governed in the form of a logical expression by its present state and those of its neighbors. Now, something like this is certain to be much more interesting and useful.

The simple logical object has been given the name *cellular automaton*. The idea of the cellular automaton was originated by the mathematician John von Neumann in 1940s[14]. Investigated by mathematicians since then, cellular automata systems were given prominence by the physicist Stephen Wolfram. Wolfram noted that many complex natural systems that cannot be reduced to simple mathematical form, such as turbulence in fluids, alignment of magnetic domains, or growth of plants, perhaps could be simulated as systems of immense numbers of cellular automata[15]. Indeed, one important work on cellular automata is subtitled, "a new environment for modeling." One of the most widely known cellular automata models, Conway's Life Game, attempts to represent the life, survival, and reproduction of unicellular organisms. In turn, this expresses a view that such systems are essentially complex computing machines, based on a vast replication of a basic pattern. The cellular automaton is essentially, as the name implies, a sort of protocomputer.

Toffoli technically defines cellular automata as "discrete dynamical systems whose behavior is completely specified in terms of a local relation."[16]. The cellular automaton is, as described above, the simplest possible computational object, having a single attribute that describes its state. This state-attribute can assume only a finite number of values -- the simplest would be binary, but larger numbers of possible discrete states are allowed[17]. The cellular automaton is of little interest in isolation. To be of use, systems of huge numbers of identical cellular automata are arranged in grids. Cellular automata models are also discrete by definition in time: they assume values only at evenly-spaced times and all cells are updated simultaneously. Relations between cells and rules for updating them (they are one and the same thing) are likewise as simple as possible and completely deterministic. The future state value of a cell depends on the current state of its nearest neighbors in the grid, as well as its own present and past values. If the cell states are binary, this can be actually expressed as a purely logical relation.

Not only are cellular automata the simplest possible objects, systems of cellular automata are the simplest possible systems, substituting sheer numbers for modeling sophistication. This has its advantages and disadvantages from a computational standpoint. The main drawback is the immense number of cells and update events (perhaps trillions or quadrillions per time step) that are required to represent any realistic system[18]. On the other hand, cellular automata have the strong advantage that they are ideally suited to parallel processing. The ideal computer for *software* cellular automata would simply be a giant parallel processing array of *hardware* cellular automata. Actual machines of this nature have been built to study, for example, the Ising model of statistics of atomic polarizations in magnetic fields.

There are many similarities between grids of cellular automata and the grid calculations of partial differential equations that so often occur in calculations of heat flux, wave motion, crystalline lattices, and fluid mechanics. What unites systems like these, and makes them attractive to the cellular automata approach, is that they consist of a large number of simple and identical objects.

Consider a simple example of a system of cellular automata. Each automaton is binary, assuming only the values of 1 and 0. They are arranged in a one-dimensional array to form a "line automaton." The relations of each cell's state to that of its neighbors obeys a "glider" rule that leads to persistent moving patterns. Figure 4-3 shows the development in time of these line automata, for random initial conditions. Each time step of the system, and thus each line in the result, can be viewed as a "generation" that gives birth to successive generations. Note the emergence of semi-ordered patterns, despite the random starting point.

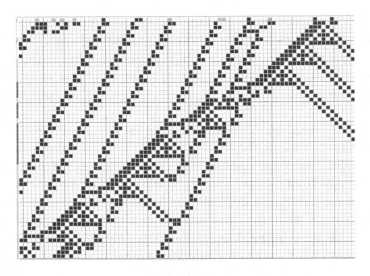

Figure 4-3. Line Cellular Automata in Action.

Figure 4-4 shows three successive time steps of a two-dimensional array of cellular automata following a rule that is a variant of the Life Game[19].

One of the most intriguing aspects of cellular automata systems is that from a set of simple objects and rules, astonishingly complex patterns can emerge. These patterns are often suggestive of patterns of fluid turbulence, of fractal geometries, or of living systems. Different pattern types can arise from the same rule depending of the initial conditions. Wolfram analyzed cellular automata patterns into four basic classes[20]:

(1) After a finite number of generations, the pattern converges to a single state that is endlessly repeated.
(2) The pattern becomes a number of unvarying or repeating subpatterns.
(3) The pattern never develops any structure and appears chaotic.
(4) The pattern develops complex localized subpatterns, some of them long-lasting.

This last class is obviously the most interesting to the modeler, and it is significant that only small minorities of automata assume and stabilize such patterns.

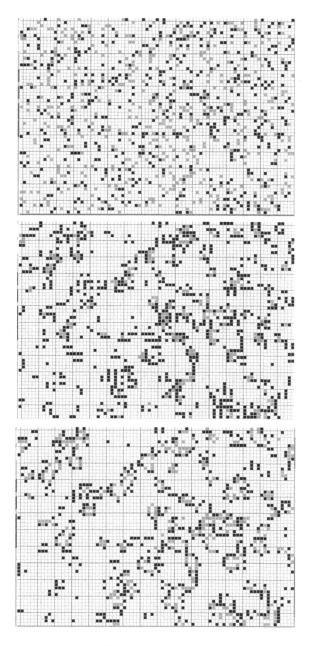

Figure 4-4. 2-D Cellular Automata and the Life Game.

The tantalizing aspect of cellular automata systems is that their complex patterns could provide the key to other complex patterns in nature. In other words, they will make otherwise intractable phenomena understandable through computer simulation. For systems where basic "rules of the game" are both simple and deterministic, this is a realistic hope. A good example is the description of turbulence in fluids, which cannot be modeled effectively using ordinary fluid modeling techniques. A turbulent fluid has a complete spectrum of currents and vortices all intermixed and nested within each other. Cellular automata seem to offer a way to model such phenomena. A more far-fetched hope is that cellular automata will show possibilities of self-organization or the emergence of order from chaos. By combining vast numbers of cells, coherent larger entities will develop. There is a problem with this, and it is that the cellular automaton can only change according to its basic deterministic rules. The Rule hovers over any system of cellular automata like a Platonic form. No pattern can emerge from it that cannot be ultimately traced to its rules and initial conditions. Any coherent pattern that does emerge is, in essence, like a trick billiards shot, carefully defined by its initial set-up. Of course, one could modify the rule adaptively through several simulations to obtain coherent patterns, but this implies providing information from without that goes beyond the cellular automata themselves.

# Chapter 5

# The Crossroads of Theory and Experiment

We return now to a thread of discussion begun in the second chapter: the relation of models to empirical reality. Anyone can build computer simulations -- every computer game is a kind of simulation. The question here is: how do we *validate* computer models and simulations? Can they be a source of knowledge about reality? Models and simulations as scientific tools depend on the answer to these questions.

The status of models as a source of knowledge remains controversial. It seems that models are neither experiment nor theory, but a combination of the two. That is because the model, as abstract image, involves both empirical data and general laws. Every theory has its roots in some model; every experiment is akin to a simulation. In fact, the model is actually the *crossroads of theory and experiment*, the point where they come together. The analogy between modeling and observation, on the one hand, and between simulations and the predictions of theory, on the other, was no accident.

A consideration of what models mean takes us directly to the heart of the scientific method. For the engine that drives science is precisely the unending reciprocal motion between experiment and theory, between observation, laws, and prediction. The two halves of the scientific understanding of the world — the empirical and the theoretical — are both necessary to its advance.

The empirical half is the data-collecting part of the scientific endeavor. It measures, tests, unearths, captures, photographs, collates. To it belongs all scientific observation, experiment, and exploration. It gets at the "facts." These facts are a *direct* characterization of the real — they are the footprints of the real world, whether they are the plants of the Amazon jungle or the orb of the night sky. Observation can uncover entirely new and unexpected phenomena that confound existing theories. At the same time, however, these "hard facts" are never entirely certain. Measurements always have an error. The same experiment never gives exactly the same result twice, and all trees are different in detail. If I observe the sky through a telescope, no two nights are exactly alike. And there always are a finite number of data points based on finite data: data is always "sparse" and taken from a certain perspective. Perspective introduces a (highly restricted) subjective relativism into science. Data is thus *an uncertain image of the real*. Even in the clearest scientific air, there remains a trace of haziness.

The theoretical half of science is the explanation and understanding of the data: it encompasses all mathematical laws, all categorizations; in other words, it contains all "meaning." It is an explanation of the existing data, a hypothesis. Theories do not merely explain existing data. They go *beyond* the data in that they make predictions that point to future observations. Theories can make stunning predictions of phenomena that empirical data-fitting would never lead to. Perhaps the best example was the famous prediction of Einstein's general theory of relativity that gravitational fields bend light rays. No one had even thought of looking for such a thing until Einstein predicted it.

Theory, when compared to observation and experiment, at first seems ethereal and somehow unreal. Now, theory certainly deals with the *ideal*. Theories are constructed in the mind of the scientist in order to understand the data. Yet, in one very important sense, theories have more reality (or more objectivity) than data. Theories are exact and precise. They do not vary from day to day. Even though constructed in the mind, they need not be subjective or dependent on a particular scientist's state of mind.

Observation and theory are both essential to the scientific method. Take away either and the wheels of science will brake to a halt. However, while vast efforts may be expended in scientific observation, theory is science's ultimate object. Science seeks the *laws* that govern the entire natural world, *not* isolated factoids or tables of properties. Conversely, without a discoverable order in reality, empirical facts or data would be entirely meaningless. There are an infinite number of facts. Scientists do not study the exact shape of particular rocks; they seek to know the laws of falling bodies or the chemical composition of minerals. Experiment is the taking of data under controlled conditions to answer specific questions; it is not *random* observation. In other words, natural science uses experiment and observation as a means to get at the nature of things.

The dynamic of science leads not only *outward*, but also *upward*. Scientific explanation progresses toward unity and simplicity. New and improved theories yield simpler and more elegant descriptions of phenomena. The next chapter, for example, examines the progress of celestial mechanics models in detail. Each step of that progress, from Ptolemy through Copernicus to Newton and beyond, moved towards greater simplicity, unity, and generality.

Theory is an explanatory construct – freely constructed in the mind as an explanation of what is given in data. It is the notion of *explanation* – of having grasped the causes of the phenomena, of being able to *understand completely* why something occurs – that makes theory attractive. Such allure lay at the beginnings of science. Why, for example, was the Pythagorean theorem worth bothering with?[1]:

"Why should it be so important to devise a proof which adds nothing to the empirical knowledge already available? What distinguishes the Greek philosopher from the careful observers in Egypt? The answer is: Through his act a theory was born; the surface of mere correlation was broken, subsurface explanation had begun."

For the pragmatic Egyptian surveyor, approximate formulations were good enough, but would always fall short in particular cases. But the Greek mathematician grasped not the properties of this or that right triangle, but those that belong to *all* triangles, without exception. Having the essence of all triangles, the properties of any particular triangle could be deduced.

The scientific method is not, however, like mathematical or logical deduction (although it involves deduction) – *it is a dynamic*. In it, theory and experiment are able to guide each other, converging on the truth of reality. What drives science forward is this dynamic, iterative *relation* between theory and experiment. Scientific method is nothing more than the reciprocal motion between theory and observation. Without it, experiment would drift into aimless researches, and theory would degenerate into an irresolvable thicket of competing ideas. It is precisely this dynamism that made modern science possible at all. It allowed science to break out the box of theories based only on everyday observations (e.g., Ptolemy's earth-centered universe) and to keep observation on the path of truth (e.g., the growth of chemistry out of alchemy). This dynamism gives the scientist confidence in the truth of the scientific method: that theories, although constructs of the human mind, do correspond to the actual order of the world.

## Models and the Synthesis of Data and Theory

From the above discussion, it is easy to see the many similarities between models and simulations, on the one hand, and the scientific method, on the other. Seeing how observation, explanation, and prediction all work together, we can now examine further their connection with modeling. In fact, the model, as an abstract image, is the meeting point or synthesis of data and theory. This is why the model has been inadequately understood in the past. The computer model is the crystallization of the relation of theory and data in digital form. It is neither theory nor experiment: *it is the relation itself.*

It should be clear that computer modeling and simulation do not constitute experiments in the proper sense of the term. Computer simulations are often referred to as "numerical experiments" and their results as "data"[2]. They are used to test theories, just as experimental data is. Any modeler strives to make the model reflect the data to the best degree possible; a model, to be worth anything, must be able to reproduce the data when queried from without by the same observational conditions. And like data, the results of computer simulations can be characterized by statistical error. Yet they cannot be experiments in the ordinary sense of the word, because they do not involve measurements or observations of actual, physical things. They are, when all is said and done, calculations. The danger is when the results of computer models and simulation are blithely treated as if they were actualities, similar to substituting an image of something for the thing itself.

It seems that modeling and simulation should be classified as a branch of theory instead. There are certainly several similarities of the two. Computer models are often based on theories; it is a point of pride for the computational scientist to say that one's models derive from theoretical first principles, rather than being merely an empirical replica.

Yet the term model implies a *description*, as opposed to theory, which explains the causes of things. Consider the following discussion of atomic models from a quantum physics text[3]:

"J.J. Thompson proposed a tentative description, or *model*, of an atom according to which negatively charged electrons were located within a continuous distribution of positive charge."

In other words, Thompson's empirical "plum pudding" model did not *explain* the atom; it only *described* certain observed features of it (i.e., the fact it had electrons in it, bound together by some sort of positively charged field). But scientists become restless with mere models, if only for the reason that so many models have proven mortal, made obsolete by the newest data. This was the fate of the first atomic model. A new picture of the atom with a nucleus orbited by electrons like miniature planets was envisioned by Bohr, and transformed into an actual theoretical explanation by quantum mechanics. Quantum mechanics gave not only a picture of the atom, but also an understanding of *how* all its parts fit together.

In the model, there need be no full understanding of the forces or causes at work in the subject system. All that is required is that observed phenomena are accounted for and that no established scientific laws are transgressed. Previous chapters explained that models are usually incomplete, based on a particular purpose or perspective. And so the model seems to lack the solidity and objectivity of theory, at least in the hard sciences. It was true for the atom; it was also true for the cosmos. We know the earth-centered universe of Ptolemy and Aristotle to be theoretically false, but it was an entirely adequate *model* of the heavens if one's aim was to describe the apparent motions of the sun, moon, and planets. It was not inaccuracy, but the strange and complicated artifices of the Ptolemaic model, such as epicycles, cut off from any known causes, that led to its downfall. Modern science began when Copernicus, Galileo, Kepler, and Newton were able to replace that model with an understanding that was not only simpler, but was based on a *theory* of gravitation that explained why the planets moved as they did.  It was an explanation that formed a *system*, and its laws and implications were universal, quite unlike the Ptolemaic epicycles.

The process is also an analysis of the order of the phenomenon being studied, progressively peeling the onion of orders, from the most obvious to the most subtle.  For example, suppose we examine a very large number of crystals of NaCl, table salt. We will find they are cubic. If we average the measured shapes of salt crystals, we would have something very close to a cube.  So we see the ideal figure -- the model -- of a cube in the imperfect figures of actual salt.  This leads us to suppose that there is an intrinsic ordering principle in salt that causes it to be cubic: the perfect salt crystal would be cubic and any divergence from that form is accidental.  No particular salt crystal I select will be a perfect cube. There will always be scratches or nicks or another crystal growing off its side.  Even a seemingly perfect crystal reveals defects under the examination of a microscope.  By seeing a cube in each imperfect salt crystal, I am abstracting what I consider to be the most important aspect of its form.  And this supposition turns out to be correct, because the crystalline lattice of salt, the arrangement of the sodium and chlorine atoms, is indeed cubic.  Even if our initial guess could not explain fully the causes of the cubic structure, *it led to it*, and that is the essential thing.

If models seem so definitely inferior to theory, then why use them? The question from Chapter Two is raised again in a new context.  The answer comes precisely from the fact that models are not so pure and universal as theory.  If they reach to the theoretical skies, they also have their feet firmly planted on the ground of reality.  They are essentially mediators between theory and data: as abstract, they are pure like theory, but as images, they can replicate particular situations.

This points to the most important distinction between the model and theory, and this time very much in the model's favor.  The model — including, of course, computer models — can reproduce the *specificity*, the particulars, the details, of a given situation.  No theory can.  Theory, of its nature, deals with general laws.  Consider, for example, a model of a suspension bridge.  A small physical model built of plastic and wood would be effective in showing what the bridge looks like or how it fits into its surroundings. But suppose we are interested in studying its structural aspects: how far it would sway in gale force winds, whether it could survive a magnitude 8 earthquake, or how large its foundation needs to be. Difficult to study with pencil and paper or with a plastic architectural model, it is ideally suited for computer modeling. Suppose, then, that we construct a computer model of the bridge. We would include, most importantly, all the girders, cables, and piers that compose it, the distribution of weight throughout the structure, and so on. The model would certainly draw upon theory: it would use the laws of physics to calculate loads, flexing, stress and strain for all parts of the structure. So the model, to be of any use, would certainly be an application of theory. But at the same time, we see how the model is not theory as such. It is not a model of suspension bridges in general: it is a model of *one particular* bridge. Unlike theory, it can represent, to a level of detail limited only by our computer's memory and speed, the specificity of the building. This is not only true of the overall design (e.g., we are modeling the Golden Gate Bridge), but of the details themselves: the model accounts for the fact that the girders are made of a particular kind of steel with its own particular properties, and likewise for its support cables and concrete foundations. Our model, then, is like an image of the bridge and not an ordinary photograph, but an x-ray picture. It shows us the entire system, and its specific details, just as a picture would. It also tells us how the bridge will behave dynamically, thus it is like a series of pictures.

This is why the model is neither theory nor experiment, but a synthesis of the two. It contains *the expression of general laws in particular things*. Because they are based on the theoretical laws that are supposedly the underpinnings of the observed phenomena, the model can be extended and manipulated to answer questions about the system being studied that are not given in immediate data. They can extend knowledge. Unlike data alone, models can make predictions that can then be tested. The unity of theory and data that models provide is also what makes them a tool for designing new things. We can reliably take the properties of known things and project beyond them to compose new things.

The topic of how data and theory are brought together — the synthetic aspect of science — is not normally discussed beyond a statistical discussion of "goodness of fit" of theoretical predictions. The synthesis of data and theory normally takes place in the mind of the scientist or engineer. The model, but especially the computer model, is a means of representing this combination. The model, because it contains the relation of universals to particulars, mediates between theory and observation, between the general laws and specific data. The abstract image has an epistemological solidity that derives from ties to both empirical observation and theoretical law.

The problem of model validity is really the problem of *induction*. Induction is how science goes from data to theory, from particular events to general laws. From a series of observations of falling objects (even an apple falling from a tree, if need be), the physicist determines the laws governing gravitation. The hypothetical laws can then be tested by further experiments and observations. Scientific theory builds models of reality, and continually revises and refines those models on the basis of new information. It is the endless cycle of theory and experiment as was discussed earlier. But the validity of this cycle, and hence the validity of science as a whole, depends upon induction[4]. How is it that a general law can be expressed in, and discerned in, a set of unique and individual events? This is really the age-old philosophic problem of the relation of universals and particulars in scientific guise.

Empirical data is inducted into laws which form the basis of every model: the mass and shape of a bird's wing, the half-life of a radioactive isotope, the Young's modulus of an automotive shock absorber, the rate at which a particular strain of yeast ferments beer as a function of temperature. These facts in turn form the basis for more general laws – aerodynamics, mechanics, quantum theory, biochemistry – which also form the basis of any model. In other words, the reliability of models can rest firmly on a foundation of scientific laws. The validation of the components of a model means replicating the data as closely as possible. If the components of a complex model are based on laws and empirical data, then we can have confidence in the predictions of the model as a whole. The assumption is that, if we get the basic properties of objects and the laws governing their interactions expressed properly in the model, then the model should produce valid results for a system of any size: the solar system model could be adapted easily to model the planetary systems of other stars, the dynamics of galaxies, or investigate the stability of Saturn's rings.

We discern something else about models here. And that is while the "primary models" which capture the specific properties (state variables) of objects are simply empirical data, the relations of objects in a complex system and any dynamic system presuppose going beyond simple observations to using laws that combine many observations. Such interactions must represent a multiplicity of possible states as a related whole – a property as a function of time or position or other condition – and this is possible only through a law. In other words, the synthesis of the basic components of a complex model into a single system depends on the existence of laws of some sort. Without laws, there is no way of treating the system as a whole: it falls apart into effectively disjoint pieces. This is how theoretical laws get manifested in models, and they are just as necessary to models as empirical measurements are. The model in turn provides a way of testing theory through its predictions, since it can do easily what no general and abstract theory can: represent particular situations in their completeness. This is especially important for complex systems where a multitude of physical laws are involved. For example, we can calculate directly the dynamics the earth and moon, but a consideration of the entire solar system (as a many-body problem) requires a simulation. Simulation alone in such cases allows theory to make predictions – if forming a model is analogous to induction, then every model simulation is the equivalent of theoretical deduction.

What gives us confidence in any model (as with any theory) is to make predictions outside the scope of the original model data, and verify these predictions in new observations. Comprehensive validation of models means not just replicating present data, but a continuing process of validation of model predictions against new data. Theory (as the next section explains) of its nature points beyond present data to future possibilities. Models do this as well. They do not just replicate, but extend, human knowledge.

Computer modeling and simulation represent the ultimate extension of the scientific understanding of the world. They are now essential to modern science and engineering, because they provide a means of grasping patterns in complex phenomena that are inaccessible to simple calculation or unaided human visualization. Even in physics, the most mathematical of the natural sciences, only relatively simple systems can be calculated directly. Computer simulation is essential in understanding such complex problems as the earth's atmosphere, ecosystems, global commerce, complex molecules, fluid mechanics, turbulence, and many-body systems. Without computer models, such phenomena could only be described (not understood or explained) in an approximate, qualitative sense. With models, it is possible to test theories against complex data in a way that the unaided theorist could never attain.

By crystallizing or representing the junction point between theory and data, by containing their synthesis, we can use models to understand phenomena where the relation of theory and data is too complicated -- due to numbers of objects in the system and the intricacies of their interrelations -- to be held in the mind of a single researcher. The real promise of computer modeling and simulation lies here. It means the emergence of the synthetic aspect of science as a distinct endeavor. The computer modeler synthesizes theory with experimental data. The synthesis, the joining of theory and data, is something as important in extending knowledge as making observations or positing theories.

### Induction, Deduction, and the Socrates File

There is thus a clear family resemblance between the modeling process and the scientific method. The reverse analogy, however, also holds. Understanding models shows how scientific knowledge comes about, and what its possible limits are. Considering this takes us deep into the question of the roles of induction and deduction in both models and science.

At first glance, the problem seems straightforward. On the one side, there are empirical measurements: sizes, masses, velocities, locations in space, durations in time. On the other side, there are theories or laws describing the relations of these quantities to each other -- location as a function of time, for example. The theories or laws are conceptual or abstract in character. They are constructs of the mind. The fundamental question that "induction" seeks to answer is: *how are theories derived from data?*

In the classical theory of induction, upheld by Francis Bacon, as the researcher collects more and more data about any natural phenomenon, the theory or law emerges automatically. It stood the deductive approach to phenomena, typical of thought before the scientific revolution, on its head. From Bacon, too, ultimately derives the stereotype of the scientist as a passive data accumulator, approaching the facts with no preconceptions, whose mind is the blank slate on which Nature will write her laws through the intermediary of careful measurement.

Conversely, deduction is what allows theories to make predictions and discover linkages between different theories. Theory, too, is a field of discovery, and here, in contrast to the passive observer, is the image of the scientist as heroic genius, wresting something entirely new from old data.

Yet nearly all would agree that scientific knowledge, to be meaningful, must start from some data. Theorists are not permitted to speculate in a data vacuum, since this results in theories like astrology that, however logically self-consistent, have no relevance to the world we live in. (We can *imagine* a world where astrology is true, and someone could build a computer game simulating it, but it is not *our* world.) So the root of all science must be the data, and laws derived directly from the data, using induction. And the test of validity of any theory, regardless how ingenious and high-flown it is, must be the predictions it makes against existing and future data. Modeling and scientific methods are in complete agreement here. Induction is the linchpin of all natural science. Remove it, and science falls apart into two disconnected halves: isolated observations that yield no wider results and theoretical constructs that can never be validated.

The contrast between deduction and induction can be seen from a purely logical angle. In deduction, we argue from known premises to a conclusion implied necessarily by those premises. To use *the* famous example, given that all men are mortal and Socrates is a man, it follows that Socrates is mortal. Seen comprehensively, the deduction tells us nothing new — the fact that Socrates is mortal is contained in the fact of his humanity. The deduction simply fills in more details that we already knew, as if we were opening a previously compiled dossier on Socrates. The deduction proceeds from the general to the specific, in that mortality, an attribute of *all* men, is deduced to necessarily be an attribute of *one particular* man, Socrates. Induction puts this process in reverse. Induction argues from sets of particular instances to general properties or identities[5]. To continue with the example, an induction regarding Socrates might assert: Socrates is mortal, therefore Socrates is a man. It's obvious this inference is a paralogism. Socrates might be an angelfish or a Sequoia tree or any other living being. Being a man is merely one possibility.

If the problem were left at this point, it would clearly be hopeless and no one would assert any value for induction at all. But the theory of induction goes further. As we collect more and more data about things, we can get a steadily clearer picture of what their properties and interrelations are. Induction asserts that *in the limit* of infinitely detailed data, inferences will pass from possibility to necessity.

Along these lines, too, we see that induction is really a sophisticated process of elimination -- not so much saying what something is as saying what it is not. If we say that Socrates is mortal, we are not able to necessarily assert he must be a man, but we *can* infer that Socrates is not a rock or a planet or a new model of automobile. Since the question of mortality is irrelevant for them, we can eliminate them from consideration and narrow down the possibilities. In other words, the inductive method of verification is really one of falsification. This points to Karl Popper's famous falsification criterion – meaningful theories are those capable of being falsified in data.

Process of elimination works perfectly nicely when the number of possible explanations is finite and some way exists of reducing the possibilities with present or future data. The mortal Socrates must be either plant or animal; further investigation will tell us which. If I am walking along a path, my next step may be upslope, downslope, or level — it must be one of these three possibilities. Only rarely, however, are we presented with a finite induction scenario. Usually, there are an unlimited number of possible outcomes.

Ponder for a moment the lines or curves passing through points: any two points, to be precise. The simplest line through the points is, of course, a straight line. But it is not the only such line; in fact an *infinite* number of possible curves pass through the points. It seems that any induction is perfectly meaningless here. But looking deeper, we see something else. There is also an infinite family of lines *ruled out* by the two points. Now, suppose the two points were data and we are attempting to fit the points with a curve on a piece of graph paper. The two points automatically divide the possible curves into two groups: the possible and the impossible. The two points act as constraints that eliminate an entire family of lines from consideration. At the same time, the lines that *do* pass through the points both extrapolate and interpolate from the sparse data to give us a *complete* set of possible explanations. This serves to remind one that, while induction proceeds by elimination, it really is a process of extrapolating beyond present to possible outcomes. This is something we do informally every day. Repeated occurrences of a given sequence of events leads us to believe that such will always be the case, and we act on such assumptions accordingly. This is both the utility and the main problem with inductive methods.

Adding more points or constraints shrinks the family of allowed curves. If the line must be straight, then just two points uniquely determines that line, just as three points will determine a curve of second order, and so on. We need not have an infinite number of points. Suppose we wish to reveal an arbitrary curve to someone else point by point. As each point is uncovered, the number of possible curves steadily decreases -- the answer converges to our curve by a process of elimination. At the limit of infinite points, the smooth curve emerges entirely.

Or consider the more down to earth problem of a falling object (pun intended). We carry out an experiment of measuring the time of fall from various heights. The drop is repeated several times at each height to minimize statistical error. We notice that each measurement is slightly different. To obtain even the raw data, we average over all the measurements for a given height, and assign an appropriate error, based on the scattering of the measurements. If our instruments are imprecise, the error will be large. If we plot the height versus the time of fall, we notice that there is a definite pattern, one that is closely proportional to the time squared. Assuming there is some pattern or law behind what we observe, as we make more and better measurements, the data should converge to line of the law. At the limit of infinite data, we should be able to "lift" the law right out of the data regardless of how complex it is. At less complexity, this can be done for a finite number of points. This latter point is important, because to have an authentic induction, we must be able to grasp a general law based on a *finite* amount of data. In practical terms, data is always more or less sparse[6].

## The Limits of Empiricism, Or, Will the Sun Rise Tomorrow?

The classical heritage of philosophy and natural science in the West, as represented by the Aristotelian school of thought, had a strong preference for deduction. One obtained certain axioms from experience and then deduced their consequences[7]. All well and good in logic, but mostly fruitless when it came to the study of natural phenomena. The birth of natural science in the West in the 16th and 17th Centuries brought to prominence two new ways of looking at the order of the world that had been downplayed in previous thought: the notion of the world being ordered mathematically and the notion of empirical research as the grounding of theory. Mathematical physics — the first of the modern sciences — was born when Galileo was able to tie these two lines of thought together.

But the relation of mathematical theory and empirical data was problematic from the first. The first intellectual salvo of thought's new world was launched by Descartes, and it was one of a purely mathematical and deductive science, certainly less empirical than its Aristotelian rival. Cartesian science proved as barren as its predecessors, but the methods of the advance of science were coming out of scientific work itself. The entire notion of induction was formulated by Francis Bacon on the basis of that work. Bacon was not a much of a scientist himself — he was really the first science popularizer – but he codified the central point of the scientific method, and turned the viewpoint round from mathematics to empirical data[8].

This essentially empirical view was reinforced by the success of Newton's physics. The success of the new science found a philosophical expression in Locke, which in turn spread far and wide in popularized forms (e.g., Fontenelle and Voltaire). Newton assumed that the order of nature was essentially mathematical; he was a brilliant mathematician as well as physicist. Science obtains its laws by induction, and these laws are formulated in mathematical terms, and phenomena can then be explained deductively from these laws. So was Newton a "pure" empiricist? Not really, since he assumed that behind the empirically derived laws was an order of Nature that was simple, uniform, and universal, and this universal order (and here Newton concurred with Descartes) had a divine guarantee[9].

That a purely empirical (or anti-theoretical) view of induction wobbles on its foundations can be seen in the thought of John Stuart Mill, the clearest exponent of induction in the 19th Century. On the one hand, Mill is a strict empiricist: we cannot attain absolute truth, and all generalizations are revisable in principle[10]. He returns to the famous "Socrates is mortal" syllogism — how do we *really* know that all men are mortal? On the other hand, he differentiated, rather like Bacon, between properly scientific induction and "slovenly generalization." Behind the induction from sparse data and a finite number of instances to a universal law, there lies the principle of the uniformity of Nature[11]. Induction, to be truthful, *depends on assumptions before one even approaches the data*. Mill is surely correct in this. Without such principles as the uniformity of Nature, induction merely results in a handy summary of empirical data, rather like the views of Comte or Mach or the Vienna Circle positivists, for whom scientific theory had the same status as a telephone book or a railway timetable[12]. The spectacular successes of physical theory in the 20th Century (e.g., Einstein's Theory of Relativity) lead one to suspect something is wrong with this view, but if science is considered in a completely Baconian fashion, plodding naively from one data set to another and hoping that general laws will emerge all on their own, the criticism is true enough.

Thus we have the paradox that "since the time of Hume, the fashionable scientific philosophy had been to deny the rationality of science"[13].

Induction's problematic nature is illuminated by a deceptively simple example, taken from David Hume himself. Hume asks us: Will the sun rise tomorrow? And our natural reply is, "of course it will — what a silly question." But he says to that — in essence — *not so fast*[14]:

"The contrary of every matter of fact is still possible ... That the sun will not rise tomorrow is no less intelligible a proposition, and implies no more contradiction, than the affirmation that it will rise. We should in vain, therefore, attempt to demonstrate its falsehood."

Now, why do we say the sun will rise tomorrow? Principally because we have always experienced it to rise each day: a classic inductive situation, since we extrapolate from what we *have* experienced to predicting what we *will* experience in the future. And, after a moment's reflection, we can think of numerous situations and causes, all perfectly plausible (if unlikely), that might result in the sun *not* rising tomorrow: the sun might become a nova and burn up the earth; the earth might be struck by an asteroid so it stops rotating, or the universe might suddenly come to an end just as it once suddenly came to be. Or we could consider a far simpler case: we live just above the Arctic Circle and tomorrow is the winter solstice. In other words, there is nothing, on the purely logical and conceptual level, that gives us an ironclad assurance that the sun will rise tomorrow.

We can think of other instances where induction seems to mislead us, such as the famous *post hoc, propter hoc* fallacy of the rooster's crowing causing the sun to rise: simply because we observe the crowing is followed by the sun's rising does not allow us to infer it *causes* the sun to rise. As one philosopher of science (who, unlike Hume, was certainly not a skeptic) observed[15]:

"a whole realm of familiar facts has been overlooked by philosophers who strove to justify science by ascribing a unique reliability to the *inductive* method. Constant conjunction would lead to absurd predictions ... Our expectation of life does not increase with the number of days we have survived."

Such are the dangers of a pure or naive empiricism. The fact that we act upon the inductive method in a practical sense — what is and has been, will be — is no guarantee of its validity in an absolute sense.

At the same time, the mind revolts against the implications of skepticism toward induction. Not only does it set practical reason in conflict with theory[16], it would be completely destructive of all science, reducing experiment to disconnected observations and cutting speculative theory off from any possible roots in reality. It seems absurd that the sun's rising could be arbitrary and capricious. Indeed, our understanding of its rising is *not* based *merely* upon the observation of repeated risings. We say we understand it by reference to the rotation of the earth, the relation of the earth to the sun as two massive bodies, the revolution of the earth about the sun, and so on. The physical principles applied to the system of the earth and the sun also happen to describe and predict the behavior and appearance of the moon and other planets -- both with respect to the sun and to the earth. Such general laws can be drawn from, and apply to, not just the earth and the sun, but all physical systems. Now this is the mark of scientific induction: a general law obtained from observation of some particular case finds application whenever similar causes appear.

Not only do these physical principles explain why the sun rises, they also comprehend why the sun might *not* rise. Setting aside any detailed consideration of the laws themselves (such as gravity), we notice something about our explanation. We are explaining in terms of an earth - sun *system*. We separate this system from its "background" of the other planets and other stars, in order to study it alone. We abstract from the sun and earth, considering them only as extended bodies with mass. We discover the laws governing this system. We can say, with complete confidence, that the sun *will* rise tomorrow, *unless* something intervenes from outside. The system operates on its own laws, and will continue to do so, until disturbed or until it ceases to be. It is this notion of a physical system, governed by laws, that distinguishes dynamics from mere kinematics (e.g., an animated film of a sunrise). Put differently, the question "Will the sun rise tomorrow?" has a different meaning for us than it did for Ptolemy. For us, the solar system is truly a system, governed by universal laws.

The whole notion of the sun rising on its own is impossible without an order or system. We could never understand the earth and sun as we do unless there was some system of recurrences. In point of fact, we are not given the earth and the sun separately; we are given them both together, and the analysis is performed by us. In other words, we do not mentally glue together earth and sun to form a system. Far from it: whenever we observe, or measure, or experiment, we abstract the system from its context and then analyze it into components — *just as in modeling*. That is why in a scientific experiment, one tries to isolate the system being studied to the highest degree possible. We see here again, too, the sort of assumptions that modeling and simulation discover: the assumption of an isolated system. In other words, assuming a system both makes induction possible and defines its limit. It is limited to the degree that a system cannot be abstracted from the background phenomena. Whenever theory and data meet, there must be similar assumptions.

This implies, then, that a naive and unaided induction yielding absolute laws or ascending to universality is impossible. They yield what is probable, not what is certain. Authentic realization of theory cannot proceed *merely* by induction in this sense -- which is to say the generalization of many acts of perception[17]. Theories, in other words, do not automatically spring out of the data. Inductive inference is not a substitute for true science. In other words, there can be no such thing as "pure" induction, if induction is to be a meaningful source of truth at all. In fact, in any induction there are already idealizations or abstractions or categories at work; in every supposed pure induction, theory is already present in some form or another, to make the induction possible at all.

The model, as we have seen, contains the combination or synthesis of theory and data. It follows that some sort of model – explicit or implicit – is necessary to both induction and prediction. Models, of their essence as abstract images, mediate between theory and empirical laws and make comparison of data and theory possible[18]. This can be understood by returning to the analogy of model and map made in Chapter 2. The map is an abstraction and symbolization of a land and its features. At the same time, it is possible for a map to act as the basis of a theory. Consider a detailed map of ocean currents, for example. Generally, such a map is a finite set of arrows (straight or curved) imposed at regular intervals upon an outline map of the ocean or sea. The arrows point in the direction of the current, and their lengths may indicate a current's speed. What such a map embodies is a model; it represents velocity vectors as arrows at a grid of locations. It would be possible to calculate the theoretical prediction of ocean currents at each of these locations and compare them.

The role of model as mediator can be seen from the side of theory also. The model is that system to which a theory applies perfectly, rather than approximately like empirical data[19]. The simple mechanics problem of a thrown object following a parabolic trajectory is an example of this: the object is an idealized mass-point and the parabola it traces out is a perfect expression of Newton's laws of motion. This idealized picture can then be applied to an actual trajectory, which will neither be exact (due to inherent errors of measurement) nor perfect (due to air drag, the fact the object is not a mass-point, etc.). It is the model that makes possible both the prediction of new observables and the comparison of predictions with data.

Models, as Graves asserts[20], really function as "ontological hypotheses" for the scientist, capturing in ideal form the salient features of a system. They provide, at least, a conceptual way of approaching a real system, starting out abstract and progressively becoming more detailed. The previously mentioned mass-point and extended body of classical physics are examples. A large number of physical systems can be modeled (at a very abstract level) as harmonic oscillators. In fact, very abstract models such as the harmonic oscillator point to another important role of models in scientific knowledge – their transferability. A model that arises from the analysis of one kind of phenomenon may find application to completely different phenomena. The corpuscular hypothesis (atoms as tiny "billiard balls") originated as a theoretical artifice, but it bore fruit in the kinetic theory of gases and quantitative chemistry. On the other hand, a specific "black box" model of a system or phenomenon is not likely to be transferable. Transferability of models is a measure of their universality and objectivity. Such universality is usually had only at the abstract level.

Importantly, however, we must not regard models as static. Rather, as an embodiment of scientific method, they will continually develop and improve. They will crystallize in many ways the current state of the science. In physical models, for example, the mechanical notion of extended bodies, mass-points, and absolute space gave way in the 20th Century to the modern physical notions of quantum wave-packets and relativistic space-time. The next chapter will provide an extended example of how models dealing with the same phenomena change and evolve over time.

## Summary: Modeling, Simulation, and the Dynamic of Discovery

Within modeling and simulation there is a dynamic, the dynamic of the scientific method itself. Our investigations of the world give rise to a network of "laws" that are at work even in our simplest experiences. That which appears enigmatic at first is progressively and gradually explained. Scientific induction and prediction is a long process of narrowing down of possibilities and convergence. It rarely sorts out rival hypotheses at one stroke, but over a long period of time. As the possibilities narrow, the predictive ability of theory sharpens and may suddenly become dramatic and universal. The movement closer to the true order is a hunt, an adventure, and this is what drives science onwards.

A valid theory defines not a *single* existence, but a whole class of *possible* existences, of which the real world is one. As science progresses, the field of possible existences is narrowed, but it is never entirely reduced to the singular. The relation of theory to reality is thus one of "resonance" with a certain aspect of reality. And this is what models really represent, the linkage of ideal form with several actual possibilities.

So induction is a process in that we start out with little data and vague explanation (or multiple explanations) and end up with much data and convergence to a single explanation or a limited number of explanations. It is this process of convergence that validates any particular induction along the way. It is convergence that gives scientists and philosophers confidence in the scientific method. One or another individual generalization may be doubtful, but the process is not[22]. The mediator of the convergence for both induction and prediction is the model. In addition, the model represents the expression of general laws in particular things. It allows theories to make specific predictions.

We can now summarize the close similarities between the modeling process and that of the scientific process:

(1) The model assumes it is dealing with an isolated system, which can be abstracted from its "background", its connections to a wider world. There are no interventions from without the model needs to consider or, if they are, they are completely known ahead of time.
(2) It assumes the objects modeled can indeed be reduced to a system, governed by deterministic (preferably mathematical) laws.
(3) It assumes the system can be analyzed as to its properties, and if it is a composite system, then analyzed into components, which can further be analyzed into subsystems.
(4) It assumes that models are based on complete enough data; laws governing the models are inductions. The quality of the model here can be known through the normal statistical measures of data quality. Completeness also means inclusion of all factors that affect a system.
(5) It assumes we can extrapolate and interpolate from the model, through simulations, to predict possible new data.

The key question for any simulation here is one of prediction: does the replication of known data by simulation mean that prediction of future data is necessarily possible? If the above conditions are met, the answer will be yes. Conversely, to the degree the conditions are *not* met, predictive quality will necessarily degrade. The model may be capable only of making very general predictions, perhaps so general as to be essentially worthless.

# Chapter 6

# Modeling the Appearances

The intent of this chapter is to expand upon the theme of the last, but more importantly, to descend from theoretical discussion with a real-life example. It is meant to answer the "Missourians" in the audience who demand: show me. The example has been already alluded to: the progression of celestial mechanics models from the ancient Greeks to the present day.

Celestial mechanics is ideally suited to this purpose. No topic in modeling has a longer history or can better illustrate how models both capture present knowledge and help extend it. The study of the motions of the planets is the oldest natural science. It was also the principal catalyst for the emergence of modern, mathematical-empirical science as we know it. It richness of topics, in areas like nonlinear dynamics and the many-body problem, has still not been exhausted. Many of the greatest minds in mathematics and physics, among them Galileo, Kepler, Newton, Laplace, Poincare, and Einstein, have in some way either pondered celestial mechanics for their own sake or used them as a laboratory to test physical theories.

The models and topics examined here will be: Ptolemy's geocentric model, the heliocentric model of Copernicus, the crucial contribution of Kepler in understanding planetary motions, Newton's theory of universal gravitation, the application of Newtonian dynamics in the discovery of the planet Neptune, and finally the famous precession of the perihelion of Mercury's orbit as a test of Einstein's general theory of relativity.

The intent is certainly not to present a history of astronomy, or even of celestial mechanics as such. Instead, it is to examine critically how the motions of the planets, sun, moon, and earth were represented at each stage and what changed in the succession of models. In this, I do not purport to add anything to what has been said by historians and philosophers of science, or scientists themselves. Rather, it is to unroll the history of the models and in that history to make clear what has changed, what has persisted, and what constitutes progress in modeling.

Among the points this extended example should elucidate are:

(1) The intimate relation between model-building and the scientific method.
(2) The essential role of underlying assumptions and preconceived notions in both modeling and scientific induction: the isolated system, the constancy of laws, and so on.
(3) The convergence of the model representation to the answer, and moreover, the kind of convergence: toward greater unity, simplicity, and depth.
(4) The attributes of each celestial mechanics model in turn.
(5) The amenity of celestial mechanics to treatment by modeling methods (that is, its conformity to the modeling paradigm) in comparison to other systems.

On this last point, there is no doubt that celestial mechanics are a nearly perfect fit to the modeling paradigm – in many respects, it is the source of it. The solar system, separated as it is from other stars, with only a very weak gravitational influence from the galaxy as a whole, is one of the closest approximations to a closed system we know of[1]. Its observable dynamics are entirely explained through the forces within the system itself. Also, the solar system is readily analyzed into point-like objects (i.e., the sun, the planets, and their moons), interacting entirely through the single force relation of gravity. The dynamics of the solar system do not depend on the details of the objects involved, just their masses, locations, and velocities. Finally, the dynamics of the system, on the whole, are not complicated. They are dominated by the gravitational forces of the sun, with the interactions of the planets among themselves far less important and in fact ignorable in a first approximation. (It is not entirely ignorable, however, as the section on the discovery of Neptune will explain.) All the planets except Pluto (or all of them, if we now exclude Pluto from the planetary club!) follow orbits that are close to being circular and all orbit the sun in nearly the same plane of revolution. This is not the case, for example, for our nearest neighbor in the galaxy, Alpha Centauri. Alpha Centauri is a triple star system with the primary and secondary in eccentric orbit about one another. Planetary orbits in such systems could be very complex or unstable. A Copernicus on Alpha Centauri III would perhaps confront a puzzle too difficult to solve.

## Observables for Celestial Mechanics

Another interesting fact about celestial mechanics is that the observable data remained remarkably stable for centuries – essentially from the time of the Babylonians up to the discovery of the telescope. The observables were those available to the naked eye and with simple measuring instruments such as the astrolabe. Both Ptolemy and Copernicus were working from the same data despite the separation of fourteen centuries between them. It is important to keep this in mind, as the birth of modern astronomy with Copernicus, Kepler, and Newton was not due to the sudden appearance of new data that overturned the old hypotheses (in good Baconian fashion), but to the reinterpretation of the same data in the light of new models. These basic observables for astronomy are summarized in Table 1. All this observational data is available to anyone with a view of the sky and a way of taking the angular measurements.

The observables are essentially a collection of appearances, of the motions of luminous objects in the sky. Some patterns, such as the apparent daily rotation of the heavens or the monthly movements and phases of the moon, were obvious even to prehistoric peoples. The cycles of the year and the general motion of the planets through the fixed stars of the zodiac were ascertained almost as easily. Others, such as the anomalous movements of the planets or the precession of the equinoxes, required a great amount of painstaking observations over a long period of time. The Babylonians in particular stand out among ancient peoples in the pre-scientific (which is to say, pre-theoretical) era of astronomy in their careful accumulation of observational data.

Table 6-1. A Summary of Basic Observables for Celestial Mechanics.

| | |
|---|---|
| Types of objects observed | Point objects<br>Fixed stars<br>Planets (regularly moving)<br>Irregularly moving or appearing: meteors, novae, etc.<br>Extended objects<br>Sun and moon (regularly moving)<br>Earth (apparently fixed)<br>Milky way as part of the fixed stars<br>Irregularly moving: comets |
| Object attributes | Apparent brightness<br>Angular location (as a function of time)<br>Angular diameter (of extended objects, such as the moon)<br>Phase (moon only) |
| Measurements (non-telescopic) | Brightness (relative scale only)<br>Position<br>With regard to the fixed stars<br>With regard to the earth's horizon<br>Size: angular diameter only (moon's diameter varies)<br>Radial information<br>Moon eclipses sun and is nearly the same angular diameter.<br>Moon occults stars and planets<br>Earth eclipses moon<br>Earth is a sphere of a radius measurable from the variation<br>    of latitude versus surface distance<br>Venus and Mercury have a maximum elongation from the<br>    sun |
| Motions | Daily day/night cycle – all objects<br>Monthly lunar cycle – moon only<br>Yearly cycle of apparent solar motion and the seasons<br>Planetary motion along the ecliptic<br>A regular motion modified by additional retrograde or<br>    apparent looping motions.<br>Precession of the equinoxes |

The observations showed that the sun, moon, and planets had regular, constant, cyclic motions that could be predicted. Events like solar eclipses could be calculated to great accuracy. (Apparently irregular or non-recurring motions, such as those of comets, immediately fell outside the scope of any primitive empirical astronomical model.) But, in addition to these general cyclic motions, there were seemingly anomalous (still predictable and recurrent) retrograde and looping motions of the planets as they travel along the ecliptic. Explaining these "anomalies'" was to be a major task for celestial modelers.

## Ptolemy and the Circular Motions of the Heavens

The *Almagest* of Ptolemy (Claudius Ptolemaeus) is the only completely comprehensive treatise of Greek astronomy that survived the downfall of the Greek and Roman world. Written around 150 AD, it can be viewed as a summing up of many centuries of ancient astronomical work[2]. His hypotheses on the nature of the cosmos were the point of departure for virtually all later astronomy in the West. In combination with Aristotle's natural philosophy, the Ptolemaic astronomy provided both a scientific picture of the world and also – through its very success in modeling actual data – a serious intellectual hurdle to be overcome by modern natural science as we know it.

For Ptolemy, as for all Greek astronomers, the task of the astronomer was to "save the appearances." By this is meant, in a minimal sense, to reproduce the apparent positions of the planets in sky as a function of time, to accurately predict lunar and solar eclipses, and so on. This is, of course, the minimal requirement of any model; it must be able to reproduce the data on which it is based. The tabular calculations of the ancient Babylonian astronomy saved the appearances in this sense, and could be viewed as a "black box" model that provided predictions without explanation. But for the Greek astronomers, to "save the appearances" went beyond this to what we properly understand as modeling. The apparent planetary data had to be explained according to a rational theory for the appearances truly to be saved[3]. It was not enough to reproduce *present* appearances; there had to be a model that saved the appearances for *all times* past and future.

By the time of the Greek astronomers, centuries of observations had been accumulated in tabular form. The Hellenic contribution did not lie in adding more data, but in its theoretical interpretation. Behind the appearances and the empirical data of planetary locations, there had to be an explanatory set of causes. In other words, the Greeks went about systematically building, for the first time, a model of celestial mechanics based on mathematical hypotheses. It meant not only seeing the same data in a new way, but seeing it as the product of an orderly and rational set of realities that caused orderly appearances. Moreover, the Greek models of the heavens were truly inductive, in that they were based upon abstracting patterns found directly in the data.

In antiquity, astronomy was the only natural science to have assumed a fully mathematical form[4]. The mathematical basis of astronomy pointed beyond a purely "black box" model, since it posited the apparent motions of the sun, moon, and planets were caused by cyclic motions that could be measured and predicted. Behind the moving spots of light in the night sky, there was a mathematical reality. What was that reality for Ptolemy? On what basic hypotheses and assumptions was Ptolemy's model of the heavens based?

The first hypothesis – really the key to all Greek astronomical theory – is that the planets move uniformly in circles, and this is the only kind of motion allowed to them. Thus, the observed motions of the sun, moon, and planets must be accounted for by a circular motion at its own rate (around the earth, as it turns out, for Ptolemy). It follows also, from observational data, that the heavens themselves must be spherical, as proven by the circular motions of stars around the pole[5]. Ptolemy's cosmic model is one of concentric spheres rotating uniformly. This accounts for the principal motions of the heavens. However, a *single* uniform circular motion is not adequate to explain every aspect of planetary motion. In addition to the daily rotation of the heavens about the earth, there was also the motion of the sun, moon, and planets along the ecliptic – that is, the zodiac. There is, as was pointed out above, the fact that the planets appear to have looping and retrograde motions. Moreover, it was observed that the planets Mercury and Venus never strayed far from the position of the Sun. The Greek astronomers had two ways of accounting for such anomalies without breaking with the essential doctrine of uniform circular motion. The first way was the notion of an epicycle, a secondary and smaller circular motion imposed upon its principal motion. The second was to suppose that the planet's circular motion could be eccentric – that it moves about a center that is not the center of the cosmos (i.e., the earth). Either the epicyclic or eccentric models could be applied recursively to any required complication, piling circles on circles until all the observed motions are accounted for[6]. In several cases, either an epicycle or an eccentric could explain the observed appearances. However, in other cases, as for the sun and moon, a combination of both epicycles and eccentrics is required to replicate the observational data. Figure 6-1 shows Ptolemy's model of lunar motions around the earth. It is obvious that to save the appearances in the full sense, the Ptolemaic model rapidly becomes very complex.

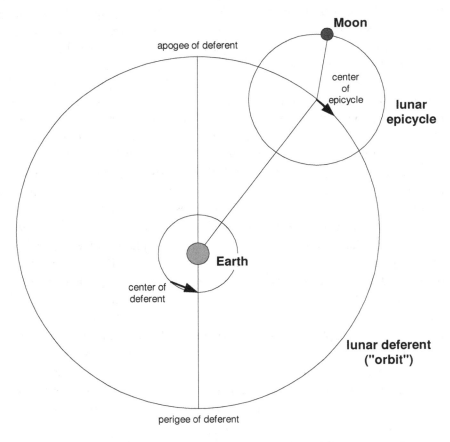

Figure 6-1. The Motion of the Moon According to the Ptolemaic Model.

The doctrine of uniform circular motion is closely related to the assumption that the earth is a sphere, albeit much smaller than the heavenly spheres as a whole. The radius of the earth is one of the few aspects of the Ptolemaic model that was measurable. (From the angle of the Sun at the solstice at two different points on the earth's surface, it was possible to derive the earth's diameter.) It was in keeping with the general tone of the model assumptions as a whole.

The second great assumption of the Ptolemaic model, and of great import for later thought, is the geocentric hypothesis: the earth is a spherical object at the center of the heavens. Moreover, it is completely stationary, moving in neither a translational nor a rotation way. We would tend to ridicule this assumption from the standpoint of modern knowledge, but as a matter of fact, it is the simplest way of accounting for appearances. For the stars, sun, moon, and planets do *appear* to be moving around us, and not us around them. (Thus, the simplest theory is not always the best one: you can cut yourself with Ockham's Razor if you're not careful.) It is also important to keep in mind that Ptolemy's geocentric hypothesis was not the only cosmic model known to the Greeks, or even at times the most accepted[7]. The Pythagoreans supposed the motion of the earth, and Aristarchus of Samos upheld a heliocentric theory more or less equivalent to that of Copernicus.

Ptolemy's arguments for an earth-centered cosmology were in fact based not on geometry (as for the rest of his model), but on Aristotle's physics and cosmology. Aristotle's universe was a giant organism with the earth as its heart and the "prime mover" beyond the sphere of the fixed stars as its mind. Aristotle drew a sharp division between physics of celestial and terrestrial entities. The planets, as celestial, were imperishable and self-moving always in cyclic fashion[8]. The earth, in contrast, was a realm of generation and corruption where things obeyed very different rules. An "astrophysics" for Aristotle would have been a contradiction in terms, since physics (the study of mutable being) applied in the strict sense only to earthly things. Plus, there was the fact, obvious to common experience, that heavy objects naturally fell downwards toward the center of the earth and light objects (e.g., fire) moved upwards away from the earth. Thus, reasoned both Aristotle and Ptolemy, the earth had to be the center of the entire cosmos. Moreover, there was almost a cultural tendency at work here: the Ptolemaic-Aristotelian earth was the cosmic equivalent of the Greek *polis*, a discrete and different realm at the center of it all[9]. It took an entirely new physics to finally dislodge geocentrism.

We can now assess the strengths and weaknesses of the Ptolemaic system from a modeling point of view. The weaknesses stand out most clearly to us today.   The most obvious weakness was the model's complexity, even though it started from the simple assumption of uniform circular motion.   The problem was, to account for all observed planetary motions, a distressingly large number of interlocking circular deferents, epicycles, and eccentrics were required – upwards of 76 in all. This was seen in the diagram for the moon above, and each planet had similar complex motions, to a greater or lesser degree.   In several cases, the corrections to the circular motion were almost as large as the principal circular motion itself – this was particularly marked in the cases of Mercury, Venus, and Mars; for the latter two, the size of the epicycle is two-thirds as large as the circular deferent (orbit).   The model's complexity would ultimately be its downfall, as we shall see, and the piling up of corrections to account for anomalies generally indicates that a simpler model is not only possible, but necessary.

Part of the problem was the doctrine of uniform circular motion: it was imposed on the system by *a priori*, theoretical fiat.   Certainly, planetary motions were a combination of cyclic motions and the circle was the simplest geometric figure capable of accounting for such cyclic motion.   This does not mean it is the only possible one, as Kepler was to point out much later on.

Second, in Ptolemy's model, each object in the system is in essence its own model, moving along a set of epicycles, deferents, and/or eccentrics particular to itself.   Other than the doctrine of uniform circular motion, there is no unity to the model.   The moon, sun, planets, and stars "suffer no influence from without; they have no relation to each other; the particular motions of each planet follow from the essence of each planet and are like the will and understanding in men.   One might almost say that the law of universal gravitation is expressly denied, and reserved only in a very particular form for bodies on the earth's surface"[10]. In many respects, each planet in the system was its own "black box" model, accounting for the observables, but incapable of explaining them or providing a unified view embracing all heavenly objects. In particular, the earth stood outside the rest of the system as a very different kind of object. And, like all black box models, the Ptolemaic planetary model was not extensible; it cannot be applied outside the domain of the observables on which it was based. In other words, it could not predict entirely new phenomena to be confirmed in future observations, as a true theory is capable of doing. It can only repeat the cycle of its original data.

Third, the disunity of the model, when combined with its doctrine of uniform circular motion and geocentrism, leads to some other interesting deficiencies. For example, any objects that cannot be fit within the framework of uniform motions – comets and meteors, for example – fall completely outside the model. The model assumes the order of the planets based on the speeds of their motions – the slower objects were further away from the earth than faster ones. The slowest moving object – the "sphere of the fixed stars" – was furthest away, followed by Saturn, Jupiter, Mars, the Sun, Venus, Mercury, and the Moon. As it turns out, this assumption is approximately correct, but it is entirely arbitrary -- which reinforces the fact that each planet is its own model. In fact, there were an infinite number of possible distance arrangements for the planets. Ptolemy admits as much: except in the case of the moon (whose distance can be measured from lunar parallax with respect to the earth's diameter), the ancients had no way of measuring distances to the planets, since they had neither observable eclipses or parallaxes[11]. This kind of "multiple equivalent hypotheses" that can reproduce the same data is a typical symptom of a partial or black box model. It is one of the principal deficiencies that Copernicus will remedy.

Despite its problems, we must keep in mind that the Ptolemaic model truly produces meaningful and useful results. With a few exceptions (such as the apparent diameter of the moon) it does a fine job of saving the appearances in a coherent and rational fashion, and can be used to calculate planetary motions, eclipses, and so on, just as effectively as the models of Copernicus and Kepler. In this, the Ptolemaic model certainly passes both verification and validation as a model. It also abstracts the most important features of the observed system to be modeled: distinct objects with cyclic motions. Despite the ultimate deficiencies of his particular approach, this abstract notion of cyclic motion and distinct objects will be carried on by every celestial mechanics model to the present day. In this, the Ptolemaic model was a real advance over simply interpolating and extrapolating tables of observational data. The model also assumed the stability of laws governing the system, even if each object obeys its own set of laws. Finally, although we have seen that there are multiple possibilities – multiple equivalent hypotheses – the Ptolemaic model did winnow down the possibilities, as any model should. The motions of the planets should be based on cyclic motions, which rules out all other kinds of motions. This assumption, when held at the abstract level (rather than concretized into an array of epicycles, deferents, and eccentrics), points the way to the truer models that emerged later. For example, the various centers of the deferents and eccentrics, when transformed by Copernicus, will emerge in the model of Kepler as the foci and centers of the elliptical planetary orbits with the Ptolemaic ratios preserved[12].

Finally, as an interesting sideshow of intellectual history, although the geocentric Ptolemaic model was an essential prop of the pseudoscience of astrology, the model in fact rules out astrology. For the planets, even though considered as "intelligences", had no relation to one another nor to the earth, which was at any rate governed by entirely different rules than the incorruptible celestial realm. Thus, it was absurd to suppose that the motions of the planets had any mysterious influence on the fortunes of earthly beings, and those non-mysterious influences the sun and moon did have, such as tides and the seasons, would be entirely explained later by the new physics and astronomy.

## From Ptolemy to Copernicus

Having explored the Ptolemaic model of the heavens, the shift to that of Copernicus in 1543 is both less and more profound than it is remembered in intellectual tradition. Less profound, since the heliocentric Copernican system is merely a geometric transformation of the geocentric system of the ancients. The only really important thing that changed is the center of the system, not the basic assumptions of uniform circular motion and so on. And we have seen that certain ancient astronomers, such as Aristarchus, had also proposed heliocentric systems with a moving earth.

So why did the heliocentric transformation of the model by Copernicus excite such intense resistance? This brings up the reason why the "Copernican revolution" was in some ways more profound than commonly realized. For that change of center, however advantageous it was from a modeling point of view, not only violated the physics and cosmology of the day – that of Aristotle – but overturned it completely. To quote the historian Herbert Butterfield[13]:

"if you grant Copernicus a certain advantage in respect of geometrical simplicity, the sacrifice that had to be made for the sake of this was nothing less than tremendous. You lost the whole cosmology associated with Aristotelianism – the whole intricately dovetailed system in which the nobility of the various elements and the hierarchical arrangement of these had been so beautifully interlocked. In fact, you had to throw overboard the very framework of existing science"

Indeed, Ptolemy himself remarked that although the heliocentric hypothesis saved the appearances as well as the geocentric, Aristotle's cosmology demanded an unmoving earth at the center of the world. For Ptolemy, this tilted the balance in favor of geocentrism, which was not only geometrically valid, but physically true according to Aristotle[14]. Despite the gains in simplicity of the Copernican model, it really required an entirely new physics to cinch its case, and that new physics would not be forthcoming until Galileo and Newton.

We know, of course, that Copernicus was right and Ptolemy was wrong. The move to simplicity correctly anticipated a new physics and cosmology, even if it was not capable of stating it. Here is a very important factor in the progress of modeling: the simplest model *on the abstract level* is likely to be the true one. The straightforward assumption of simplicity, which failed in the valley of concrete particulars, was entirely vindicated on the abstract heights. Copernicus, by making a change of perspective away from an earthbound point of view, was able to make a simpler model taken as a whole.

Copernicus himself certainly did not regard the heliocentric hypothesis as a mere calculational device, despite the disclaimer by

Osiander in his introduction to *On the Revolutions of the Heavenly Spheres*. To the contrary, he regarded the earth's mobility as a fact as physically certain as its sphericity, and classed his opponents with Lactantius, the ancient writer who denied the existence of the earth's antipodes[15].

How and why was the Copernican model simpler than the Ptolemaic? By placing the sun at the center of the system, and allowing the earth to rotate on its axis daily, an entire set of motions and epicycles were eliminated. The cosmos no longer revolved daily around the earth, for example, and the sphere of the fixed stars really was fixed. Of the heavenly bodies, only the moon still moved around the earth. Copernicus still required epicycles in his model – in fact, the moon and some of the planets had strange dual epicycles – but far fewer of these anomalous motions were required than by Ptolemy, and their sizes were much smaller. Recall that in Ptolemy's model, the epicycles of Venus and Mars were nearly as large as their deferents or "orbits". The Copernican model is in fact the simplest possible picture of the solar system based on purely circular motion.

The heliocentric hypothesis had another advantage, not immediately obvious, that was seized on by Copernicus. By placing the sun at the center, and allowing the earth to move around it with the other planets, it becomes possible to measure the distances and orders of the planets, as well as their orbital periods (i.e., their "years") around the sun. All these were immeasurable and essentially arbitrary in Ptolemy's model – the only body whose distance could be measured was the moon, using the yardstick of the earth's diameter and the geometry of parallax. The Copernican model opened up similar possibilities using the parallax of the earth's orbit to measure planetary distances. In fact, the same method is still used today to measure the distances to nearby stars.

Now, this method only provided distances in terms of the earth-sun distance (the astronomical unit), which could still not be known. Nonetheless, the order of the planets was now known unambiguously, and the distance ratios were known[16]. The simpler Copernican model, by rearranging as it were the model attributes of Ptolemy (for Copernicus was working from essentially the same observational data as Ptolemy), was able to unify several separate attributes of each planet (the large epicycle and yearly anomaly) into a single new attribute: the distance from the sun to the planet[17]. This unification was the key to the ultimate success of the Copernican system. The relation of distance and orbital period became comprehensible for the first time, and the notion of a planetary "year" became meaningful, since the epicycles remaining in Copernicus were truly only minor corrections of a much larger orbital motion. In contrast, there was no relation between motions and distance in Ptolemy's model. In fact, the ratios of the distance and the period of each planet in Copernicus's model, even working with the data available to Ptolemy, are remarkably close to Kepler's law. Copernicus, by a simple geometric change of center and assuming the rotation of the earth, extracted the crucial new information that was necessary for the steps to be taken by Kepler and then Newton. There could be no Keplerian formulation in a geocentric model like that of Ptolemy.

The Copernican model was unified in a way that Ptolemy's was not. All the planets – including the earth – obeyed the same law of circular motion and the same sort of relation between distance from the sun and the length of year. It was a unified system ordered by a single law. True, the sun seemed to have replaced the earth as a specially privileged body at the center of the cosmos. (And much of the rejection of Copernicus was based on the fact that he "demoted" the earth from the unique status it enjoyed in Aristotle's cosmology. In fact, the whole Aristotelian division between terrestrial and celestial physics had been removed. The earth was no longer a sovereign city-state for man at the center of the world. It was merely one subject in a kingdom with laws governing all bodies). But no longer was each planet a separate "black box" model as in Ptolemy.

For these reasons, the Copernican model was extensible in a way that Ptolemy's never could be. The soon to be discovered moons of Jupiter and Saturn could be comprehended, as could any newly discovered outer planet or asteroid. (Comets, on the other hand, would not fit into either the Copernican or Ptolemaic models, due to the assumption of circular motions.)

This said, the Copernican reorganization of the cosmos from geocentric to heliocentric form still lacked conclusive force. Ptolemy's model was still *possibly* correct geometrically, and if Aristotle's physics and cosmology were valid, then Copernicus's model was impossible. The intellectual establishment of the day (and of any day) hesitated to throw out the entire basis of natural science just for an improved picture of the solar system, and ease of astronomical calculations.

In fact, alternate models were not only possible, but continued to be offered. The most prominent of these was the compromise model of Tycho Brahe, which kept the earth at the center of the system, but placed all the other bodies (save the moon) in orbit around the sun, and the sun in orbit around the earth[18]. Tycho's model had all the astronomical advantages of the Copernican, but did not disturb the motionless earth from its Aristotelian place in the middle. It even found a way of comprehending comets as bodies in the system, and correctly concluded that the crystalline spheres of Aristotle's celestial realm could not exist, since the comets would smash through them.

The modern reader may find it disturbing, but there was no possible way, based on data available to the earthbound observer with naked eye and simple instruments, to decide between Ptolemy, Copernicus, and Tycho. Conclusive proof of the earth's rotation required observation of the Coriolis effect or the motions of Foucault's pendulum[19]. Proof of the earth's revolution about the sun required measuring such minuscule effects as the aberration of starlight and the parallax of stars relative to the earth's orbit. To be a Copernican in the year 1600 was to place a bet that simplicity and abstractive unity represent progress in modeling. What was required to pay off the bet were Kepler's ellipses and Newton's physics, but handsomely paid off it was. This historical fact, above all, should convince one that models are in fact capable of extending human knowledge and not merely representing it.

## Kepler, Galileo, and the Extension of the Heliocentric Model

It was entirely possible that the heliocentric model of Copernicus would have languished, like the very similar model of Aristarchus of Samos, as one of several alternate models of the sun, moon, earth, and planets. But, as we know, this did not occur. Copernicus's work represented the beginning of modern natural science. It was the take-off point for an entirely new cosmology and physics, and the pace of new theories and discoveries quickened rapidly.

Most of that story must fall outside this chapter. But it is worth noting two particularly important mileposts on the way from Ptolemy to Newton. And these are the contributions of Kepler and Galileo. It is due to them that the Copernican model is now viewed in retrospect as a revolutionary occurrence, the spark that lit a trail of inquiry, rather than just an alternate geometric formulation of celestial motions. Both Kepler and Galileo were vocal adherents of the new Copernican view. More importantly, each in his own way provided a key theoretical insight that was able to anchor the Copernican model on firmer foundations and provide a necessary bridge to Newton. In fact, without their work, the physics and celestial mechanics of Newton would not have happened.

Johannes Kepler was a strong advocate of the advantages of the heliocentric model, yet at the same time, he proposed crucial changes to it that were nearly as important as those of Copernicus himself. Kepler proposed that the ancient assumption of uniform circular motion of the planets be abandoned. He replaced it with a new geometric formulation, where the circles are replaced by ellipses. The advantage gained by this change is small, but theoretically immense: all the remaining epicycles of the Copernican model were gotten rid of – the last "black box", object-specific laws of the model were gone. All the anomalies that epicycles were invoked to explain are dealt with by ellipses. Kepler's elliptical representation of orbits still provides the mathematical basis for celestial mechanics today.

The import of the elliptical orbits was twofold. For the first time, all planetary motions were governed by a single law of motion. Each object's motion was along a single ellipse, with no special corrections by epicycles. Second, the ellipse is a generalization of the circle; the circle is merely one special case of an ellipse. A Keplerian orbit can indeed by a circle, as the ancients supposed, but can also be of other closely related shapes. So Kepler's model represented a move towards both generalization and complete unity of laws governing the system. Also, a formulation akin to Kepler's was impossible for the alternate geocentric models of Ptolemy and Tycho.

Kepler also broke with the doctrine of the uniform motion of the planets. But he replaced it with a new law that was much more solidly grounded. The uniform motion law held only for a circular orbit. But for the more general elliptical orbits, this law had to be replaced with a new, more general law: Kepler's famous equal area - equal times law. As a planet moves along its elliptical orbit, the orbit sweeps out an equal area between itself and the sun in an equal time, regardless of what distance the planet is from the sun at any instant. For a circular orbit, this is a restatement of the law of uniform motion. But for a highly elliptical orbit, such as that of many comets, it means that the orbiting object moves slowly when distant from the sun, but very rapidly when nearby.

Kepler's two changes to the Copernican model turned out to be of immense importance. He was already getting close to Newton's law of gravitation. For Kepler supposed that the motions of the planets had something to do with the influence of the sun at the center of the system, and that the solar influence was proportional to the inverse square of the distance from the sun to a planet. Kepler cited Gilbert's work on magnetism and supposition that the earth is a lodestone in support of his more general theory that all the planets and the sun are also lodestones[20]. The solar *system* was just that: a dynamic system, bound together by magnetic attraction, and also driven by the sun as its motor at the center. As it turns out, of course, the solar system is bound together by another force – gravity – that is nonetheless of an inverse square nature.

The most important point to grasp here is that Kepler's ellipses may still be an entirely kinematic formula, but that he was trying to transform this kinematics into a dynamics by positing a new physics. It was no longer enough to save the appearances; they must be entirely explained. Leaving aside some of Kepler's wild theorizing about astrology and the nesting of regular solids in the planetary spheres, he correctly saw that a new physics was needed, and the general shape of the law of gravitation that would be central to that physics.

Notice also that about this time the "sphere of the fixed stars" has essentially fallen out of the model. It is something so remote that it has no obvious dynamic connection with the sun and planets. The sun is even viewed as one star among many; Bruno's far-fetched speculations (rather like some of Kepler's) nonetheless pointed towards a new way of looking at space. By the 18th Century, the universe was viewed as an infinite three-dimensional container full of a limitless number of stars, a view that would last until Einstein and 20th Century cosmology.

In sum, Kepler's model was both simpler and more comprehensive in scope than that of Copernicus. It provided a single, unified view of all planetary motions. And, in addition, Kepler addressed one of the main objections to the Copernican model – the fact that it ran against Aristotle's physics. For Kepler flatly rejected Aristotle's physics, and under the banner of mathematics and the new science, partially pointed to the way to what this new physics must look like.

But Kepler was an astronomer, not a physicist. The story of modern, mathematical physics begins with Galileo – a story that touches ours, but is not central to it. In addition to inventing physics as we know it, Galileo also made the first published and scientific telescopic observations of the heavens. What he found and reported in the *Starry Messenger* in the space of a few nights of observing provided the first really new astronomical data since the days of Ptolemy. For example, not only did Jupiter have a finite disk (just like the moon and sun), it also had several moons orbiting it. Galileo called them the "Medicean Stars" in honor of his patrons; we know them better as Io, Ganymede, Callisto, and Europa. Galileo not only discovered their existence, he also observed them over a period of time in an attempt to determine their orbital "months" and distances from Jupiter, an observation that was confirmed by Kepler. It turned out that these matched the times and distances predicted by Kepler's laws. In other words, not only did Kepler's theory of planetary motion predict other data, it was extensible to entirely new phenomena (Jovian moons) that Copernicus and Kepler could not have suspected the existence of[21]. The basics of Kepler's laws would be extensible not only to other moons, but to binary star systems – in fact, to all dynamic systems obeying an inverse square law of attractive force. It is this kind of extensibility and universality that is the mark of a true model.

Galileo also drew the correct physical conclusions of the new Copernican astronomy: the old Aristotelian distinction between terrestrial and celestial nature was erased, since the earth was one planet among many. The mathematical nature of celestial mechanics, combined with the Archimedean mathematical statics, was moved down to earth and gave birth to physics as we know it. Objects no longer moved in circles or verticals with respect to the earth inside an organic cosmos, but along inertial trajectories in an infinite space. The challenger to Aristotle's physics was now ready[22].

## Newton Completes the Classical Model

With the work of Isaac Newton, not only was a new, comprehensive, mathematical physics completed, but the entire framework of science that endures to this day laid down. But as with Galileo, we are not concerned with Newton's physics as such. What is important is that the combination of the new mechanics and the inverse square law of gravitation offered a complete explanatory framework for the Keplerian orbits. Newton's physics completed the classical solar system model, providing the explanatory theory that fully replaced Aristotle's cosmology. The basic Newtonian picture of the solar system is that which we still have today.

It is important to keep in mind that Newton's physics added nothing to the predictive ability of the model of Copernicus and Kepler – in practical terms, it was exactly the same. Newton was not motivated by a stream of new data to be explained.

Rather, the change is all on the theoretical underpinnings of the model. With Newton's work, Kepler's laws of elliptical orbits and the equal-time equal-area relation were explained by a scientific and universal theory of gravitation and motion, whereas before they were only empirical models. Kepler's laws were now seen as the necessary consequence of gravitational fields and the law of inertia. They became a dynamics rather than just a kinematics. Moreover, all physical objects, both terrestrial and celestial follow the same law: physics and astronomy are unified for the first time.

From a modeling point of view, we see that Newton's universal law of gravitation grew largely out of reflection on existing models, rather than directly on empirical data. It was an attempt to explain the elliptical orbits that led to the gravitational law. Kepler's model was a necessary preliminary to Newton, providing the abstract mathematical image that could then be equated with other mathematical images belonging to the rest of Newtonian mechanics. In other words, the law of gravitation could never have been found based on Ptolemaic model; Kepler's intimations of some solar influence on the planets proportional to the inverse square of the distance made Newton's theory possible.

With Newton, the classical model was completed and had converged toward unity, simplicity, and comprehensiveness. All objects obey the same laws; there is a single law (and no "black box" special laws for each planet), and all the planets form a single system united by gravitational attraction. The solar system truly became viewed as a system in which everything is explained and everything is predictable. To predict a future set of solar eclipses has a different meaning for Newton than Ptolemy, even though their models might arrive at the same sets of dates, times, and durations. For Ptolemy, the predictions may be accurate, but remain ultimately unexplained. Classical mechanics can explain why the eclipses must occur.

This fact raises still another modeling issue. We may ask: is the Newtonian picture of the solar system still a model at all? Since it has passed over to theoretical explanation, should it not really be considered a full-fledged theory instead, having left behind the hovel of approximations for the mansion of exact science? And after all it deals with planets only in the most abstract sense, as gravitating objects with mass, location, and velocity.

Yet it is still a model. The particularities of the solar system – the masses and distances and orbital inclinations and so on of each individual planet – must be included to actually make predictions. In this, we see once more the typical role of a model as an abstract image mediating between empirical particulars and theoretical generalities. Newton's laws deal with generic and abstract conceptual entities – objects with mass. But the solar system model is a set of particular parameters plugged into those laws, and moreover, we can make a picture of it, which we cannot do with the laws themselves. Moreover, we see all the typical assumptions of the modeling paradigm as preconditions of the Newtonian theory: analysis of the system into discrete parts, the assumption of an isolated system, and so on.

## Extending the Newtonian Picture: The Discovery of Neptune

The solar system model of Newton and Kepler assumed, mostly for the sake of calculational simplicity, that the only important gravitational interaction was that of the sun upon the planets; the only exception being made for the case of a planet attracting its moon or moons. Yet, explicit within the universal law of gravitation was the fact that all bodies in the solar system were acting upon each other.

Fortunately, these many-body interactions are relatively weak, and in practical terms could be ignored. Even today we can exactly solve only two-body mechanical problems, and a few special cases of the three-body problem. The exact solution, even in classical mechanics, of more interacting bodies remains intractable. However, if the interaction between the objects is relatively weak (in comparison to the main two-body interaction between the sun and the planet of interest), it is possible to approximate the many-body interactions using perturbation theory – the mathematical complexities of which we will not go into here. Of course, nowadays one would just simulate the system on a computer, but point is that perturbation theory offered a practical approach to solving the many-body problem before the invention of digital computers.

Where this enters our story of modeling the solar system is the possibility of new planets other than the six classical planets of Mercury, Venus, Earth, Mars, Jupiter, and Saturn. The planet Uranus was discovered telescopically by Herschel in 1781, and its location beyond the orbit of Saturn was confirmed soon after by Lexell[23]. Between 1801 and 1807, the four largest asteroids – Ceres, Pallas, Juno, and Vesta – were discovered. This led to suspicions there were yet other planets out there. This suspicion was heightened in 1821 when the mathematician Bouvard discovered that Uranus was falling behind in its orbital position as predicted by a pure two-body sun-to-Uranus interaction. One possible cause of the orbital shift was that Uranus was being gravitationally attracted by another, as yet undiscovered, massive planet at some distance yet further out from the sun.

Independently, the mathematicians Adams and Le Verrier both investigated the hypothesis of a new planet perturbing the orbit of Uranus[24]. Their thorough calculations indicated that an unknown planet could indeed account for the anomalous behavior of Uranus's orbit. Although it turns out they got the mass and orbital parameters of the new planet wrong, they did predict its location with close accuracy. On the basis of these detailed predictions, the astronomer Galle telescopically discovered the planet Neptune in 1846. Analogous calculations of the orbits of Neptune helped lead to the later discovery of the planet Pluto in 1930, and even today there are hints that yet other planets may lie undiscovered beyond Pluto's orbit.

The importance of this for the classical solar system model was immense. Based purely on Newtonian mechanics and the existing model, a correct prediction of new existents that *should* belong to the system was made – from one component of the interacting system, it was possible to infer both the existence and attributes of others. The model was not only extensible; it could point out to the researcher how it ought to be extended. From the empirical parameters of Uranus's orbit and Newton' s laws, one could predict an entirely new member of the system. It was as if Neptune had been a part of the model all along, latent in it – rather like a missing piece of a puzzle that we are led to by the negative shape of its surrounding pieces.

Another point of importance for modeling is that a more complete, more strongly interacting, many-body gravitational model could only be a simulation, and could never be calculated directly. The solar system is dominated by the massive sun at its center, but consider the opposite possibility where the interacting bodies are all of roughly similar mass. Examples of this latter case occur in the dynamics of galaxies and star clusters. Another possibility is where the dynamics of the system are governed by two or three massive bodies acting on many smaller ones. This is relevant, for example, in the influence of Jupiter and the Sun on the asteroid belt, planetary influences on comets, or the possibility of planets in binary star systems such as Alpha Centauri. Without a model (in addition to empirical data on the one hand and theoretical equipment on the other), the study of such systems would be impossible.

## Einstein's Theory of Relativity and the Precession of Mercury's Perihelion

The early $20^{th}$ Century witnessed an earthquake that shook up the staid world of classical physics.  And, as in so many cases, there was a synergy between new discoveries in physics and those of astronomy. The cosmos was a ready laboratory for the predictions of Einstein's new and revolutionary theories of relativity.  In fact, celestial mechanics was to provide one crucial test of the gravitational force predicted by general relativity.

To understand why this is so, it is important to grasp that the stability of Keplerian orbits is very sensitive to the slightest variation from the inverse square law of gravitational attraction.  If the exponent of the distance were -1.95 or -2.05, no planetary orbit would have been stable – the solar system would have flown apart or collapsed upon the sun eons ago.  (An exponent of -3 produces what are known as Cote's spirals – the object spirals smoothly in towards the center.)  The known stability of the solar system over a period of billions of earth years means that the exponent must be extremely close to -2.0.

In the context of Newtonian physics and a 3-dimensional Euclidean space, the exponent should be exactly -2.0.  But what if space were not perfectly flat and Euclidean?  One of the most fascinating aspects of the general theory of relativity is that it predicted that space was curved. Moreover, the curvature was due to gravitational fields (or, put another way, gravity was a consequence of curved space).  This also meant that the law of gravity was not exactly proportional to the inverse square of the distance.  Newton's inverse square law was an approximation valid in the limit of low masses or large distances.  Einstein's new law of gravity was a much more complex function derived from the space curvature; we need not state the equations here.  For practical purposes, however, it can be approximated closely by the inverse square law plus a small correction factor proportional to the $-4^{th}$ power of the distance[25].

The existence of this small deviation from the inverse square law must have an effect on the orbits of the planets.  The question is, was it large enough to result in a measurable effect?  For the Earth, the quartic

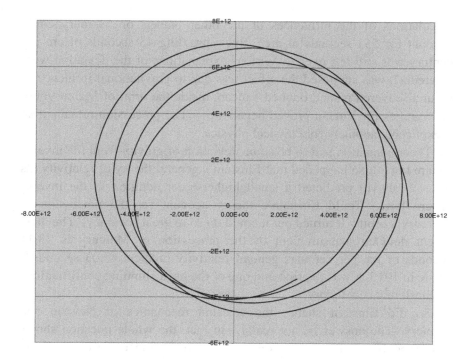

Figure 6-2. The Precession of the Perihelion of Mercury's Orbit (effect exaggerated).

correction factor was only 11 parts in a billion, far outweighed by not only the influence of the moon, but also Jupiter. However, the relative strength of the effect grows as one gets closer to the sun. Could the effect be measurable for the planet nearest to the sun, Mercury?

As a matter of fact, there was a behavior of the orbit of Mercury that Newtonian mechanics and gravitation could not account for. One result of any small deviation of gravitation from the inverse square law form is a gradual precession of the major axis of an elliptical orbit, as shown in Figure 6-2. Over time, the axis will gradually rotate around the sun – or, put differently, the orbit is no longer a true ellipse, but a daisy-shaped curve.

The planet Mercury has a measured precession of perihelion amounting to 574 seconds of arc per century. Detailed perturbation calculations of the influences of the other planets on Mercury could account for 531 seconds of arc. But a puzzling 43 seconds of arc per century was still left over[26]. Various explanations of the deviation were offered. It was supposed the effect was due to gravitational influence of an undiscovered planet, dubbed Vulcan, inside the orbit of Mercury, but all searches for Vulcan proved negative[27]. The precession remained an inexplicable anomaly for classical physics.

The explanation had to be some deviation of gravity from the inverse square law. It so happened that Einstein's general theory of relativity (as we saw above) predicted a small higher-order addition to the inverse square law. Could Einstein's theory account for the precession of Mercury's orbit? It turned out it could do so to great accuracy. The most recent detailed measurement of the precession of Mercury is 43.11 seconds of arc per century; general relativity predicts 43.03 seconds[28]. Made in 1915, it was the first and one of the most stunning confirmations of Einstein's new theory.

So did Einstein shatter the celestial mechanics of Newton and Kepler? The answer is, not really. In fact, the whole question shows how models progress. The relativistic formulation of mechanics and gravitation did not overrule Newton's physics; instead, it showed it to be a low velocity and low mass limit of a more general set of physical laws. In a way, the step from Newton to Einstein was analogous to the step from Copernicus to Kepler. Kepler showed that circular orbits were merely a special case of ellipses; Einstein showed that the inverse square law of gravitation was a special case of a more complex curved space formulation. In each case, there was a move to a more general and comprehensive perspective. In each case, the anomalies of previous models (epicycles and anomalous precession) were explained completely by the new more general theory, and the domain of the unexplained continued to shrink.

## Summary: How Models Progress

From the preceding examples, one can definitely see that the sequence of celestial mechanics models from antiquity to the present is a progression.

They show both how models crystallize knowledge and how they advance it.

The salient points that emerge in that progression – and in analogy the progression of any model – can be summarized as follows.

(1) <u>Conformity of celestial mechanics to the modeling paradigm</u> was key to the ability to model the solar system. The solar system is, on time scales of interest, a closed system that can be modeled disregarding external influences. Furthermore, it is a nearly perfect example of a system that can be analyzed into a set of discrete objects (sun and planets) with spatial relations. The inherent simplicity of the solar system from a modeling point of view was one reason why the Copernican model could act as the midwife of modern science.

(2) <u>Convergence</u> of the model occurred on several levels. Convergence in terms of matching data occurred even with Ptolemy's model, in that it reproduced the observed measurements (i.e., "saved the appearances"). But the number of adjustable parameters in Ptolemy's model (e.g., the epicycles) was very large. Another convergence can be seen in the steady reduction of the number of such "free" parameters and their replacement by laws – the number of anomalies in the model decreases. In the transition from the circles of Ptolemy and Copernicus to the ellipses of Kepler and Newton, the remaining parameters (major and minor elliptical axes, planetary masses) are both fewer in number and more universal. A third kind of convergence is that the number of multiple alternate explanations steadily decreased. For example, in Ptolemy's model, the distances of the planets from the earth was largely arbitrary; by the time of Kepler it is not arbitrary at all and is fixed on a single set of values. And, moreover, what remains open to multiple explanations or what is unexplained steadily decreases – what was unexplained by the time of Newton was far smaller than in antiquity.

(3) <u>The models progressed in generality, universality, and coherence</u>. The many rules applying separately to each planet were replaced by a single rule governing all planets. The empirical "black box" aspects of the model, such as epicycles, recede from the picture and are replaced by laws that explain the anomalies of old models. The disconnected planetary models are unified into a single system with a

single law. Moreover, the new models subsume the old ones. We saw how the circle is seen to be merely one kind of ellipse, and the inverse square law of gravitation merely one limit of a more general law. We also saw how, at the dawn of modern science, that celestial and terrestrial physics were unified.

(4) <u>Simplicity and abstraction</u> become more apparent with successive models. Copernicus's model was the simplest possible with circular orbits. This simple geometric change of perspective also yielded an important unification of model parameters, giving a meaningful orbital distance and orbital period for each planet, relative to the distance of the earth from the sun. That the model is an abstract image and that models advance in abstraction is also clearly seen. The abstract idea of circular motion in Ptolemy provided the key to the advance to the more abstract idea of elliptical motion in Kepler and finally the notion of abstract point masses in Newton's physics interaction through gravity.

(5) <u>Extensibility</u> of the model is a key measure of its progress and its generality. The model of Kepler and Newton could encompass previously inexplicable phenomena such as comets and meteors; it could deal with new discoveries such as Jupiter's moons. The case of the discovery of Neptune showed it could predict new objects that should belong to the model. The model was also extensible on the conceptual level. It could incorporate new physics such as relativity theory without the model being destroyed or cast aside (as was the case with the Ptolemaic system), but instead by moving to a more general viewpoint.

(6) <u>Models emerge as a source of knowledge</u>. Physical theory emerged from the model, not models from the theory. Celestial mechanics based on Newton's physics was an explanation of the abstract Keplerian model, not of raw empirical data. It was refinement of the model that made the theoretical breakthrough of Newton possible. The model acts as mediator, as synthesis, of theory and observation, and is essential to the emergence of a theoretical explanation. Moreover, as the model progresses, it gains steadily more explanatory power. It becomes less of an empirical description and more the embodiment of theoretical explanation.

Finally, we note that models of the solar system crystallized a number of underlying assumptions, which were central to physical science as it emerged in the 17th Century and have endured as assumptions to this day. The laws governing the system are invariant and universal, affecting all objects in the system the same way at all times. The laws have a mathematical character – one of the key sources of mathematical physics was Galileo's insight that dynamics could be mathematically described, thus unifying celestial and terrestrial physics. There was also an isolation, a bracketing, on the conceptual level: since the birth of modern celestial mechanics, questions regarding the meaning of the cosmos ("final causes") and the like were excluded as outside the scope of natural science. All these assumptions allowed Western science to reap its overflowing harvest in the centuries that followed. Yet they also represent a crucial limitation of the applicability of models, as we will see in the next chapter.

## Chapter 7

# Laplace's Mirage, or the Impossibility of the Exact Calculation of the World

From the preceding, it seems possible we might exactly simulate the world process. True, any particular model of the world and its parts might be doubtful at present. But the progressive advance of scientific understanding would steadily pare down and eliminate uncertainties, converging to a clear and distinct picture of the world. Then, having captured the world in the bottle of our computer, we would be able to calculate any past or future state.

The computer model would realize the dream of 18th Century French mathematician and physicist Pierre Simon Laplace[1]:

"An intelligence which knows at a given instant all forces acting in nature, as well as the momentary positions of all things of which the universe consists, would be able to comprehend the motions of the largest bodies of the world and those of the smallest atoms in one single formula; provided it were powerful enough to subject all data to analysis. To it, nothing would be uncertain, both future and past would be present before its eyes."

Laplace held that all phenomena could be reduced to a mathematical or mechanical model. It was an idea of common intellectual currency in his age, and it is scarcely less widespread in our own. For Laplace, the world was a machine governed by Newton's physics, with laws that are both deterministic and easily integrated. The inference follows straightaway: since we know the laws, all we need are the initial conditions to calculate the outcome. The framework of this vision inspires mathematical physics yet and also the computational modeler. It is at the root, for example, of the search of the physicists for a unified field theory (or "theory of everything"). As one molecular modeler remarked[2]:

"From the time of Newton to the present day, this deterministic mechanical interpretation of Nature has dominated science. ... we remain undeterred from Laplace's dream ... and Laplace's universe has given way to model universes"

The notion that reality is entirely reducible to physical laws, and that physical law is reducible to mathematical relations, goes by the modern label of *reductionism*. The reductionist views physics as the root science, from which all the others are built. Chemistry is the physics of the outer electrons of atoms; biology is nothing more than the chemistry of complex organic molecules, and psychology and sociology in due time will be reduced to biological forces. The world is a giant machine full of little machines. Physics in turn is viewed as simply a set of mathematical relations, so the reductionist (in essence) views the world as mathematics made visible, a sort of super-modern Pythagoreanism[3]. This is not the place to dispute the truth or falsity of the reductionist hypothesis, only to point out a couple of important consequences for modeling and simulation[4].

First, computer models are most at home in the reductionist universe. It is almost a working assumption of theirs – a set of objects interacting through mathematical laws is the computer model's birthplace and home territory. This points to a natural division of possible limitations on any model – those that lie within the bounds of reductionism and those that do not. Some examples of the latter include organicism (the notion that complex entities, such as living beings, are not simply reducible to the sums of their parts), the possibility of authentic freedom or randomness, and so on.

Second, even within the bounds of reductionism, the assumption of an underlying set of deterministic laws does not guarantee that a computer model will be able to exactly predict phenomena, due to the inherent limitations of models themselves.

Regardless of the reality, there are certain limitations built into the modeling paradigm from the very beginning. The model assumes an isolated (or isolable) system, governed entirely by deterministic (preferably mathematical) laws, composed of a set of distinct objects with distinct relations, with clearly characterizable (again, preferably quantifiable) properties. Every model, in other words, relies on the set of "categories of object-oriented reason" discussed in Chapter 4. These are the keys to the success of modeling, yet they are also irremovable, *a priori*, self-limitations, analogous to Kant's categories of pure reason for the human mind. What conforms to the modeling paradigm can be modeled; what does not, must in some way escape the modeler's grasp.

The above requirements are *intrinsic* limiting factors of modeling. Equally important are *extrinsic* limitations, such as incomplete and erroneous data. Models are ultimately only as good as the data on which they are constructed. To the extent the data is doubtful, the model constructed upon its foundation will also be doubtful, especially when predictions extrapolate the model beyond the region for which data exists into new phenomena or future occurrences. These restrictions become more important if we require the model data be quantifiable, since the intrinsic model limitations (mathematical reduction) are introduced into the model data itself.

The importance of these limiting factors depends largely on the model's purpose. For a model with a specific purpose – for example, a crash test dummy – then the purpose itself so restricts the amount of information required that building a model that is "good enough" is attainable. Such a narrowing of perspective also serves to restrict possible uncertainties.   A crash test dummy reproduces certain observables (the size and mechanical properties of the human body) and does not care about the rest of the subject. Here, "black box" models that simply replicate system properties without complete understanding of underlying forces ("results without explanation") are perfectly adequate.

It is another matter entirely for models that attempt to be complete, representing every property and behavior of its subject. Instead of a crash test dummy, suppose we want to represent a human driver completely in every respect. Or suppose instead of an approximation of tomorrow's weather, we demand an exact prediction of the weather for any time in the future. The whole notion of a complete model assumes subject fits within the bounds of the modeling paradigm. It also assumes adequate data and theory, so that by degrees, the partial black box models of system parameters can be transformed into complete explanatory models of the phenomena. This is none other than the notion of convergence of data and theory discussed in the previous chapter. In such cases, both the intrinsic and extrinsic limiting factors of models loom large. Any place where the subject cannot be fit into the modeling paradigm or where there are data errors will throw the model off. The model will fail to be a complete and perfect model, even if it is the best possible and entirely adequate for practical uses.

On reflection, it becomes clear that *Laplace's dream is in fact an illusion.* It is a mirage. It is a very attractive image that has danced on the horizon of Western thought for centuries, but the exact calculation of the world cannot be performed. And the more the phenomena under consideration diverge from the modeling paradigm, the less possible it is. There will never be a computer (apologies to the late Douglas Adams) cranking out the answers to life, the universe, and everything. Indeed, no supercomputer will ever exactly predict tomorrow's weather, even if given complete data – very accurately perhaps, but not exactly.

Since the computer model represents the ultimate extension of scientific understanding of the world, it means that science itself (regardless of how well the laws governing the world are understood) will never be able to predict all details of phenomena. It can manifest the laws of gravitation, but will never exactly predict the moon's orbit – even if it can predict it with extraordinary accuracy. It can understand the laws governing the growth of trees, but it will never be able to say why the branches of the old oak tree in my yard are exactly the shape and size they are. It can understand the causes of earthquakes, but cannot predict exactly where and when the next earthquake will strike along the San Andreas Fault. Such are the limitations imposed on both models and science like these when they descend from the mountaintop of theoretical perfection into the valley of particular things.

## Intrinsic Limitations of Models and the "Categories"

To restate, all models are intrinsically limited by their assumptions. Models, as abstract images constructed by human reason, are always idealizations to some degree. The previous two chapters discussed how those idealizations are the key to the success of the modeling paradigm, but also an ultimate barrier beyond which models cannot go.

Chapter 3 introduced them as the modeling paradigm, and Chapter 4 expanded them into the "categories of object-oriented reason", which can be summarized here as distinctions of:

(1) *system and background* – the isolated system assumption.
(2) *object and relations* – analysis of the system into interrelated parts, as well as the assumption of a finite number of parts.
(3) *entity and attributes* – analysis of the system into a container for attributes (essentially the old substance versus quality distinction).
(4) *cause and effect* – distinction between states and transitions between states, as well as an assumption of deterministic state transitions.
(5) *object and class* – the "is a" relation between an entity and the class that stands for it, as well as the "is a kind of" relation between classes.

Each of these "categories" imposes its restriction on the ultimate quality of any model. For practical reasons, once again, such limitations may be of little importance. But if we set our sights as high as Laplace and wish to model the world as a world-machine, they add up to a serious concern indeed – even when the phenomena are completely deterministic and mathematical when considered separately.

The first, and perhaps most basic and important of these categories, is the distinction between the system and its background. To model something at all, we must abstract the system from its surroundings. The model behaves like an isolated system. To the extent interactions between the system and its environment exist, they must be clearly characterizable as a set of "events" or "stimuli" impinging on the system and a corresponding set of "responses" or "actions" by the system in return. We want to identify the system's boundary conditions in space and its initial conditions in time. In this way, the system's environment is reduced to a set of interactions through a clean interface. There is a clear distinction between what is "inside" and what is "outside" the system. This distinction assumes the interactions of the system with its environment are much less strong than the interrelations within the system itself – in other words, that the system is not overwhelmed. If this condition is not met, the system will not cohere, but will be broken apart by its environment. We could not reliably identify a system, except on short time scales.

To abstract a system, we need first to identify it. In practical terms, system identification can be difficult for several important reasons, which can lead to both mistaking a non-system for a system and overlooking a real system[5]. A system's functioning can be split up among different entities that have no obvious connection. This is usually not the case when dealing with physical systems, but it is common with human ones. Conversely, it may be difficult to distinguish the essential components of a system from those that are extraneous or merely redundant. It can also happen in living and human systems that the same entity plays an integral part of two or more functionally distinct systems, as when a human being is simultaneously part of political and economic systems. Finally, the system may simply be too big to be easily seen as a system (the forest and the trees problem), or it may be so imperfectly realized as a system that it is not even recognized as such.

In other words, the model paradigm's natural home is that region of experience where there are distinct boundaries between systems and their surroundings. This requirement is usually met in the physical sciences, at least on short enough time scales, or when the internal binding forces of the system are sufficiently strong. It is another matter entirely for human systems. Here, the limit of the system is more functional than physical – i.e., that systems are distinguished by the various functions they carry out rather than by spatio-temporal separation. The assumption of "crisp edges" falls down.

Suppose, then, the model successfully abstracts the system from its environment. Now, in accordance with the modeling method, we perform the twofold analysis of the system into its parts and it attributes. Each of these analyses imposes its limits on understanding, even when the system in question is reducible to mathematical physics.

The object/relation dichotomy, to recall, arises from the analysis of the system into its component parts. Applying the analysis recursively yields the "part of" hierarchy that for the elements of the system and its subsystems. Connecting the parts of the system are relations of varying strengths; these relations hold the system and its subsystems together. But underlying the analysis are two important assumptions: (1) that one can identify distinct and separate parts and (2) that there are a finite number of parts. Negatively, the challenges presented to the modeler are those of *continuity* and *multiplicity*.

The problem posed by continuity is as follows. The world is of continuous extent in space and a continuous flow of time. But if the world is continuous, any simulation of it is not. A model divides space into distinct objects and relations. When the modeler is confronted by a continuous subject, like a fluid or a force field, the response is to use a grid -- to divide the continuity up into finite sections and impose a set of virtual objects and relations on the continuity. Indeed, without such techniques, fluids and fields could not be modeled. Grids are used in field calculations, weather prediction, and in studies of aerodynamics with great success. Grids or finite element arrays may contain millions of cells and links. Yet a fluid could be modeled exactly only using a grid with an infinite number of cells (i.e., an infinite intension) and this is clearly impossible. And so for any system that cannot be reduced to an object/relation or "billiard ball" nature. Anything smaller than the calculational grid mesh will escape the model's notice and becomes an unknown for the model. A model cannot replicate the exact state of a continuous system for any "ripples" that are smaller than its "data buckets" or bins. The mesh size is like the size of smallest units on a ruler; that size determines the error of the measurement. In many cases, we assume processes smaller than the model's spatial scale are essentially unimportant, consisting of random fluctuations that cancel out on a larger view. This is often a valid assumption. The model makes predictions that are confirmed within experimental error (the measurements of the modeled phenomena are not perfect either). But the assumption that "small causes lead to small effects" is not always true, as will be discussed at more length below. And it represents an important limitation on the truth of models.

We have seen, for example, how models are built around the assumption of isolated and closed systems, with clear and distinct boundary conditions. We have also seen how this methodological assumption represents a serious limitation, even within the bounds of reductionism. The fact we can build models at all on the basis of closed systems is more an accident of the "lumpiness" of the physical world than anything else. As the physicist Henry Margenau pointed out[6],

"The occurrence of closed systems is no means to be expected on *a priori* grounds. It is occasioned by such contingent facts as the rapid decline of all mechanical forces with increasing distance between interacting particles."

In other words, all systems in the world are really only *relatively* so. The notion we can decompose anything into completely isolated systems (i.e., separable parts) is part and parcel of mechanism, but even in physics, the notion of extended force fields begins to break down this notion. The "isolated system" is only an abstraction; what nature *really* presents us with is a continuous network of relations, some as strong as steel cables and others as diaphanous as cobwebs, but all relations nonetheless. When we encounter a particularly tight knot of relations, we call it a "thing" or a "system" and mentally extract it from its background of much weaker relations.   When this is impossible — wherever closed systems cannot be found — the modeling paradigm breaks down, and models increasingly become approximations.

Chapter 3 explained why simulations must divide time into finite steps. The reason is very similar to that for space: a time step is like a grid in space.  For this reason, phenomena that are changing more quickly than the time step can account for will be lost. The flow of time is not broken up into convenient instants for us. The larger the time step relative to the rate of change of the system, the worse the error, and the effect is cumulative.  It can snowball and lead to the collapse of the model, computationally speaking.  Normally, however, the cumulative effect of time-stepping errors leads to what is called *numerical diffusion*, the tendency of predictions to blur out. In fact, any calculation involving real numbers will lead to rounding or truncation errors, and hence to numerical diffusion. Weather forecasts degrade with time for this reason. Tomorrow's forecast is more accurate than that for the day after tomorrow, and so on.  Finite time step errors a very important constraint on the predictions of all computer models, whether we are talking about models of molecular interactions or models of world climate.  The way to get around this is, of course, to use a finer set of time steps. But to remove it all together, we would have to use an infinite number of time steps, which is, as for an infinite number of spatial cells, impossible.

The finite time step error is equivalent to the sampling problem in measurement. For example, to record a certain frequency of sound, we must sample the waveform at least the rate of half a wavelength -- the Nyquist critical frequency. (Figure 7-1) For a slower sampling rate, the wave escapes the notice of the recorder and appears as seemingly random noise or an erroneous pattern instead.

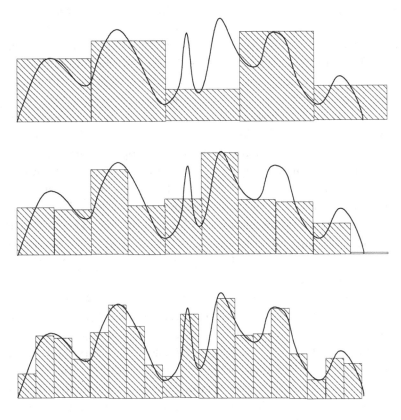

Figure 7-1. Illustration of the Sampling Problem.

One temporal factor that was irrelevant for space is the nature of the interaction between objects. Some interactions are easily integrable in time and others can be intractable. For a large set of objects interacting through a nonlinear field, the motions of objects will no longer be exactly calculable. They will form a mathematical manifold that can be calculated numerically to great accuracy, but no longer exactly. For the simulation must still take finite time steps, and thus approximate a curve by a polygon. Indeed, this is the best analogy of the space-time limitations of modeling. Finite time steps and spatial grids are akin to inscribing a circle with a regular polygon. The more sides to the polygon, the more closely we will approximate the circle, but we will never entirely reach it. Of course, if we know the formula for the circle, we can plug it into our model and make an exact calculation[7]. The point is, however, that a complex, nonlinear system that cannot be approached in this way – it can only be simulated. One added difficulty of time in comparison to space is that, in space, we can at least visualize the continuity. Continuously extended objects are part of our everyday visual experience. To make time "thinkable," we spatialize it, breaking it into a series of discrete states, just as a computer model would. This is an important conceptual limitation the chapter will return to.

The finite sieves with which any model must approach both space and time are crucial limitations, even if the phenomena modeled are entirely reducible to mathematical laws. These limitations are unified by the *Courant criterion*, a general measure of the spatio-temporal quality of a model[8]. Grid type models of physical phenomena are usually governed by differential equations: to calculate the value for a given cell at the next time, a model includes not only the state of that cell, but also those of its neighbors. (Without this, models could not treat flows of materials from cell to cell.) In the actual phenomenon being modeled, there is a certain flow rate or speed of information exchange. Multiplying this speed by the time step yields a distance, and if the distance exceeds the grid cell spacing, the simulation is unstable and will produce useless results. It follows that for rapidly changing phenomena, one must use either a more intensive grid (a larger density of cells) or shorter time steps.

In sum, the problems inherent in numerical calculations are often far from trivial. As the systems theorist Foster Morrison pointed out[9]:

"In many models, even seemingly simple ones, the loss of numerical significance of extending the predictions rises so rapidly as to reduce their value to almost nothing. This was not totally unanticipated, but almost no one expected it to happen until the number of variables became large, certainly not as small as three."

Morrison touches here on another problem: the large number of free parameters required in many real-life simulations (especially ones that have a large number of parameterized model components) also leads to a proliferation of numerical errors.

There are some interesting similarities between the numerical limitations inherent in computer simulations and the famed Heisenberg uncertainty principle of quantum physics. The uncertainty principle states that the product of the uncertainty of position and the uncertainty of momentum can never be reduced beyond a minimum value -- meaning that physical measurements have an inherent, irreducible uncertainty in them. This is not the place to explore theories on the uncertainty principle, but it does have some implications for the limits of modeling, too. Positional uncertainty is due ultimately to the scale size of any measuring probe relative to what is measured. For a wave probe, it means one cannot discern objects smaller than half the wavelength; for a particle probe, it is the extent. It is the sampling limit and is thus analogous to a grid size. The first reaction to this constraint is to attempt to decrease the scale size of the probe (the wavelength or extent) as much as possible, but this can only be done by using higher and higher energies. But as the energy increases, the more the probe disturbs what is measured in process of making the measurement itself; we cannot "query" an object without disturbing it. This disturbance leads to the uncertainty in the momentum, and the shorter the scale size (i.e., the less the positional uncertainty), the greater the uncertainty in momentum becomes. In modeling, it is as if the product of the grid size and time step had some maximum number. Practically speaking, this will always be true, due to the finite size of any computer (limited number of cells) and finite computing time (limited number of time steps). The more cells used, the more computational cycles are needed to advance the model grid by one time step.

This leads directly to a second inherent limitation on all models and simulations: multiplicity or extent. We can't exactly calculate even physical phenomena because we cannot always deal with everything in a system. Computers, being of a finite size, can hold only a limited number of modeled objects. No model can extend across the spatio-temporal whole. A model treats an isolated part, limited in extent and duration. We don't model air flow around a wing, for example, by simulating every air molecule as it interacts with molecules of the wing material. Even a cubic centimeter of air contains more molecules than all the memory spaces of all the computers ever built. In practical terms, the multiplicity limitation may matter little — the model makes simplifications and still obtains an adequate, usable answer. But in theoretical terms, it leads to some interesting facts. *The computer required to model something must always be larger than what is modeled.* To simulate the universe, in every detail, the computer required to represent it would be *bigger than the universe itself* — which is to say that such a model, an authentic and complete "mirror world," is *impossible.* To put the world in a box, the box must be bigger than the world. The substrate of any model (including virtual realities) must be at least large as the subject.

In reality, any model leaves out unimportant details and/or external influences. But this is, once again, a *pragmatic* assumption, based on our usage of the model under particular circumstances. In more comprehensive terms, the necessary finiteness of models in space, time, and number, means all models are more or less approximate, except in those few cases where direct calculation is possible. This leads to the optimization problem of all models. The optimal design of a model is like the optimal design for a vehicle. It all depends on what it's used for: the ideal sports car is very different from the ideal dump truck, just as the ideal jungle cat is very different from the ideal buffalo. If one optimizes a model for detail, it will necessarily sacrifice extent and/or speed. If one optimizes for speed, the results will be of lower quality, and so on. It is here computer modelers exercise the most cleverness, but again, rather like the uncertainty principle in physics, there is always a theoretical limit beyond which model quality can never go.

One major problem is that the limitation of the model parameters based on pragmatic concerns of calculability can lead to unexpected and anomalous predictions by the model. This tendency may be abetted by data aggregation, the lumping together of many different sets of data on which the model is based, incorrectly reducing the number of model parameters[10]. To anticipate the next chapter on climate modeling, the simplifying assumptions of early computer models of the atmosphere actually led to the discovery of chaos – in this case, as an artifact of the simulation itself.

In addition to the analysis of the system into parts, there is also the analysis of the system into a set of essential attributes or state variables. Attribute analysis also applies recursively to the component entities of the system. Chapter 3 observed that relevant state variables are those that affect external interactions of the entity with others, and thus lead to observable results. Failure of attribute analysis leads to parameterized or "black box" models which reproduce empirical data within a model domain, but have no underlying explanatory law. In other words, the essential behavior of the system, the rule that governs all transitions of state variables, is not available. As for analysis into parts, attribute analysis may be of little consequence for models of narrow scope and limited purpose. It is another matter for a complete model that seeks to capture a phenomenon in its entirety. Such a model cannot merely "save the appearances." To the contrary, the model must completely represent the laws that govern the phenomena. It must comprehensively understand all the rules that govern state transitions within the system.

The modeler's relevant question is: how can we be sure the model includes the *essential* attributes of the system? How do we distinguish necessary attributes from those that are superfluous? And can we really be sure the modeled attributes are the true ones, and not merely appearances behind which lie other, more important attributes? Part of the uncertainty is due to external factors, such as data error, to be discussed in the next section. But of greater importance, the intrinsic limits of all models appear once more. We naturally see an object as a container for attributes – as a "coexistence of qualities," to use Locke's terminology. What is *not* given to the model is the object in a holistic sense. For example, I perceive a cardinal bird in a nearby tree and list its properties: it is mostly red; it has a distinctive song, a pointed crest on its head, and so on. To build a computer model of the cardinal, I would take a "bird" class which I have already built (which has, for example, the attribute of birds having wings) and extend it to model the cardinal's properties. The only problem is how to be sure I have really captured the essential features of the cardinal. To say that a cardinal is a red bird found in North America with a certain call helps me *identify* one should I see or hear it, but it is far from building a model that captures every aspect of the bird. The attributes, such as color, that are useful in identifying the bird could be accidental and meaningless to a complete model of it. Nor is the set of attributes necessarily unambiguous: a "North American red bird" could also refer, for example, to a scarlet tanager.

Closely related to attributes are the conditions imposed by the organization of concepts or classes – the "is a kind of" hierarchy. The object-oriented modeling approach implies every system has a supreme class encompassing all entities and relations in the system, a single apex of the conceptual pyramid. The question is, what should this root class, from which all other classes are derived, contain? In object-oriented analysis, two classes are unified to find a common base class, the base class contains only those attributes and methods the two classes have in common, a reduction to a common denominator. In set-theoretic terms, it is the intersection of the two sets of attributes. This approach implies the root or base class of the entire system will have the fewest attributes of all, since it only holds those occurring in all other classes in the system. In other words, it is the most generic and most impoverished of all classes. Also, only the classes at the "leaves" of the conceptual tree are concrete, i.e., have instances. The more generic classes are typically abstract and can never have instances. Socrates is an instance of the class "Man" and Man is a kind of Animal, but there are never generic instances of Animal, only instances of particular kinds of (i.e., species) of Animal.

But is the above procedure the only way to construct an "is a kind of" hierarchy? It is not. Consider, as an object-oriented example, the relations of various shapes to their base classes. A circle is a kind of ellipse, but ellipses neither have fewer attributes than a circle nor are they abstract. A circle is simply one specific kind of ellipse – an ellipse whose major axis is the same as its minor axis. The ellipse class contains a formula which can define any particular ellipse, including circles. The ellipse class encompasses and explains any possible ellipse or circle.

Such formulations are typical of mathematics. They represent a depth of understanding that every class hierarchy would like to attain. A complete model of something must be able to produce such a structure. But, in reality, the model is usually limited to a class hierarchy that only captures common attributes.

## Extrinsic Limitations

Extrinsic limitations arise from the fact that we don't know and can't know particular situations perfectly. Data is sparse. This impacts any model in several different ways. It affects every aspect of the model, but particularly the characterization of attributes and behaviors of the system. And the closer to a specific reality, the more detailed, a model, the larger the impacts of extrinsic limitations become.

Models, and in particular their state variables, are always based on imperfect data, and are thus in some way doubtful. The model is like an induction, and has all the limitations thereof. Even when run on the best imaginable computer, model results will still only be as good as the empirical data on which the model is based. The model — however true in a generalized or statistical sense — will always fall short of a complete replication of its subject. Models can be greatly improved with better data, and we can understand statistically the amount of inherent experimental error involved. But we can never take data for all possible conditions and an unlimited amount of data for each condition. So we can have confidence in a model so far as its data goes — beyond it, we can't be sure. Even a mature science like physics has its interstices[11]:

"Even the most fundamental sciences have causal gaps. The difficulties of the many-body problem leave a possible doubt regarding the exact lawfulness of the moon's motion; our ignorance of nuclear forces veils precise nuclear laws; the chemist, if he insists, can make a point of the random character of molecular actions so long as detailed forces between molecules have not been calculated."

Now, before the reader dismisses this with a wave of the hand as something esoteric and irrelevant, he should keep in mind that it was the exploration of exactly such "causal gaps" that gave birth to both Einstein's theory of relativity and the quantum theory. Neither of these invalidated old data, nor really even old theories — they showed that the old theories were really a limiting case of a more general description. And so also with any model. New information may not just mean an adjustment of some detail of the laws governing the model; it might mean going completely beyond the existing model. An old model might not be invalidated at all in its zone of applicability, just as the mechanical engineer gets along entirely adequately with Newton's laws, and can ignore Einstein and Planck. Rather, it may be that to extrapolate the model beyond its current frame of reference is not only wrong statistically (e.g., our line misses data points beyond its bounds), but is too limited *conceptually*, like trying to understand a three-dimensional object by modeling its shadows. Certainly, one could develop an adequate model of this or that shadow. But a true and complete model requires a conceptual leap beyond two dimensions.

We also lack perfect knowledge of what is *outside* of any model. Suppose, for example, we had a perfect model of some entirely deterministic phenomenon, such as celestial mechanics. As in Laplace's thought experiment, given the locations, velocities, masses, and forces of objects at any one time, we would be able to calculate any future or past state of the system. Now suppose that we wish to simulate an actual system, such as the earth and sun or of an arrow flying on its way a target. Could the model do it? It could only with perfect and complete knowledge of the initial conditions, and that we do *not* have. So even a perfect model is still not guaranteed to exactly replicate reality, since the initial conditions are partly unknown. This is a common problem faced by the meteorologist. Weather models are based on well-understood laws of fluid mechanics and thermodynamics, yet weather predictions are in error. Why? Because the meteorologist does not have complete data, even with satellite photographs and the like, (a knowledge of the complete state of the atmosphere) at any given time, and thus lacks the exact initial conditions for a weather simulation.

There is also, once again, the problem of systemic isolation. A model could be perfect, but the system it models is still cut out of the world and placed in isolation, conceptually speaking. As long as outside influences are unimportant, the model would produce valid results. But whatever comes into — or, just as importantly, leaves — the model is essentially an unknown.

So our necessary ignorance of all conditions affecting an actual system mean that any model (an idealized system) will necessarily fall short of complete accuracy and truth, even if it could perfectly replicate the laws governing an entirely deterministic system. These unknowns function as effectively random factors, meaning that model predictions must be at variance with reality to a lesser or greater degree. In fact, stochastic variables are introduced into models to account for such external unknowns, such as a rate of incoming phone calls. There is a decoupling between the deterministic laws governing a system, and our ability to model and predict that system[12]. *Even in a reductionist scenario, Laplace's dream remains an unreachable goal.* No model can perfectly replicate the world, or any piece of it, just as no machine will ever draw absolutely perfect circles.

It is the model's unique capability, as opposed to theory, to get close to particularity, as a sort of "moving picture." Yet the closer we get to the particular, to the irregular, even the nonlinear continuity, to the interconnected, the more chance the model will break down. There must always be a certain fuzziness to answers on the exact level, regardless of their truth on the generalized level. In simulation, an uncertain prediction is tested against more or less uncertain data. This is a two-edged sword for the modeler. On the one hand, the data does not invalidate the model. On the other, we can never be entirely certain that the model's predicted outcome is the one that will actually occur. This is fully in keeping with the previous chapter's argument for the generality of induction. Just because we can attain certainty on a general level does not guarantee perfect and complete understanding of specific results.

Consider, for example, the seemingly simple mechanics problem of a falling rock[13]. If we compare a number of instances of falling rocks, we can obtain a law governing falling objects in general. But the more we concern ourselves with the investigation of *one particular* fall, in all its details, the less applicable general explanations will be. We cannot, for example, ignore the exact shape of the rock, the density and temperature of the air through which it falls, the exact way it was dropped, and so on. In other words, the more exact we wish to be, the less we can tear a system out of its web of interconnections to the rest of the world.

Let us consider just one more weather example. There is near my house a park that I enjoy to walk in. It is an unkempt park of dirt trails, prairie grass, cattails, and scattered copses of oak and cottonwood. A few years ago, a tornado tore a swath through the park. In some places, it snapped huge old trees in two like dry twigs, while just a few yards away other trees were completely untouched. Such are the peculiar ways of tornadoes. Suppose I had sought to predict this tornado and its effects. Also suppose I had all the information and computer models that were available to the National Weather Service at the time. I could have reliably predicted that the day was ripe for thunderstorms and tornadoes. But even with the best models available, I could not have predicted that *this particular* thunderstorm would have appeared and produced *that* tornado, at such a place and such a time. Suppose instead that I locked a detailed weather model onto the thunderstorm and the tornado at the exact moment it spun down from the clouds. The model would doubtless give a good prediction of the general track of the storm and the path of the tornado. But could it predict that Tree A would be blown down by the whirlwind, while Tree B, not five feet away, would be unharmed? The answer is simply, no. The model is not detailed enough, nor is the data upon which it is based.

This small example is just one event in a bigger one. Consider a hundred square meters of this park, right where the tornado ripped through. Suppose we were challenged to build a model of this hundred-meter wood. At first, it seems fairly straightforward -- to describe the trees and animals and soil as an ecosystem. But then we discover we must account for many things that act on our system from without, like the weather, like unexpected tornadoes. The more we probe into the details of the wood, the more we find ourselves drawn into its interconnections with the whole. The wood was once, only a few decades ago, the verge of a farm, and before that clearing, another, older woods, probably with a different variety of trees. A complete model would draw in the entire human and natural history of the region.

## Reductionism, Determinism, and Reality

Computer models extrapolate or continue already known rules and conditions. If the model's subject is effectively isolated, or forms a closed system, and continues along on its own laws, then we may predict its future with accuracy. But in the real world, as previous examples show, we can never be entirely sure of that. The model, in and of itself, can never account for the unexpected. All is not lost, however. Assuming the reductionist hypothesis, and that reality is entirely governed by deterministic and mathematical laws, we can still fall short of perfect prediction and have a clear understanding of why the prediction fails. Indeed, we can often characterize it statistically.

It is otherwise for any phenomenon that falls outside of reductionism. The inherent limitations of models run closely parallel to the typical tendencies and limitations of conceptual reasoning. When investigating the world scientifically, we strive to reduce it to a closed system governed by mathematical laws or mechanical analogies, just as a computer model would. As the philosopher and scientist Emile Meyerson emphasized, "Mechanism is not the fruit of science, for mechanism and science were born at the same time. ... It finds our minds prepared, it seduces them, and is immediately adopted, unless contradicted by very evident facts."[14] Mathematical formulae are to the modern mind the most perfect kind of knowledge, quantitative and objective. And scientific theory usually proceeds *as if*, behind the iron mask of data, nature *really is* mechanical and mathematical. It is a methodological assumption that has proved extraordinarily fruitful in physics, its natural home. But when stretched beyond physics into other areas, reaching an antipode in human affairs, the mechanical or reductionist approach becomes increasingly questionable.

We can look at this from the angle of the type of system being modeled. As summarized in the discussion of the modeling paradigm at the end of Chapter 3 and in Table 3-2, Foster Morrison has organized dynamic systems into five basic classes depending on the degree of difficulty of modeling them[15].

Systems of Morrison's types Zero or I, such as simple mechanical problems, can be solved directly and no numerical methods are required. Type II systems, such as the many-body celestial mechanics problems of the previous chapter, will always introduce some degree of approximation and can only be approached by a simulation or through perturbation methods[16]. These systems can be treated as solvable over a certain period of time, but errors in the calculation are unavoidable and can never be reduced to zero. Type I and II systems often have either cyclic or constant rate growth behavior.

Type III and IV systems – those with chaotic or random behavior – obviously cannot be modeled exactly. Any model results for such systems, as will be discussed below, are valid only in an average, aggregate, and statistical sense. Exact prediction of individual states as Laplace would have hoped is not possible.

The dilemma for the computational model-builder is that the only systems that clearly fall into classes zero, I, and II are of a physical and usually linear nature – essentially those of physics, chemistry, and engineering. Other systems can be approached only at an abstract and/or statistical level, even if they are assumed to be entirely deterministic on the microscopic scale.

It seems fairly obvious there is a progression here. In the most physical and quantitative of the sciences, like physics, astronomy, chemistry, geology, and so on, we are usually able to identify systems amenable to computer modeling. Ascending in complexity to biology, psychology, and human society, however, the less meaningful models and physical analogies become. In those areas, we cannot represent the subject in terms of a closed mechanical system with a set of simple relations. To abstract such a model from the subject becomes steadily less meaningful. It reliably captures less and less as the subject ceases to conform in an obvious way to the modeling paradigm. The fact that such subjects have often proven intractable to models, except on the most superficial level, is evidence that reductionist assumptions must at least be adjusted in practical terms.

Reductionism also asserts that all experience is ultimately governed by necessary and deterministic laws. This is not the place to argue whether there are authentic freedom or random phenomena. If they do exist, however, they represent a serious problem for the would-be Laplaces of the computer age. They are both essential unknowables for the model — something that, by definition, cannot be modeled. If human freedom exists, within the limits it is authentic, it is unpredictable from the "outside," however meaningful human actions and intentions may be in a retrospective. Freedom does not, of course, concern us in the domain of modeling the physical world. But even here there is the tantalizing, and still very much unresolved, question as to whether there is authentic *randomness*. It is a problem that lies at the basis of discussions of phenomena like entropy and it was thrust to the forefront of modern physics by the quantum theory. As is well known, only a few simple problems can be solved exactly in quantum mechanics, such as the harmonic oscillator and the hydrogen atom. Even in those cases, the calculated results are really only a statistical average.

Quantum physics raises the possibility of true indeterminacy[17]. In classical mechanics, a given set of initial conditions always leads to the same result: A is always followed by B. In quantum mechanics, this is not so. For a given set of initial conditions, there can be different outcomes, each with its own probability. A might be followed by B 50% of the time, C 25% of the time, D 15% of the time, and E 10% of the time. The "choice" of an outcome *appears* entirely random to an observer. For every move made, dice are thrown. And the lifetimes of quantum states also appear to fluctuate randomly: two identical uranium nuclei, for instance, will persist for different durations before disintegrating; all the physicist can do is characterize an average "half life" for uranium. In other words, there appears to be a real indeterminate element in quantum physics. It is clamped within the narrow limits of the atomic and subatomic world, of course, but it is real nonetheless, and has important consequences for the systems built out of those seemingly random building blocks.

One of the fathers of modern quantum theory, Werner Heisenberg, emphasized the difficulties of fitting quantum phenomena into the framework of mathematical concepts derived from classical mechanics[18]:

"Instead of asking: How can one in the known mathematical scheme express a given experimental situation? the other question was put: Is it true, perhaps, that only such experimental situations can arise as can be expressed in the mathematical formalism? The assumption that this was actually true led to limitations in the use of those concepts that had been the basis of classical physics since Newton."

In other words, the mathematical modeling "categories" used by the physicist and in measurement are crucial limitations even for purely physical phenomena. Is the randomness merely apparent (e.g., an artifact of the measuring process) or really there? That is still an unanswered question.

True randomness is also implicit in the notion of entropy. Entropy is a measure of the order of a system. A well-ordered system (such as a crystalline lattice) has low entropy, while a disordered system (such as an ideal gas) has a high entropy. Even if the systems described by entropy can be understood on the microscopic level in a thoroughly mechanical fashion (e.g., atoms as so many little billiard balls), the famous Second Law of Thermodynamics, or law of the increase of entropy, proceeds *as if* there were true chance in reality. The entropy of a system always increases to its maximum allowed value. An ice cube immersed in warm water melts until the water is uniformly cool. The net thermal energy before and after the ice cube melted is exactly the same: what has changed is the degree of *order*, the distribution of the energy. The orderly cube of ice has disappeared into a random and tepid uniformity.

The notion of entropy is completely general. It is a property of any complex system. Entropy is abstracted from complex systems just as inertia is abstracted from simple ones. So the Second Law has implications far beyond the scope of mechanics (one famous application has been the theory of information entropy). And that law raises another problem for the modeler — namely, the possibility of irreversible processes.

Time in classical mechanics is reversible. A movie of the motions of colliding objects — balls on a pool table, for example — makes just as much physical sense whether the film runs backwards or forwards. Cause and effect can be transformed into one another just by rewinding. In other words, there is a complete identity between cause and effect. This is the sort of world Laplace was thinking of calculating. Relativistic "space-time" only reinforces this: time is transformed into a fourth spatial dimension. It is in such a mechanistic world that time travel would make the most sense. Traveling in time would be like traveling in space. Pure mechanics means the nullification of time, its reduction to a scan through a predetermined geometric space.

Irreversible processes, in contrast, cannot be "rewound" and still make physical sense. They have a true "arrow of time"; the system moves only one way. The famous example of an irreversible process is the ink drop experiment. A blue-black drop of ink falls into a clear glass of water. It begins as an ordered sphere or teardrop and even once in the water, it is relatively concentrated. But as time passes, the ink is diffused uniformly. Diffused ink in water never spontaneously concentrates itself into a drop. Diffusion of the ink is irreversible: it always moves from the more ordered to the less ordered state, as the second law stipulates. On the microscopic level, the water molecules diffuse the ink molecules in what, from the ink drop's point of view, is a random process (because the exact motions of the water molecules are an unknown). But the law of entropy increase assumes they are truly random, and connected with this is the notion of a true irreversibility. In theory, the diffusion of the ink drop could be modeled by solving the equations of motion for the ink and the water molecules. In reality, this would mean solving on the order of $10^{23}$ equations, which in practical terms is impossible[19]. Thus, some kind of stochastic and collective approach is required. But such an approach of its nature precludes exact prediction.

Models can, of course, simulate random phenomena through stochastic state variables. They also have a tendency to introduce a false randomness through numerical diffusion. But that is just the point: to the extent something is random, we can't predict it. Any deterministic model, considered by itself, can be thrown into reverse, just like a classical mechanical system. Randomness is either due to the faults of the model or a consciously introduced random factor.

There is something else to discern with regards to simulations, randomness, and time. Models have only a single time-track. But an indeterminate world has a curious structure: it is not unilinear, but branching. Each present instant radiates several possible futures, of which only one will be actualized. Models can deal with branching realities (multiple outcomes) by Monte Carlo or random walk procedures, where every possible branch is explored in turn. Or they can explore each branch simultaneously, spawning parallel universes until the computer runs out of memory. But what they cannot do, by definition, is predict the *exact* outcome of any particular event, even when given a complete set of initial conditions.

Another roadblock confronting the modeling paradigm is that of organism. There is no inherent problem with modeling organic systems, if we see them simply as systems of interacting parts, each with a different function. Indeed, computer models are very useful in understanding such systems. But the notion of organism in its full sense stands in contradiction to the reductionist assertion that things are simply the sums of their parts. An organism is more than the sum of its parts, and conversely, the parts cannot be understood apart from the whole. In other words, the theory of organism cannot see entities as machines, composed of a set of spatially extended parts, each with a separate and distinct location. That organisms have extended bodies can simply be seen as a consequence of the fact that they act and interact in the physical world, and must therefore not violate its rules. They can indeed be understood mechanically in an operational sense on the "micro" level. It also implies that the forces (or "fields" or "forms") at work in organisms as a set of simple two-body forces as those of physics are. Rather, there are forces at work on the organism as a whole, n-body forces, collective phenomena. The "parts" of the organism could really be seen as subfields, which (unlike mechanical parts) can occupy the same spatial location and penetrate into one another. At the same time, there is the notion of saturation of forces, forces that act on specific components and no others[20]. Indeed, the notion of a universality of forces — the same forces acting exactly the same way everywhere — breaks down.

Whether such organic phenomena do really exist, in life, society, or the mind, is not our concern here. The point is, if they do, they represent an almost insuperable barrier to the modeler, if the goal is exact prediction. The problem is not so much one of determinism versus indeterminism (an organic system can be entirely deterministic in nature), but of characterizing the system to begin with. If there is an organizing principle at work on a whole, we cannot understand it by analyzing the system into its parts, characterizing each part separately, then seeing the whole as the sum of those parts. Because of this, the modeler cannot be entirely sure that all forces have been accounted for.

An example of the difficulties involved can be found in the problem of protein folding[21]. An unfolded protein will fold up again much more quickly than molecular simulations would indicate. In fact, the folding speed is so much quicker than the calculation that it leads to what is called Levinthal's Paradox: there are so many intermediate states in the folding process that even if the protein spent only one-trillionth of a second in each of these states, the entire folding process would require a time longer than the age of the universe! Somehow, the protein molecule "knows" its final state and goes directly to it – a phenomenon that would have delighted Aristotle, but fills the modern biochemical modeler with consternation. Teleology, like randomness, even if only apparent, falls outside the modeling paradigm.

This points to a related problem: there are many cases where data are not easily reducible to mathematical form. Or it may be impossible to easily grasp a complex system due to the nature of the data. This is often the case, for example, in biological measurements[22]:

"Measurement for the life sciences is complicated by the fact that there is a very considerable variation in result from subject to subject, no matter what parameter is being examined. ... Even when measurements are made on the same subject, but under different environmental stimuli, variability of the same order can be expected."

In other words, the modeler in such situations must labor under the fact of the difficulties of characterizing the system because of the inherent limitations of the data itself — rather as if one were asked to model an automobile engine strictly on the basis of a recording of its sounds and a photograph of its exterior. Data becomes more like a sense-quality, like color or tone. One may reduce color to a numerical representation, for example, but that numerical representation alone is not the color. It is the symbol of the color in a specific system of representation, just the way that letters represent sounds.

Measurement may be impossible because it disturbs or destroys the system being studied. This occurs even in physical measurements due to the uncertainty principle: as was discussed, we must interact with something in order to measure it, but the very process of interaction changes the measurement. This fact becomes more important in studies of living beings, the mind, and society, where the measuring process could destroy the subject being measured.

## Between Order and Randomness: Chaotic Systems

One universal assumption of systems modeling is that "small causes lead to small results." The modeler tries to characterize the major forces at work in a system and either excludes the smaller ones or deals with them as needed for a particular problem. In other words, modeling assumes a linearity of forces, an assumption that arises from our common sense experience of the world. If we exert a small force on an object, it only moves a little, and with increasing force, there is increasing movement.

But such assumptions do not always and necessarily hold true. Small forces can have big effects, in the case of a catalyst or nonlinear force. A huge explosion can be set off by a tiny spark. A pencil balanced on its point can be tipped over by the tiniest breath of air. The common property of such systems is an extreme sensitivity to the details of initial and boundary conditions, usually combined with non-linear forces and feedbacks. Such systems will often demonstrate chaotic behavior (Morrison's Type III systems) or undergo the sudden, unpredictable transformations studied by catastrophe theory. Although earlier researches into non-linear systems hinted at chaos, their definite recognition in 1963 belongs to the meteorologist E.N. Lorenz[23]. The discovery arose from his attempts to model the atmosphere, a complex non-linear fluid system. Notably, the chaotic solution appeared (as was discussed previously) from the simplifying assumptions made to render the problem tractable on the computers of the day. Lorenz also coined the term "the butterfly effect" — the flapping of the wings of a butterfly in the rain forest causes changes to the atmosphere, however minuscule, that have huge and incalculable results elsewhere[24].

Fluid mechanics is rich in non-linear problems that lead to chaotic results. One of the best examples is found in the phenomenon of turbulence, which has been called one of the last great unsolved problems in physics. Yet turbulence can be of great importance in many systems studied using computer simulation, such as airflow around wings, mixture of hot and cold air in combustion, and weather systems.

Turbulence means the breaking up of the smooth flow of a fluid into innumerable vortices of different sizes and strengths. A tiny irregularity in an object (e.g., an aircraft wing) can cause a flow to churn itself into a tangled mass of turbulence. Turbulence is ultimately due to the non-linearity of the laws governing the fluid. Even if the laws are well-understood, that is no guarantee of the ability of the modeler to calculate turbulence. Fluid flow is modeled on grids, and can reliably model only those phenomena that are the same size or larger than the grid mesh. But turbulence typically has an infinite spectrum of vortices, and a great deal of the energy of a turbulent flow can reside in subsystems smaller than the grid size. Despite the great ingenuity that has been applied to modeling turbulence, it cannot be modeled exactly. It becomes a random factor in the calculation, no matter how fine a grid mesh we use. Turbulence also shows how the modeling paradigm of distinct objects and relations can break down. The grid, to recall, is essentially a set of virtual objects and relations imposed on a continuity. In turbulence, continuity matters – it is continuity's revenge on the modeler's finite mesh.

Chaos theory has been invoked as a way of modeling turbulence[25]. Chaotic modeling approaches turbulence by seeing it as a size spectrum of structures, ranging from the largest turbules down to the tiniest vortices, and understanding this spectrum as a product of the nonlinear fluid forces. However useful this is, however, it does not provide a means of predicting the *exact* behavior of a fluid. That is, the modeler can use the results of chaos theory to provide a general characterization or system average of the state of the fluid, but not to predict its specific configuration at any one time.

Yet we need not turn to systems as complex as turbulent fluids to discover chaos. A simple pendulum driven outside the range of small oscillations or the collisions of balls on an asymmetric billiards table are also capable of exhibiting chaotic behavior[26]. The curious fact about such systems is that they are entirely calculable at each step of their motion, yet their extreme sensitivity to initial conditions renders exact prediction of their behavior practically impossible for long time frames.

Chaotic behavior has even been detected in the realm of celestial mechanics, the paradigm (as the last chapter showed) of deterministic systems. As explained by Ivars Peterson in his book *Newton's Clock: Chaos in the Solar System*, clear evidence of chaos has been found in the motions of asteroids, the erratic tumbling of Saturn's moon Hyperion, and in the orbit of Pluto[27]. In fact, even the orbits of the Moon about the Earth and the Earth about the Sun have small chaotic contributions that degrade the predictability of their positions on very long time scales. The reason for such chaos in the solar system is that, while celestial mechanics problems are exactly soluble for two point-like bodies, the extension to three or more bodies introduces a non-linearity and sensitivity to initial conditions. Depending on the conditions, motion in such many-body systems is sometimes regular and sometimes chaotic[28]. Many-body problems, like fluid mechanics, are an area with many chaotic solutions.

An additional complication for modeling is, as was shown, that chaos can be an artifact of the modeling process itself. Lorenz's climate model first brought this out, but any kind of numerical diffusion in a model can enhance chaotic behavior[29].

In sum, chaotic systems provide a curious example of systems that are often calculable, yet provide no detailed predictive capability. They are ordered, yet disorderly. Models of such systems, like stochastic systems, can provide only statistical averages.

## Summary: Laplace Humbled, but Not Destroyed

To summarize: we must conclude that Laplace's dream is an illusion – to the chagrin of the computer modeler. It fails even within the bounds of physico-mathematical reductionism, which the modeling paradigm follows so closely. And for those areas outside the modeling paradigm, it must fail altogether. We therefore cannot exactly calculate the world. Once theory descends into reality in the shape of a model, it is hedged in with all sorts of limitations. On the other hand, the computer model is far from worthless. To the degree that the reality modeled conforms to the modeling paradigm, it can produce complete success.

Moreover, even in the case where exact prediction is not possible – as for chaotic and stochastic systems – statistical approximations are still possible. Such approximations can provide useful forecasts of average behavior over a restricted time frame. The most familiar example of such statistical forecasting can be found in weather prediction, and its extension to climate modeling, that the next chapter considers.

## Chapter 8

# Climates of Fact

The first chapter discussed the three possible culminations of modeling and simulation. This and the remaining chapters of the book aim to explore those culminations or "ultimate models" in detail. The first and most obvious ultimate model would be of the natural universe: a complete simulation of physical processes. In many ways, this is by far the easiest ultimate model to build. For the universe is a system, governed by deterministic laws, most of which (at least in the realm of physics and chemistry) are well understood. Such a model would be a vast expansion in scale, but not in principle, of the simple models of the solar system presented earlier. From the behavior of one solar system, we can extrapolate to innumerable others. A galaxy, for example, can be readily modeled as a set of mass points that are its component stars.

Of course, we do not have complete information regarding distant worlds nor will we any time soon, but in general outline, it should be possible to build a comprehensive model of the cosmos. Not only would such a model provide a complete picture of the present-day universe, but one should be able to run it forwards or backwards in time to represent any past or future state: Laplace's dream once more. Moreover, the modeler would be able to modify the conditions of the present universe to investigate alternate universes.

However, before the computational microcosm can really represent the macrocosm, we must be able to entirely represent some small portion of the universe that is well known and directly testable – such as the Earth. If we can build a comprehensive model of the Earth and its processes, and have it operate before us on the computer screen just like the real world, then we have confidence that the task before us is possible.

Actually, like another stacking doll within the Earth lies a subsystem that received a great deal of attention from model-builders over the past three decades: the Earth's atmosphere, weather, and climate. Climate models – and especially global climate models – represent an excellent test of the limits of computer modeling and simulation within the purely physical realm. They are thus the main focus of the present chapter.

Climate models necessarily involve a complex set of submodels of many different interacting systems. Climate modeling has, in fact, pushed back the frontiers of physical modeling in many ways. Another factor that makes such models especially worthy of notice is that, despite their immense complexity, they involve only well-understood laws of physics and chemistry. Basically, the study of weather and climate is the study of the heating, cooling, and motions of air and substances carried by the air, such as water vapor, or systems affecting the air, such as the oceans. It is all fluid dynamics, thermodynamics, with some chemistry and transport of radiation. In other words, the study of climate involves no "bleeding edge" science, as a broader cosmological model would. Modeling climate taxes the atmospheric scientist because of its size and complexity, not because of its basic laws. Moreover, there is abundant data to validate a climate model against – great masses of weather statistics – which cannot be said of other areas of earth science. Climatologists have also gained in recent decades a much-improved understanding of the linkages between the systems that determine climate. One important example is how the oceans influence the weather both in the short and long term, as shown by steadily better understanding of the El Niño (Southern Oscillation) cyclical interaction between the Pacific Ocean and weather across the globe.

Climate and weather models (the former is really just an expansion of the latter) also provide a valuable tool for predicting future conditions. Such predictions might be as simple as tomorrow's temperature and chance of rain at my location, or as complex as gradual global climate change on a time scale of decades. The same model can also be used to understand the causes of past climate fluctuations, such as the ice ages of the Pleistocene or the much warmer global climate of the Mesozoic. Further, the basic model framework for the Earth's climate can be adapted to the study of the very different atmospheres of other planets, such as Venus, Mars, Jupiter, or Saturn's moon Titan.

Put simply, if building a complete simulated world is possible, climate models represent an excellent starting point. At the same time, climate models are perhaps the best test of the *limitations* of models in the physical world, and hence of models in general. That such models *are* limited is borne out by the simple fact that tomorrow's weather predictions are far from being 100% accurate. Our aim is to determine which limitations are due to lack of technology (i.e., a problem that can be remedied by faster computers and more data) and those that stem from inherent limits in the models themselves.

A study of climate models is also timely. Climate models improved to the point of credibility just at a time when the question of global climate change – especially the question of the role of human industry in that change – began to rise to prominence. Two possible man-made side effects, global warming through increased atmospheric carbon dioxide levels and the thinning of the stratospheric ozone layer, are increasingly important questions of public policy. But to comprehend these problems one must first understand how climate models work and whether they can give definitive answers to questions of climate change. This chapter's aim is not to stake out any particular position in the ongoing controversy, which unfortunately has become a political football[1]. One can only hope that a measure of objectivity will be restored.

Towards a better understanding, the chapter will explain what climate is and the scope of the climate system, then discuss the various approaches to global climate modeling, as well as the verification and limits of existing climate models. At this point, we will be properly equipped to understand the possible reality and causes of global warming, and the role of climate models in that prediction.

## Climate and Conceptual Models

What is climate? This question is perhaps best answered by comparing climate with weather. Weather is concerned with the day-to-day changes in the atmosphere, its instantaneous state at any particular time. It is also concerned with short-term predictions of the atmosphere, and its aspects that affect us most directly, such as tomorrow's temperature and chance of precipitation. In most of the world, weather changes rapidly, on a time scale of hours or days. Climate, in contrast, can be thought of as averaged weather. The fluctuations of the weather cancel out to yield a well-defined average at a certain place and time. At the same place at the same time, we should expect similar weather from year to year. (The whole notion of climate depends on the regularity and recurrence of atmospheric conditions – if the atmosphere continually underwent violent, random variations, one could not reasonably describe a climate.) The *global* climate is the average of local climates for the entire earth.

The most important climatic factors from a biological point of view are temperature and precipitation, as well as their seasonality. These factors determine broad regions across the world of similar flora and hence regions of analogous ecosystems. They also govern agriculture and gardening. We quite naturally see climate in terms of the contrast of desert and forest, of polar ice and tropics. On this basis alone, it is possible to develop a very useful picture of climate. The climate zones developed by the German climatologist Wladimir Köppen in 1918 (refined later by himself and Glenn Trewartha) are based on botanical factors[2]. The fact that Köppen and Trewartha required only five major categories (A = tropical, B = dry, C = subtropical or temperate, D = cool, and E = polar), as well as some modifiers to indicate the seasonality of temperature and precipitation (e.g., b = cool summers, w = dry winters), testifies to the impressive regularity of climate zones across the world.

At the same time, we see there is not a single or uniform global climate – the global climate is an average over very different local climates. These zones also point out important features of the earth's climate that models must account for: the fact that the polar regions are cold, while the equatorial tropics are hot; that, in general, the interiors of continents are dry, while the oceans and coastal regions tend to be much moister.

In fact, while climates vary greatly over the world, from ice fields and burning deserts to the wet, dense green tangle of equatorial rain forests, no climate is an island. All the climates of the world form an interconnected system, each playing its role in the global circulation system of the atmosphere. We cannot model regional climates in isolation, as the meteorologist can when predicting tomorrow's weather. Areas where the local climate is determined by local factors alone – like some tropical mountain climates – are quite rare. So, when modeling one climate, we must model the global system of climates, and conversely, to model global climate is to model all the individual climates that compose it.

This notion of a global system both simplifies and complicates the modeler's task. The atmosphere is just that: a thin spherical shell of air over a much larger earth. If the atmosphere were all at sea level density and pressure, it would be less than 10 kilometers deep – as Peixoto and Oort remark in their *Physics of Climate*, on an ordinary desk globe, the atmosphere would be only the thickness of a coat of paint[3]. This thin shell – it can almost be considered a film, like the skin of a bubble – is a thermodynamic and hydrodynamic system that is almost entirely driven from without by powerful forces. This is a very important point: the atmosphere cannot be considered in isolation at all. It is a passive medium. The atmosphere is set into motion by the external influence of solar heating, as well as the rotation and gravity of the earth. The atmosphere is like a pot boiling on the stove, while being gently stirred. All the energy is from outside.

The atmosphere is small, both in terms of its size and its energy, when compared to systems like the sun or oceans that act on it. The response time of the atmosphere and its time scale (as measured by the atmospheric size divided by the average wind velocity) is about a day, much shorter than any other component of the climatic system. The next fastest component of the system, the ocean, has a time scale of about 4 months, or 100 times longer[4]. The atmosphere is like a tennis ball being batted back and forth by systems that are much bigger and "heavier" than it is.

So much is this true that we can attempt to calculate the most important component of the global climate, the global average temperature, without reference to the atmosphere at all. We can, in fact, devise a high-level, abstract conceptual model of the climate system, and it is extremely well-defined (Figure 8-1). The objects in this abstract

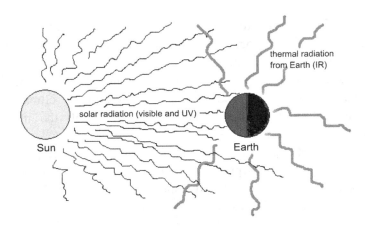

Figure 8-1. Highest Level Conceptual Climate Model: the Sun, Earth, Space System.

climate system consist of the earth, the sun, and outer space. As far as energy is concerned, the earth is a completely open system. All the thermal energy comes from the sun, and outer space acts as an infinite sink for any sunlight reflected from the earth or energy radiated away by it – more on this latter in a moment.

If open with regard to energy, the earth can equally be considered completely closed with regard to material, at least on the time scales of interest to climatologists[5]. Material neither enters nor leaves the system. It has just as much air, water, and carbon as it started out with. In other words, there is a conservation law, which is always a powerful tool for the modeler to work with.

With regard to energy, there is no systemic conservation law, but an equilibrium: a balance between the incoming energy from the sun and the outgoing energy from the earth. In fact, it must balance exactly, and the balance point depends on the earth's temperature.

Why is this so? Suppose the earth absorbed energy from the sun, but never radiated any away. The earth would steadily heat up; at some point it would become as hot as the sun and then even hotter than the sun. But this is absurd: as the earth heated up, it would begin to shine like the sun, radiating its energy away as the sun does. We are all familiar with metal heated to the point of becoming red hot and radiating sensible heat – this is what physicists call "blackbody radiation." The heat we feel from an open fire is largely of the same sort. The point to grasp is that all macroscopic bodies lose radiant energy as a function of their temperatures. Cold objects radiate at a slower rate than hot ones, but their energy is leaking away nonetheless. The rate of radiation is in fact proportional to the fourth power of the object's temperature. This means that when a steady source of energy impinges on an object (e.g., sunlight), at a certain point the energy going out is increasing much faster than the energy coming in. The incoming and outgoing energy balance, leading to an equilibrium temperature.

It should be a straightforward exercise, then, to calculate the global mean temperature of the Earth[6]. Let us assume that the atmosphere efficiently and rapidly distributes thermal energy across the globe (just as the energy in boiling water is distributed), so we can speak meaningfully of a global temperature. The sun's energy enters the climate system at a rate of about 1368 watts per square meter times the area of the earth's disk illuminated by the sun, the familiar $\pi R^2$, where R is the radius of the earth (about 6371 kilometers). Slightly complicating matters is the fact that the earth's surface is not a perfect absorber of sunlight – some of it is reflected back into space. For the earth, the average reflectivity (or albedo) is about 30%. Thus, solar energy is absorbed by the earth at a rate of:

$$P_{in} = (1 - A)S\pi R^2$$

where A is the albedo, S the solar intensity, and R the earth radius. The thermal blackbody radiation emitted by the earth can be described by an equally simple formula, the Stefan-Boltzmann law times the entire surface area of the earth ($4\pi R^2$):

$$P_{out} = 4\pi R^2 \sigma T^4$$

where $\sigma$ is the Stefan-Boltzmann constant ($5.67 \times 10^{-8}$ in mks units) and T is the temperature in degrees Kelvin. The balance will occur when $P_{in} = P_{out}$, which happens at an equilibrium temperature of:

$$T = \left[ \frac{(1 - A)S}{4\sigma} \right]^{\frac{1}{4}}$$

Plugging in the actual numbers, the model equation predicts a temperature of about 256 degrees Kelvin. How does this compare to the actual value? It's wrong by a biologically very significant amount! 256 degrees Kelvin is -17 degrees Celsius or 1 degree above zero Fahrenheit. If true, the Earth would be a giant iceball (rather like Jupiter's moon Europa), locked in the deep freeze of a perpetual ice age. So our naive first attempt at calculating the global temperature is about 32 degrees Celsius colder than the actual value.

Where did the calculation go wrong? Actually, our approach was not far off ... if we wished to calculate the surface temperature of the moon. The lunar temperature really is determined just by this simple radiation balance – rising to hundreds of degrees Celsius during the lunar day and plunging equally below zero in the frigid blackness of the lunar night. So what is the difference between the earth and the moon? It is atmosphere: but not just atmosphere as a transparent window. Something in the earth's atmosphere is holding some fraction of the earth's energy in.

We have just discovered the greenhouse effect. The analogy is, of course, to the glass in a greenhouse letting sunlight in, while preventing heat from getting out. Trace components of the earth's atmosphere, such as carbon dioxide and water vapor, absorb an important fraction of the energy radiated out by the earth's surface, reflecting it back again or absorbing it to heat the air itself. In the visible wavelengths of light, where the bulk of the Sun's rays lie, the "greenhouse gases" like carbon dioxide are as transparent as the rest of the atmosphere. But in the infrared wavelengths, where the earth's surface thermally emits, these gases are almost opaque. Without some greenhouse effect – or with too much of it – the Earth would be uninhabitable by life as we know it.

## Towards a More Detailed Model

In fact, looking at the details of the Earth's radiation balance, we discover it is astonishingly complex (Figure 8-2). And it depends on details of the climate itself, such as cloud cover and water vapor

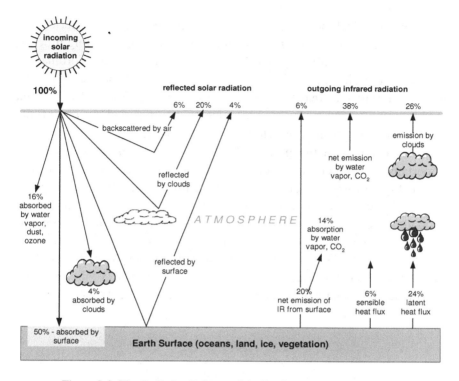

Figure 8-2. The Radiation Balance of the Earth (adapted from ref. 3).

densities, which certainly cannot be deduced from our simple sun-earth-space radiation model. So while a radiation balance occurs, and a mean global temperature can be obtained, it is not necessarily easy to calculate at exactly what temperature the balance occurs. In other words, *the details of the earth matter*. The model must account for the details of the Earth system to determine radiation balance, even though the source of the Earth's atmospheric energy is wholly external. We must model the whole complex of the Earth – not just its atmosphere, but also its oceans, topography, and so on – to model the climate.

We also know from geological and historical evidence that the earth's climate and global temperature have not been constant throughout the ages. So the equilibrium itself has changed, and the causes of the changes are not fully understood.

Thus, a useful climate model must represent all the interlocking systems on the earth that form climate. Following the modeling process, the next step is to analyze the earth into distinct subsystems. Fortunately, this is not too difficult to do. As in the earlier model, our second-order model continues to treat the sun as an external and essentially constant energy source. Also, space continues to be regarded as an infinite external sink for the energy radiated away by the earth.

What changes in the new model is our picture of the earth. It is important that each modeled subsystem have coherent behavior, reasonably uniform properties, and similar time scales. First of all, there is the obvious distinction between the Earth itself and its atmosphere. Second, there is the ocean to consider. Lastly, there are the less obvious systems of the polar ice caps and the sum total of living beings. Technically, these subsystems are termed the atmosphere, lithosphere, hydrosphere, cryosphere, and biosphere. Figure 8-3 shows them schematically, along with some of their important interactions.

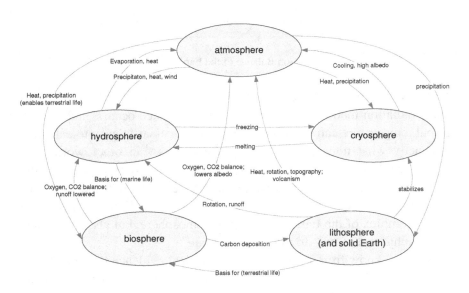

Figure 8-3. The Earth's Climatic System and its Components.

Having identified these subsystems – analyzed the climatic system – how does the climatologist characterize them? The solid Earth itself – the *lithosphere* (if we refer to the Earth's crust) – affects the atmosphere most directly through gravity and its rotation. These two are among the most important forces acting on the air and its fluid equations of motion. Less obvious influences are the tilt of the earth's axis to the plane of its rotation about the sun (responsible for the seasons as it changes the daily insolation) and the length of the year itself[7]. Equally important are the details of the earth's topography – the arrangement of continents, mountain ranges, and so on. These have a large effect not only on local weather patterns (e.g., wet conditions on the windward slopes of mountains with much dryer conditions in the "rain shadow" on the other side), but also on the global circulation. This is especially true of major mountain ranges like the Himalayas. Volcanoes represent an episodic influence on climate, due to the effects of volcanic ash and fumes injected into the atmosphere. The albedo of the Earth's surface is also included, but the albedo is usually more a function of vegetation (hence the biosphere) than the Earth itself. In other words, any global climate model must model the geographical details of the earth. The systemic relationship between the earth and the atmosphere is mostly one-way: the earth has a profound effect on the climate, but the atmosphere has very little direct effect on the earth in return.

The *atmosphere* is an "ocean of air," but that "ocean" is, in terms of mass, only a thin layer over the earth. However, the actual atmosphere extends roughly 90 km above the earth's surface because it is not of constant density (as the oceans are) but decreases in density roughly exponentially with altitude (due to the balance between air pressure and the earth's gravity) – hence, air on mountaintops is thinner than at sea level. This is of obvious importance to a climate model. The composition of the air is also important: predominately nitrogen and oxygen, with trace admixtures of minor constituents like water vapor, carbon dioxide, ozone, and argon. The major constituents of air determine most of its thermo-hydrodynamic properties – how it responds to heat and how it flows – that a model must consider. These follow well-known thermodynamic and fluid mechanical equations and can thus be incorporated into the model with confidence. Hot air rises; cooler air rushes into to replace it; the rotation of the earth swirls the wind flow. The modeling of atmospheric motion is essentially a problem in convection under the influence of rotation.[8]

Minor constituents of air can, however, have a major effect, such as the role of water vapor and carbon dioxide in the greenhouse effect. Consider ozone, for example. Ozone is a tiny fraction of the atmosphere – if all the ozone in the air above you were compressed to sea level density and pressure, it would be only 3 millimeters thick! Yet this thin layer of ozone is profoundly important (hence the controversy over the fate of the ozone), since it absorbs virtually all of the incoming hard ultraviolet light from the sun, which if it fell with full intensity on the surface would be fatal to many animals and plants, as well as dangerous to humans[9]. Absorption of UV by the ozone layer also heats the upper atmosphere, with correspondingly important effects on atmospheric structure. Equally important for climate are flows of water vapor, which not only determines patterns of precipitation, but also has a major effect on the transport of heat, due to water's large heat of condensation.

So far, the atmosphere presents the modeler with no insurmountable difficulties: it is a fluid that is heated by the earth's surface and its own absorption of radiation. Unfortunately, at this point a complication emerges, one that is both difficult to model and has a great effect on climate: cloud cover. Not only do clouds bring rain, they have a profound effect on the radiation balance. Like water vapor, clouds act to hold in radiative heat. Unlike water vapor, they are opaque to visible light, and reflect it back into space. So clouds both tend to heat and cool the earth at the same time, and complicating matters further, the balance of heating and cooling depends on the cloud type. So the effect of clouds is complex, and dealing with clouds is one of the major challenges that any climate model must deal with. Indeed, atmospheric water, because it can assume so many forms (vapor, liquid, ice) within the temperature bounds of the Earth's climates is probably the most difficult problem faced by a comprehensive climate model, since a small error can easily snowball into a major model anomaly over time.

After the atmosphere and the lithosphere, the next most important component of the climate system is the *hydrosphere*, which may be considered as equivalent to the oceans for modeling purposes. The hydrosphere is of tremendous importance to climate, but like the lithosphere, it has far more affect on the atmosphere than the reverse. Covering two-thirds of the earth, the oceans receive the majority of the solar energy that falls on the surface. Many times more massive than the atmosphere, the oceans act as a gigantic thermal reservoir, not only storing heat, but also tending to equalize it over the earth. The temperatures over the oceans and in littoral regions of continents tend to be more temperate, with less seasonal contrasts, than continental climates distant from the sea. Here also figures in the one important effect that the atmosphere has on the oceans, namely that winds tend to drive ocean currents. Without the Atlantic Ocean, and its wind-driven Gulf Stream, carrying warm tropical water northward, the climate of western Europe would resemble the continental climates of its latitude: Russia, Siberia, or Labrador. The ocean is also, of course, the major reservoir of water on the earth and the source of most atmospheric water vapor – at any one time, only about 0.001 % of the earth's available water is in the atmosphere[10]!

For short-term climate models, the hydrosphere can be included as a constant boundary condition. However, for longer term models, such as would be used for studying climate changes, a complete model of the oceans and their coupling to the atmosphere must be included, and this relation of the two subsystems is complex and in some respects still not entirely understood. This relation is unlike that between the terrestrial earth and the air, which is one-way and much simpler. The oceans, in addition to acting as a heat reservoir, also hold large amounts of atmospheric gases in solution, and thus act as a buffer for the atmospheric composition no less than its temperature. The ocean holds about 50 times as much carbon dioxide as the atmosphere does[11]. The details of the storage and release of such gases, and their dependencies on all the combinations of possible atmospheric and oceanic conditions, is obviously not simple, although a long term climate model must find some way to incorporate them.

The *cryosphere* means predominately the earth's polar ice caps, and secondarily the seasonal advance and retreat of snow cover in the subpolar regions. The cryosphere affects climate primarily through the radiation balance, both globally and locally. Ice and snow have a high reflectivity or albedo for visible light (80+ %), much higher than that of bare ground or vegetation (15 - 30 %). Thus, much more of the sun's energy is lost from the system immediately in an ice-covered environment. In the polar regions, the high albedo of ice and snow are the dominating factor in the climate[12]. Ice and snow are also almost perfect radiators of thermal (infrared) energy back into space, act as excellent thermal insulators (e.g., sea ice blocking the otherwise mitigating effects of polar seas), and require a great deal of thermal energy to melt. Thus, the effect of the cryosphere on climate is very strongly to cool it. This leads to a positive feedback effect, because once ice establishes itself, it tends to make the local climate still colder due to the reduction of absorption of sunlight and the increase of radiative outflow. The reverse effect of the atmosphere on the cryosphere is mainly through precipitation and thermal transport, which also shows strong feedbacks.

This brings us to perhaps the least obvious component of the earth's climate system: the *biosphere*, the sum-total of all living beings in the world. We have noted the profound effect that climate has on terrestrial life. The climatic variables of precipitation, temperature, and seasonality largely determine what vegetation will grow in a particular place. Being the root of the food chain, the plants act as a strong constraint on what animals can survive, and thus determine the ecosystem. Geographically widely separated parts of the world belonging to the same climate zone will favor similar agriculture, wildlife, and seasonal weather patterns. The fact that French and Italian grapes and Australian eucalyptus trees grow so well in California is no accident; it is due to the existence of a similar dry summer subtropical ("Mediterranean") climate in all these places.

If terrestrial ecosystems are merely a passive product of climate, a climate model could omit the biosphere. Instead, the biosphere has a decisive influence on the atmosphere, a fact which became completely clear only recently.

In the short term, the principal influence of life on climate is the modification of the albedo by vegetation. Forested land has a significantly lower albedo (~0.15) compared to the bare rock or sand of a desert (~0.40). Hence, vegetated land will absorb more solar energy than a desert. Destruction of vegetation can set up a positive feedback effect leading to desertification, decreasing the albedo, lowering heat and rainfall, eliminating still more vegetation.   Secondly, plants soak up rainfall, and emit it back into the atmosphere through transpiration, or absorb it into plant growth, whereas water falling on bare ground will have a greater tendency simply to run off.   The thermal and humidity effects of life thus must be accounted for in any comprehensive climate model.

But there is another influence of life on climate, and this influence involves the marine as well as terrestrial biospheres.  And that is the composition of the atmosphere itself. It has long been known that plants emit oxygen as a by-product of photosynthesis and that animals use this oxygen to help fuel themselves, emitting in turn carbon dioxide that can be used by plants.  The connection between this process and the overall composition of the atmosphere was not grasped until the past few decades: excepting the relatively inert gases of nitrogen and argon, *the present composition of the atmosphere is entirely due to life*.  Without life, the atmosphere would become completely different within a few thousand years.  And thus, far from being ignorable, a long-term climate model or model of climatic change must include the biosphere.

It is life that accounts for the anomalous composition of Earth's atmosphere in comparison to other planets, and we could not have inferred the earth's atmospheric properties from a comparison them.  The earth, in fact, has an atmosphere completely different in character from its cosmic siblings.  The pre-biotic atmosphere of the earth was, as can be inferred from geological evidence, a largely a combination of carbon dioxide, nitrogen, and water vapor.  Earth began with an amount of atmospheric carbon dioxide similar to that of Venus[13] – the Earth and Venus began their stories as sisters, if not twins.  From a common origin, their paths completely diverged.  As the Sun steadily brightened over a million millennia, sultry Venus boiled over into runaway greenhouse effect, with a surface temperature capable of melting lead.  The resulting atmosphere of Venus is a dense mantle of carbon dioxide and poisonous sulfuric acid vapor.  Mother Earth might have eventually ended up just the same, if she had not borne within her a means of changing her atmosphere, namely living beings.  It was life, first in the form of microscopic bacteria and blue-green algae, that steadily removed the primordial Earth's thick blanket of carbon dioxide and slowly replaced it with oxygen. In fact, what stands out about the Earth is its relatively *low* fraction of atmospheric carbon dioxide, and its anomalously high fraction of oxygen and water – by far the highest of any world we know of.

Where did the carbon dioxide go? It was deposited into thick beds of carbonate rocks, like limestone, and later into the "fossil fuels" of coal and oil[14]. With rising oxygen levels, the ozone layer at the top the atmosphere could form, and extend its protective parasol against the deadly ultraviolet rays of the sun. This in turn made life in the ocean shallows and then on land possible. So the atmosphere – and thus climate – that life requires is itself a product of life. Climate and life, seen in the long run, are completely interdependent, and they grew up together. It was for this reason that the climatologist Stephen Schneider could justly write of *The Coevolution of Climate and Life*[15].

For the climate modeler, this means a considerable complication. If we are simply interested in replicating the present climate, it can be ignored, other than for the albedo and hydrological effects previously discussed. On the other hand, in a study of climate change, or of climates of the geological past, it is essential to include biospheric effects. Life must be accounted for in one area in particular: the earth's carbon cycle, which controls the amount of atmospheric carbon dioxide. Being a "greenhouse gas," it in turn affects all the other components of the climate system. In several ways, the biosphere can be considered the regulative hub of the global climate system, as it is the only component capable of an active response.

It is obvious that any realistic climate model is going to be complex, a major undertaking. We have five major systems – atmosphere, hydrosphere, lithosphere, cryosphere, and biosphere – linked together by relations that are not only complex, but are also often nonlinear in character. The components of the system are different in physical composition, structure, behavior, and essential time scale. As the next modeling step, let us consider the nature of these linkages.

One way to look at the relations is in terms of the presence or absence of feedback phenomena. By feedback is meant that the effect of one system on another is cycled back into the original system and its state. If the influence is to increase the original phenomenon, it is a *positive feedback*. Examples of positive feedback include the build-up or melting of the polar ice (such feedback was surely a major factor in the ice ages), as well as desertification, which raises the surface albedo. Another example is the water vapor greenhouse effect[16]. Increasing temperature increases the humidity, which traps more infrared radiation, which further increases the temperature – heat and humidity lead to more heat and humidity.

*Negative feedback* tends to decrease the original phenomenon. Radiative balance provided an example of negative feedback – an increase in temperature leads to a much more rapid increase in energy radiated away, thus lowering the temperature. Negative feedbacks act as regulative mechanisms. There are many regulative cycles in the climatic system. With enough of them, any system will be self-regulating, able to regain its balance if disturbed. Without them, the Earth's climatic system could never have ever stabilized itself in a state habitable by life as we know it. It is the existence of such self-regulatory negative feedbacks, and the role of the biosphere in those feedbacks, that prompted the famous "Gaia hypothesis" of Lovelock and Margulis. They "see the interaction between life and the atmosphere as so intense that the atmosphere can be regarded as an extension of the biosphere. The atmosphere is not living, but is a construction maintained by the biosphere."[17] The climate system in this view is self-regulating due to the biosphere; the biosphere in turn is viewed as a unified and active, if loosely coupled, super-organism. Regardless of the truth (or degree of truth) of the Gaia Hypothesis, the fact it could seriously be posited shows how real and how important negative feedback phenomena are for climate.

Some components of the climate system simultaneously lead to both positive and negative feedbacks. Clouds, for instance, are a very complex participant in feedback relations, since they both let in reflect sunlight and absorb infrared radiation welling up from the earth's surface[18]. Even the type of cloud matters. Low and middle clouds lead to cooling by reflection, while even a thin layer of high cirrus clouds will have a distinct warming influence.

There is another angle from which we can view the interrelations of systems in the overall climate system, and that is in terms of conservation laws and cycles of materials. We have seen that the earth is a completely open system for radiant energy, but an essentially closed one for regards material. This leads to four main conservation balances that the climate linkages must obey, regardless of how complex these linkages might be in detail: the radiation balance, the global circulation, the water cycle, and the carbon cycle.

The radiation balance was already discussed in detail: the average global temperature is determined by the point at which the solar energy impinging on the earth is balanced by the infrared energy radiated out from the earth. The global circulation conservation law expressed that, for purposes of dynamics, no air enters or leaves the atmosphere, regardless of how complex the circulation patterns it sets up. In other words, atmosphere – and any climate model – can be treated as a closed vessel[19].

The water cycle expresses that the sum total of the water in the atmosphere, hydrosphere, and cryosphere must remain the same. To give a simple example, water evaporated from the oceans falls as rain on land, which runs off into streams and rivers back to the ocean again.

The carbon cycle is more subtle. Plants absorb carbon dioxide from the atmosphere and oceans (and can effectively remove it from the climate system altogether by depositing it in the lithosphere), while animals and rotting vegetation (as well as human fossil fuel burning) put carbon back into the atmosphere not only as carbon dioxide, but also as methane and carbon monoxide. Each of these cycles involves several different components of the climate system, but a conservation law is still enforced. In turn, the water and carbon cycles imply the existence of regulatory, negative feedback loops without which the cycles would not remain stable.

To summarize our second attempt at a conceptual climate model: unlike the first, oversimplified sun - earth - space model of climate, there is no simple mathematical formula that will provide the answer. We must build a detailed model, and verify it by simulation and numerical experiments, even though the physics and chemistry of the processes involved are generally well-understood on the "micro" level.

## Global Circulation Models

Despite these challenges, climate models have been built, and some have done a remarkably good job of modeling the present global climate. Climate modeling was an outgrowth of weather modeling. Computer weather models appeared in the 1950s and 1960s. Because of the complexities of the weather, it was a natural area for computer modeling. For the first time, weather prediction could become explanatory, because it was the result of a simulation. Using today's data on the state of the atmosphere, the meteorologist initializes the weather model and runs it forward in time to obtain a prediction of tomorrow's weather. And as data and computer models have improved, so also have the quality of predictions.

The study of the global circulation began in earnest in the late 1940s with the discovery of jet streams[20]. The first global circulation model was developed by Phillips in 1956. Although very simple, it demonstrated the familiar west to east flow at mid-latitudes, with the corresponding succession of high and low pressure zones[21]. In 1963, the two-level model of Smagorinsky clearly replicated general circulation features. It is not the aim here to present a history of climate models. The essential point is that even the early models could reliably replicate the overall flow structure of the atmosphere. The more sophisticated models of today have built on these early successes, adding steadily more detail. The success of models in this regard is founded on the fact that the circulation of the atmosphere can be calculated on the basis of the well-understood laws of fluid mechanics and thermodynamics. It is this physics-based nature of the model (as opposed to simply an empirical representation of the current state of the climate) that makes global circulation models such powerful tool for the study of both the present climate and climate change.

Because the atmosphere is a fluid, it is naturally modeled on a grid, a spherical grid (or section of a spherical grid), bounded on the bottom by the surface of earth and on the top by the relative vacuum of space. In a weather model, only a small region of the earth is modeled, with a grid a few hundred miles on a side, with cells perhaps a few miles across. That is because a weather model deals with phenomena, such as storm fronts, that develop on relatively short spatial and temporal scales. For a *global circulation model* (GCM for short), on the other hand, the entire globe is modeled. Global climate models are essentially scaled-up weather models. The time scale covered by a weather model is typically only a few days or a week. Unlike weather models, climate models do not extrapolate present weather conditions to future ones. They attempt to see how weather is generated from the operations of the climate simulation itself. Nonetheless, climate model results are generated by running many years of simulated weather in the model and then averaging.

To set the climate model into motion, energy enters the atmosphere from the sun and from the combination of earth rotation and gravity. Energy is absorbed by the surface as well as by the atmosphere. To account for the latter, we add gravity as a force in the fluid equations and rotate the grid (i.e. each cell in the grid stays at the same latitude and longitude as the earth rotates). Then, using the fluid advection and convection equations – there is no point in troubling the reader with the complex mathematics involved – the model atmosphere will begin to move.

The hydrodynamic equations are solved on the grid as finite difference equations. Since the model must not violate the Courant criterion, grid cell spacings are typically between 100 and 500 kilometers, with anywhere from 10 to 20 vertical levels[22]. The time step might be on the order of an hour.

The lower boundary of the model is formed by some representation of the oceans, continents, the polar ice, and vegetation. In a simplified model, whose aim is to replicate the current climate, these can be treated as static boundary conditions, which mainly act as sources and sinks of energy. The chemical composition of the atmosphere, except for water vapor content, can also be treated as a constant. Water vapor and clouds are treated as passive components of the atmosphere as far as dynamics, but their effect on energy is important. This reflects once more the fact that the atmosphere is by far the most dynamic portion of the earth's climate system – in the shorter term, the state of the atmosphere is largely a product of its boundary conditions.

In a longer-term model of climates, the effects of the oceans, polar ice, and biosphere must be included. The most important of these is the ocean. Being a fluid, it is also modeled on a grid; a sophisticated model can incorporate a multilevel ocean such as those used by oceanographers. The cryosphere, because of its longer time scales, can be modeled at low computational cost. The atmosphere, hydrosphere, and cryosphere together close the water cycle, with the sum total of water in these systems being a constant, and with precipitation balanced by runoff and ice accumulation. The terrestrial biosphere can be modeled essentially as a modification of the surface of the earth itself. It affects both the radiation balance, by changing the albedo, and the chemical composition of the atmosphere. Between the atmosphere, the biosphere, and the oceans, the carbon cycle is closed. Modeling the biosphere is crucial to any long-term climate model, but offers difficulties, since its dynamics cannot be reduced to simple mathematical relations like those of the atmosphere, oceans, and polar ice.

Any phenomenon that occurs at a spatial scale smaller than the cell size, or a temporal scale smaller than the time step – called sub-scale phenomena – must be parameterized in some reasonable way. The best thing to do with sub-scale phenomena, if possible, is to ignore them. For example, purely random motions on a small scale will cancel out and not affect larger directed motions. Unfortunately, some sub-scale phenomena are of great importance in climate, since typical cell sizes in GCMs may be hundreds of kilometers. Some notable examples are clouds, mesoscale weather systems (such as cold fronts and their associated storms), and atmospheric turbulence. These play important roles in the vertical transport of heat, momentum, and water vapor, and thus must be included in the model[23]. For example, cumulus clouds are individually small (much smaller than a GCM cell size), but collectively influence the general circulation by the release of latent heat, by the vertical flux of moisture and heat, and interacting with both incoming sunlight and outgoing infrared energy from the earth's surface. Every such parameterization means introducing a "black box" model into an otherwise physics-based model of the atmosphere, and hence a source of uncertainties.

Even the best GCM has inherent limitations. The most obvious limitation is the finite resolution of the model grid. As computers have grown larger and faster, grids can be of a finer and finer mesh and time steps can be steadily reduced, but the limitations of the Courant criterion remain in effect. To the extent that subscale phenomena do matter, they represent a potentially serious limitation on the predictive ability of any climate simulation. But at least in theory this limitation of climate models can be effectively addressed by building ever-larger computers.

A more serious limitation is presented by the sparsity of data as regards the details of the interactions between the various components of the climate system. As one standard work on climatology states[24]:

"the climatic processes are very intricate and some of them are still poorly understood. They involve various feedback mechanisms whose effects are not always known. ... the boundary conditions are not always sufficiently defined because they are based on observational data which are sometimes incomplete or not accurate enough."

Even such a key strand in the web of the earth's climate, namely the details of the interaction between the atmosphere and the oceans, is not entirely understood, especially with regard to long-term processes. On the other hand, the data relevant to climatology is steadily increasing and improving, and the missing pieces of the puzzle can be acquired in the decades ahead.

A final limitation on climate models, and perhaps the most serious of all, is the complexity of the feedback mechanisms in the climate system as a whole. Since these feedbacks are highly nonlinear, with details not fully understood, the assumption that "small causes have small effects" can break down. Because of non-linearity, an initial error can blow up to immense proportions; it can even lead to chaotic behavior in the simulation, negating any predictive ability. (And if subscale phenomena have an influence on such feedback processes, then the model must seriously be called into question.) It is for this reason that the previously quoted text continues[25]:

"the integration of a fully coupled model including the atmosphere, oceans, land, and cryosphere with such different internal time scales poses almost insurmountable difficulties in reaching a final solution, even if all the interacting processes were completely understood."

The present author is more optimistic about the possible capabilities of climate models, but the point is that non-linear feedbacks, in conjunction with lack of data and subscale processes, impose a definite upper limit on the quality of climate model predictions. It also means that it is correspondingly difficult to verify completely all the implications of any one model solution, since spurious predictions under extreme conditions are always possible, regardless of how well current conditions can be replicated.

Such inherent limits appear clearly in weather models. Weather models have steadily improved in the past several decades, but their predictive quality still degrades rapidly with time (Figure 8-4).

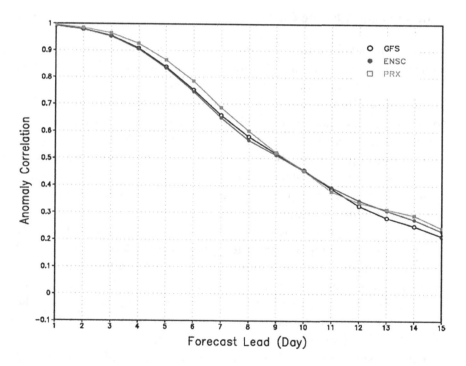

Figure 8-4. Statistical Measure of Weather Prediction Quality Over Time (from ref. 43).

It is interesting in this light to examine where present climate and weather models succeed and where they do less well. Climate models do a very good job of reproducing the overall general circulation of the atmosphere, just as weather models can reliably predict storm tracks for a couple of days in the future. But with regard to details of precipitation patterns, for example, the quality of both climate models and weather prediction is not nearly as good. There are good reasons for this: sketchy data, complex feedbacks, and subscale phenomena. In desert regions, for example, an entire year's rainfall might come from a couple of localized, highly non-average, thunderstorms. So it is not surprising models do less well here, and that is in keeping with both the capabilities and limitations previously discussed.

## Validation and Climate Change

Verification and validation of climate models depends on how well they replicate present conditions. A validated model is interesting in itself as having captured the essence of the earth's climate system. But more interesting still is to conduct numerical experiments with the model in order to replicate and understand past climates or to extrapolate the present climate forward to predict future climates. In other words, the most interesting use of climate models is in understanding climate change. Given the complexity of the climate system, it is only through simulations that we can hope to understand, rather than just describe, processes of climatic change.

Climatic change involves two possible sources. The first are the changes arising within the climate system itself, due to the internal instabilities, non-linear interactions, and feedbacks within the climate system. The second – of more interest to society at large – are changes induced by external forces, such as variations in solar intensity, the orbital parameters of the earth, and influxes of different gases into the atmosphere, whether of human or volcanic origin.

Climate simulations and their corresponding predictions of climate change are ultimately based on extrapolation of current conditions, which climate models are "tuned" to best replicate. Especially when numerical experiments study causes of climate variation, such as doubling or tripling the amount of atmospheric carbon dioxide, it means pushing climate models outside of the regime where they are known to be valid, into regions where little or no data exists. Within certain limits (and it is not necessarily clear where those limits are), we can assume their reliability, but beyond those limits, the inherent complexity of climate systems will assuredly cause the model results to be invalid. (A GCM could not, for example, be used to reliably predict tomorrow's local weather.) The complexity of the climate system, which ensures that computer simulation is the only proper approach, also ensures that we can never be entirely sure of model predictions.

Verification and validation of climate models are thus major issues for predicting future climates. Looking beyond replication of the present climate, GCMs can also study climates of the past. In fact, for a study of climate change, replication of past climates (e.g., the ice ages and their aftermath) is probably more important than perfect replication of the present climate. If the model can replicate past climate changes over a wide range of conditions, then we can have confidence its predictions of future climate.

Unfortunately, data is necessarily sparser for past than present climate, and the farther back in time, the worse the problem. However, there is also a much greater temporal record to work with. And the picture of earth climate that emerges is interesting indeed. Two aspects of the picture impress us immediately. The first is that the Earth's climate has hardly been constant throughout the stretches of Earth history. Even within the bounds of human history, there has been significant climate variation, such as the Little Ice Age of late Medieval and Renaissance times. There have also been occasional catastrophic disturbances to the Earth's climate system, such as massive volcanic eruptions and the impacts of comets and asteroids, which temporarily led to huge changes in weather conditions. This points out a second, equally impressive, feature of climate history: the self-regulation of the system. Despite variations, the climate system as a whole has remained remarkably stable for many millions of years. On very long time scales, what is most impressive is the intimate relation between the atmosphere, the biosphere, and the oceans, with the latter two acting as the main regulators of the system. It is this active regulatory system that makes the earth completely different from any other known planet[26].

The self-regulation of climate has not been perfect, however. During the Permian Age (between the coal-producing Carboniferous and the Mesozoic age of the dinosaurs), the Earth experienced its most severe known Ice Age[27]. It was so cold that most the oceans froze. The Earth came perilously close to becoming inhospitable for life and ending up as a giant ice-coated rock. Apparently, the sudden (sudden in geological terms) luxuriant growth of terrestrial plants during the Carboniferous had removed so much carbon dioxide from the atmosphere that the Earth's greenhouse effect seriously weakened and the climate cooled. Only centuries of volcanic eruptions were enough to restore carbon dioxide levels, increase the greenhouse effect, and melt the ice sheets. In contrast, the subsequent age of the dinosaurs was much warmer than today, by about 8 degrees Celsius or 14 degrees Fahrenheit[28]. Apparently, the polar ice caps disappeared altogether in the Mesozoic. In yet another reversal, the past 40 million years have seen a gradual cooling of the earth, culminating in the most recent Ice Ages. The causes of this cooling are still a matter of some controversy[29], as well as the multiple oscillations of advance of glacial ice and the much warmer interglacial periods (the present day being one of these).

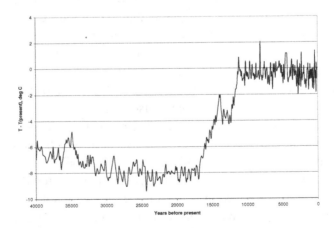

Figure 8-5. Temperature over the past 40,000 years, minus present temperature (as inferred from Vostok ice core data, ref. 45).

Climate since the end of the most recent Ice Age has experienced significant fluctuations, the causes of which are still not entirely understood. Global temperatures over this time span are shown in Figure 8-5. Global climate was several degrees warmer during the Altithermal period at the dawn of human civilization – what is now the Sahara desert was covered with grasslands and savannas[30]. It is thought by some that the sudden cooling of the global climate about 6000 BC, and the corresponding drying of the African and Middle Eastern climates, played a role in the emergence of civilization in Egypt and Mesopotamia. Climate was warmer than today in the first millennium AD, but cooled several degrees during the Little Ice Age of the later Middle Ages up to the 18th Century – an event which had wide-ranging effects, contributing to the demise of the Viking settlements in Greenland as well as the decline of the tropical civilizations of the Maya and the Cambodians.

This brings us to the dawn of the industrial age, when man acquired the means to become a significant player in the earth's climate system. There are two main ways that human civilization can affect climate[31]. The first is through changes to atmospheric composition, as when the burning of fossil fuels injects carbon dioxide into the atmosphere. The second is by changes to the earth's albedo. Deforestation and overgrazing can replace vegetation with desert, raising the albedo and removing energy from the system. The first process will on the whole tend to *increase* the global temperature, while the second will tend to *decrease* it. It is the first process, and in particular carbon dioxide emissions, that have received by far the most attention. It is the source of the now-famous industrial carbon dioxide - global warming inference. Stated in simplest form, it asserts that modern society is causing a warming of the global climate, perhaps a catastrophic warming, by its burning of fossil fuels, which raises levels of atmospheric carbon dioxide, a greenhouse gas. But how valid is this inference from a modeling point of view? For the prediction of *future* global warming ultimately depends on climate models, it is not an empirical datum. The chain of steps in the future warming inference is complex, and we will now examine each step in turn. Note that climate models do not enter the scene until Step (8).

## I. Steps in the future global warming inference: independent of models

(1) *Carbon dioxide is a central contributor to the greenhouse effect.* This is indisputable – without carbon dioxide, the earth's climate would be significantly cooler. However, it is important to remember that several different molecular species are at work in the greenhouse effect, and that carbon dioxide is not the most important contributor: water vapor is.

(2) *Carbon dioxide levels have been rising steadily since the beginning of the industrial age.* This is true beyond any reasonable doubt. Atmospheric carbon dioxide has risen about 25% since 1800 – from 260 parts per million to 340 p.p.m. in 1980 and 367 p.p.m. at present.[32]

(3) *Human civilization has been injecting large amounts of carbon dioxide into the atmosphere,* beyond what the climate system can absorb, and is thus responsible for rising carbon dioxide levels. The inference follows naturally: what changed after 1800 was human burning of fossil fuels and corresponding restoration of fossil carbon to the atmosphere (from which it had been removed eons before by plants). There are no other causes than can reasonably explain the rise is $CO_2$ – e.g., there has not been a significant increase in volcanic activity over the past 200 years. The rise in atmospheric carbon dioxide is less than the amount actually put into the climate system by human activity (about 20,000 billion kilograms per year), since the biosphere and the oceans have coped with about half of it. However, they are unable to remove it at the rate at which it is being added, so it accumulates, and carbon dioxide levels rise. One major error to avoid here is assuming that man is the only or most important source of atmospheric carbon dioxide. Actually, the annual human contribution is only about 2% of that due to natural sources[33]. But the short-term carbon cycle is almost entirely between the biosphere, oceans, and the atmosphere. Burning fossil fuels means adding carbon from the lithosphere to the carbon system and hence a net increase in atmospheric carbon dioxide. Human activity has also been responsible for increases in less important greenhouse gases such as methane and carbon monoxide[34].

(4) *Atmospheric carbon dioxide levels will continue to rise in the next century.* On one level, this assertion is simply an extrapolation of current conditions: civilizational inputs of carbon dioxide will continue at the same or higher rate. But it also asserts that nature will not be able to handle the increase through any sort of feedback effect. It brings in not just extrapolation of present conditions, but also the complex system of interactions in the climate system. This is not the place to discuss all the possible feedbacks in the system, but if some major negative feedback existed (e.g., increased carbon dioxide stimulating more plant growth, restoring lower atmospheric carbon dioxide levels), it is not apparent in the record of $CO_2$ increase over the past several decades (what processes may affect the longer term are not entirely clear). Thus, if inputs of carbon dioxide continue at their current rate, atmospheric levels will continue to rise. What is not clear is the rate of rise, especially in the longer term. For example, if the deserts of Africa and Arabia reverted to grassy and treeclad plains, due to increased global temperatures, this would represent a major expansion of the terrestrial biosphere, with a corresponding fixing of atmospheric carbon.

(5) *If strict controls are placed on industrial emissions, then carbon dioxide levels will level off and decline.* On the surface, this assertion follows the path laid out: since modern civilization is responsible for increased atmospheric carbon dioxide, the solution to the carbon dioxide problem is to stop those emissions. One complication is that the oceans and biosphere act as large reservoirs, so even a complete cutoff of $CO_2$ emissions would not have any immediate effect. Presumably, however, in the long term the carbon dioxide level can be stabilized or reversed – there is regulation at work here, but it is relatively slow.

(6) *Other human effects on the atmosphere do not counteract the effects of increased carbon dioxide.* This assertion cannot be justified. First of all, some industrial pollution, most notably sulfur dioxide, have the effect of cooling the atmosphere. (This is one of the reasons that weather after a major volcanic eruption may be cooler for a year or two – $SO_2$ is an "anti-greenhouse" gas.) Second, human activity that leads to desertification increases the surface albedo, and thus acts to cool the climate system.

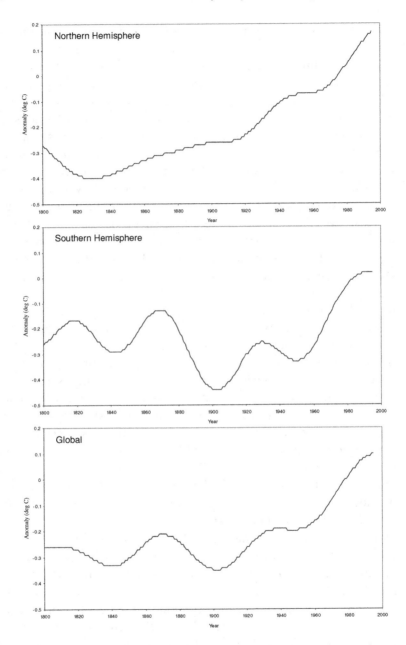

Figure 8-6. Global Temperature Trends Since 1800 (from ref. 44).

(7) *Global temperatures have been rising steadily since the beginning of the industrial age, and even more in recent decades.* No step of the global warming inference is more controversial than this one. In fact, the historical record is mixed and does not produce clear, unequivocal evidence of warming since 1800 (Figure 8-6). The northern hemisphere trend is one of general heating before 1940, cooling from 1940 to 1970, and warming since 1970. The southern hemisphere data point a warming throughout the period, but at a lower level[35]. There are also discrepancies between the trends for temperatures measured at sea versus temperatures measured on land. So a *clear and obvious* pattern of global warming thus far is not evident in the historical record, although there is suggestion of that trend.

## II. Steps in the future global warming inference: involving models

(8) *The global rise in temperatures is due to an enhanced greenhouse effect from increased levels of carbon dioxide.* Conversely, decrease of $CO_2$ will decrease the temperature. Taken strictly, this assertion is not justified. Temperatures have not risen clearly, and certainly have not risen in direct correlation with carbon dioxide levels. As one atmospheric scientist remarked[36], "Theoretically, warmings of 0.5 to 1.0 °C should have arisen over the course of this century. However, 'noise' in the form of natural influences on climate make it extremely difficult to establish the existence of an enhanced greenhouse effect. ... direct evidence that the global warming trend is attributable to an intensifying greenhouse effect is hard to discern in the temperature record. According to climatic models, enhanced greenhouse heating should lead to the most pronounced temperature increases in Arctic regions, but there is no consistent pattern in the experimental record." Another asserts[37]: "There is little empirical evidence to allow us to predict with any confidence the effects of increasing $CO_2$ on climate." So here model predictions are at variance with empirical data – they predict a rising temperature trend from increased $CO_2$ that has not (yet) been observed. Whether a clear pattern will emerge in the decades ahead as $CO_2$ increases further is anyone's guess.

(9) *No natural causes can explain the temperature rise, and they are outside recorded natural climate fluctuations.* The truth of the first half of this assertion is at present unknown. When causes of climatic epochs as important as the ice ages are still not fully understood, one should never rule out possible natural causes for observed temperature fluctuations, especially when there is no immediately obvious trend. Some natural causes of recent global temperature changes, such as variation of solar radiation, have been examined and ruled out[38]. So, to the degree a rising trend exists, the cause is likely to be human-induced, but the link is weak due to the complexities of the system. The second half of the assertion, that no natural fluctuations of the magnitude of global warming have ever occurred, is flatly false – much larger natural fluctuations than the temperature changes of the past 150 years have occurred. More on this below.

(10) *Since carbon dioxide levels will continue to rise, so too will global temperatures.* This is an inference from computer model predictions, and is hence of most interest to us here. It is also one of the key points in the dispute over global warming. Climate models do indeed predict that rising carbon dioxide levels will lead to increased global temperatures. But there is little exactitude in these predictions. According to best estimates, by 2020 global temperatures will be 1.3 to 2.5 degrees Centigrade above pre-industrial levels, and by 2100, between 1.7 and 4.9 degrees $C$[39]. And we have seen that the GCMs fail to adequately represent the temperature changes of the past 150 years. Moreover, it is important to remember that carbon dioxide is only one component of the greenhouse effect and the earth's radiation budget – water vapor and clouds are more important. The effects of the individual contributors do not add linearly, so increased carbon dioxide is not going to be reflected by a direct increase in global temperature, and temperature data bears this out.

(11) *No natural self-regulatory effect can stop global warming.* The answer to this is as yet unknown. Taken in extreme form, it means a denial of the self-regulation of the climate system and is certainly false. Given enough time, the system will restore its equilibrium –

it has done so many times throughout Earth history. The question is really the response of the entire system to a moderate rise in temperature, and it is based on model predictions. Perhaps the biggest unknown of all are the effects on cloud cover. Increased temperatures lead to both increased water vapor (a positive feedback) and increased clouds (on the whole a negative feedback). If higher temperatures and carbon dioxide mean more clouds, more rain, and more plants, then the climate system will tend to regulate itself. Other possible systemic changes from global warming are very complex. Consider the possible melting of the polar ice caps. On the one hand, this would both dramatically lower the albedo at the poles, as well as release considerable amounts of greenhouse gases like methane and carbon dioxide that have been locked in the ice – a positive feedback tending to increase temperatures still further. On the other hand, the melting ice would lead to an immense flood of cold water into the oceans, tending to *cool* global temperatures – this is apparently what happened temporarily at the end of the most recent Ice Age[40]. So there are no simple answers here.

(12) *The predicted rise in temperatures is unprecedented in earth history.* In a word: nonsense. Even within the bounds of human civilization, there have been temperature fluctuations of the predicted global warming magnitude. The Altithermal period of some 4500 to 8000 years ago was as warm as the predicted 22nd Century temperatures of global warming models. The Ice Ages themselves represented a completely natural fluctuation in the opposite direction. The Ice Ages in turn were the culmination of a 40 million year global cooling trend. So even if a human induced global warming does occur, it is not out of line with natural fluctuations that have occurred many times in the earth's history. The primary mistake here is taking the climate of the past 300 years or so (i.e., since scientific measurements of weather and climate have been made) as "normal" and all the other climate regimes of natural history as "abnormal." In fact, a dinosaur would find the present global climate hardly better than the Ice Ages and highly abnormal from its Mesozoic point of view.

To sum up, while there are clearly increasing levels of carbon dioxide, the inference of a *catastrophic* global warming, as is often presented in the press, is almost certainly incorrect. (Indeed, over the past decade, certain politicians and journalists have seized on any unusual weather pattern as supposed evidence of global warming.) The whole nature of the warming inference means plugging a relatively minor increase in carbon dioxide (by earth historical standards) into a GCM and expecting a directly proportional increase in global temperatures. But, in all likelihood, it won't work that way: the system is too complex. A moderate global warming of a couple of degrees Celsius is entirely possible and probably the most likely outcome – but only better data and better models will confirm or deny it. Present climate models, as we have seen, do an excellent job of replicating the overall circulation patterns of the atmosphere, but they do less well when asked to replicate the details of known global temperature changes. To draw an aeronautical analogy, climate modeling is well beyond the Wright flyer stage; it is more at the 1920s biplane level – certainly serviceable, but still lacking. What is needed for the solution of the global climate change puzzle is not a biplane, but the equivalent of a moon rocket: a comprehensive earth model with grid cells on a scale of kilometers rather than hundreds of kilometers, with complete models of all components of the climate system, especially the biosphere and the linkage between the hydrosphere and atmosphere. Recently, Japan's Earth Simulator computing system has taken significant steps forward in atmospheric modeling detail, with grid cell sizes as small as 10 kilometers (Figure 8-7), but in the coupled atmosphere-ocean simulation, the atmospheric cell size was 120 km and the oceanic cell size about 30 km[41]. While impressive, it still falls short of what is needed. (Analogous modeling limitations due to dynamic scales and grid sizes appear in other areas of Earth science. For example, it is estimated that a realistic simulation of the dynamics Earth's liquid metal core and the origin of the Earth's magnetic field would require up to $10^{15}$ grid cells, due to a need to model turbulence down to a scale of 10 meters[42].)

Figure 8-7. Earth Simulator Calculation of Precipitation in the Western Pacific for Mesh Size of 10 km.

In addition to larger supercomputers, more comprehensive data on the relations between the atmosphere and the rest of the climate system must be taken. None of this presents an insuperable barrier; it's just a matter of doing it. Such an improved earth simulation would doubtless cost a great deal of money. Regardless of how much it costs, it is still infinitely cheaper than guessing wrong about global climate change, which brings us back to one of the primary justifications of modeling in the first place.

## Chapter 9

# Calculating War and Peace

The preceding discussion in Chapters Six and Seven might raise doubts with regard to modeling any aspect of human affairs. There are boundaries beyond which models of physical phenomena cannot trespass, a computational equivalent of the Heisenberg uncertainty principle in quantum physics. There will always be an ineradicable fuzziness we cannot further clarify. Given such limitations in the purely physical arena, how could we hope to simulate the far more complex phenomena of living organisms and human society? If models cannot predict earthquakes, how can they predict wars? The next chapter explains why we cannot calculate the unfolding of human history as if it were mechanics – it is delusion to think we can.

Nonetheless, there are some areas pertaining both to organisms and societies where models – even purely mathematical models – have proven remarkably successful. They have not only accurately predicted phenomena like population growth, but have been an excellent aid to understanding of the laws governing such phenomena. The aim here is not to point out possible exceptions and failings of such models (that would be easy considering the complex systems with which they deal), but, to the contrary, to understand why they work at all. The key is that each of the models deals with an aspect of life that is essentially *quantifiable* (e.g., counting individuals born, dollars spent, or fish caught) and is governed by certain stable laws or constraints. Those complex living systems that Gelernter suggests could be captured by computer models – economies, ecosystems, synthetic life, businesses, transportation networks – are basically of this nature[1]. He does not suggest, for example, that we should attempt to predict future scientific discoveries or the futures of various cultures. Rather, the modeler should look at measurable and more obviously deterministic systems.

## Population Modeling

Population, from the lowest protozoans up to humans, is an example of a quantifiable biological phenomenon. It is thus amenable to modeling. At first glance, this might appear impossible: we naturally think of our attitudes toward our children, and how could all this be calculable? Yet one of the greatest successes of mathematical models in biology has been precisely the prediction of the growth, stabilization, oscillation, or decline of populations. Indeed, in many respects population models are the most basic sort of biological model. As one ecologist remarked[2]:

"Few would disagree with the proposition that nature is immensely complex. However, if we wish to understand this complexity, we will be well advised to abstract relatively simple facts from nature and examine these first. Species-habitat interrelations could be considered, or interactions between species within communities; but before they are, we must examine the basic components: single-species populations."

It is a relatively simple, quantitative nature that makes population amenable to modeling. Consider the population at a given location and time. It is a count of the individuals of a given species (for very large populations, a density rather than absolute numbers is used). The change of population is equally simple. Population is increased by births of new individuals, as well as immigration of existing individuals to our location. Population is decreased by deaths and by emigration. Figure 9-1 shows this graphically. By analogy, we can think of a population as the level of water in a tank. An inflow of water represents births and immigration, and an outflow corresponds to deaths and emigration. If the inflow exceeds outflow, the population increases. Given the current population, and the rates of birth, death, immigration, and emigration, one can calculate future populations. For an isolated population, the rates of immigration and emigration will be zero, so the population level depends only on the difference of birth and death rates. Such a single-species model is remarkably simple, but it is also accurate – if we know the rates involved.

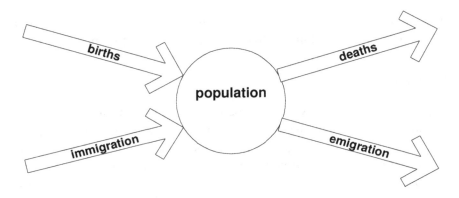

Figure 9-1. Basic Population Process Model.

The rates for any actual species in a given habitat are determined empirically and may require meticulous observation. In addition, it may require building a model of the life process of the organism involved, what is called a life table[3]. For example, each plant of a certain species of plant produces N seeds, of which a fraction $x$ germinate, and of those that germinate, a fraction $y$ survive to grow into mature, reproducing plants. If the plant is an annual, the population P(t) of this year will lead to a population P(t+1) next year equal to P(t) times $Nxy$, and a rate of change of ($Nxy$ - 1). The life table, or model of populations at each stage of the plant's growth, is fairly simple. Life tables can be very complex, however, for insects that have several different phases, or for colonial animals such as corals that reproduce both sexually and asexually, or for plants, where the decisive life stage factor is usually size rather than age.

Many organisms, including humans, are capable of breeding continuously, so the logical unit to model is the cohort, a group of individuals born during the same time interval. In human terms, a cohort is a generation. Each cohort will have its own birth and death rates. A weighted average over all cohorts will give the birth and death rate for the species. This can be simply expressed as: N(t+1) = R x N(t), where N is the population at a given time, and R is the rate of increase or decline. If we integrate over time, we obtain N(t) = N(0) $R^t$.

Now, suppose there is an isolated population with a birth rate exceeding the death rate, yielding a net rate of continuous increase, without any constraints. The resulting population will grow exponentially, just like compound interest on a bank account. For a rapidly reproducing population in isolation – whether bacteria in a test tube of nutrients or rabbits on an empty island – the population will essentially blow up. It will consume and grow without end: hence the term "population explosion." Suppose we start with a population of 1000 individuals that increases at a rate of 3% per year. In one year, the population will be 1030; in ten years, it will be 1324; in 100 years, 19,219; in 500 years, 2.62 billion, and in 1000 years: 6.87 quadrillion! Figure 9-2 shows this population compounding diagrammatically.

This exponential rate of increase in population is called the Malthusian Law, after its discoverer, Robert Malthus. Malthus supposed that human beings, like any animal, would reproduce themselves without limit if given the chance, absorbing all available resources. Malthus was a pessimist about the human condition, but pessimists can be right when actions are unconsciously governed by natural impulses.

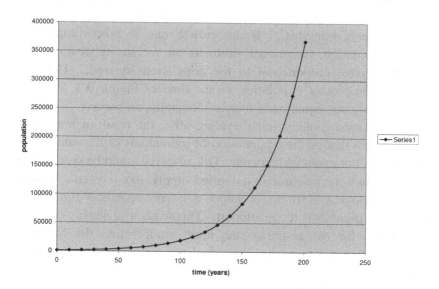

Figure 9-2. Population Growth of an Initial 1000 Individuals at 3% per year.

Consider the global human population, which has been increasing throughout the 20th Century at a rate of approximately 2% per year. In 1960, the world population was about 3 billion; now, at the turn of the 21st Century, it is 6 billion. If population were to continue to grow at this rate, in 2050, there would be 16 billion people, in 2100, 44 billion, and in 2200, a whopping 328 billion. Extrapolating the calculation further, by the year 2635, there would be so many people that each individual would have only one square foot of space[4]! Just like compound interest, population growth keeps building on itself, growing faster and faster in absolute numbers.

In the real world, of course, populations reach a limit. In a test tube full of microorganisms or on the rabbits' island, sooner or later the expanding population will consume all the available nutrients. The population, whose level had been growing at an accelerating pace, will collapse. More realistically, when the resources the organisms consume are renewable (such as water and sunlight for plants, or plants for herbivores), the population will level off.

Just as population growth in ideal conditions was modeled by a remarkably simple mathematical relation, the mathematician and biologist Verhulst discovered that a small addition to that relation could describe the leveling-off[5]. If the growth rate is proportional to the current population, the model subtracts an increasing death rate (or emigration rate) proportional to the population squared. The result, shown in the plot of population versus time of Figure 9-3, is what is termed the logistic equation or more colloquially, an S-curve.

In population ecology, such leveling-off is the result of intraspecific competition – that is, the competition of individuals of the same species for a scarce, but essential resource. This resource could be space or food or mates, but not a resource in unlimited supply, like oxygen[6]. Since the essential resource is finite, it imposes a corresponding limit on the numbers of organisms it can support. This leads to a density-dependent competition for the resource: the more competitors, the higher the probability that any particular individual will not survive and contribute to the next generation. In other words, the death rate increases in proportion to the number or density of organisms. At some point, a

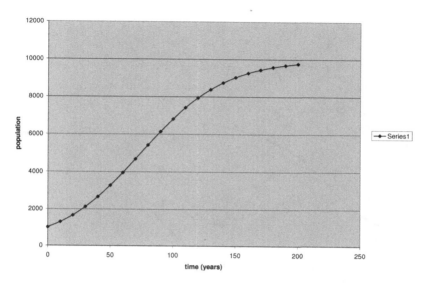

Figure 9-3. The Logistic or S - Curve of Growth.

maximum population is reached. This population limit is called the *carrying capacity*. An isolated population at carrying capacity has reached equilibrium with its resources: birth rate balances death rate.

This can be expressed mathematically as

$$N(t+1) = \frac{N(t)R}{(1+aN(t))} \quad \text{where}$$

$$a = \frac{(R-1)}{K}$$

and $K$ is the carrying capacity[7]. In other words, we now have an effective birth rate that declines with the increase of N. Suppose we apply this model to a more realistic population modeling scenario with variable conditions[8]. Starting with a population of 1000, the animals increase until the carrying capacity is reached. Suppose also that a random fluctuation of conditions, hence carrying capacity, is included. Figure 9-4 shows the result this more realistic population simulation versus time.

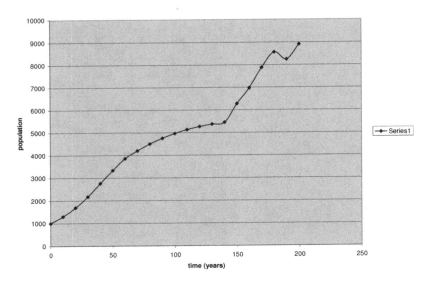

Figure 9-4. Population Model versus Time: Logistic Law with Fluctuating Conditions.

The population rises rapidly at first, and then begins to steadily level off. Finally, the population reaches its carrying capacity and can increase no further. The cause for the leveling off is that the animals have reached the maximum that the natural resources can support – any extra and some must go without and die of starvation.

Using more sophisticated models, it is possible to replicate fluctuations and oscillations in the equilibrium population. In fact, in certain cases, even a single species population model can result in chaos – a seemingly random fluctuation of population. Certain natural examples seem to bear this out[9].

Single-species population models can shed light on the different responses or life strategies of species to different habitats. Every organism's life strategy is a compromise between its own survival and the survival of the species, because reproduction decreases the survivability of the individual. There are two extreme reproductive strategies among living beings[10]. The 'r' strategy maximizes the reproductive growth rate (hence 'r') of the species by producing vast numbers of young, with small size and short generations. The other extreme is the 'K' strategy of producing a small number of young, of larger size, with careful parental care, intense competition among individuals, and long generations – but also populations close to the carrying capacity (hence 'K' strategy). The 'r' strategy is favored in habitats that are unpredictable and fluctuating in favorable conditions, because the species must take advantage of good conditions quickly while they exist. Conversely, the 'K' strategy is favored in environments that are either constant or predictably seasonal, because the species has, in essence, the luxury of looking ahead.

## Predator-Prey Cycles

Populations of individual species are, of course, never alone in the real world. They interact and compete with other species. And competition between species is by no means an unimportant factor in population models. Return to the logistic model for a moment. In the natural habitat, the limiting factor on the population of voles, for instance, is not so much the availability of food as the action of predators. It is in fact the central limiting factor: without predators like owls or hawks, we would be infested with plagues of small rodents.

Population ecologists note six basic types of interspecific effects of one population on another, depending on whether the effects are beneficial, neutral, or negative[11]. For example, if the effects are mutually beneficial, there is a symbiosis or mutualism, like that between bees and flowering plants. This mutualism will tend to increase the populations of both organisms involved. The reverse is that of interspecific competition: two functionally similar species competing for the same ecological turf. Such models are applicable not only in biology, but also to economic competition and warfare. Interspecific competition leads to what is known as the competitive exclusion principle: one of the competing species will eliminate or exclude the other from the available niche.

But here we will consider in more detail those interactions that benefit one species at the cost of another: a *predator-prey* relationship. A mathematical approach to the predator-prey problem originated in the 1920s, when the Italian biologist Umberto D'Ancona noted that, during the First World War, there was a great increase of sharks and like marine predators in the Adriatic Sea – not only in numbers, but relative to their prey[12]. Commercial fishing had decreased during the war, but why was the decrease in fishing more beneficial to predators rather than prey? Unable to explain the phenomenon, D'Ancona challenged his mathematician father-in-law, Vito Volterra to solve the puzzle. Volterra solved it admirably by noting how the populations of predator and prey are indissolubly tied together. Remove the predator, he reasoned, and the population of the prey fish will increase exponentially according to the Malthusian law of population growth. Conversely, any decrease in prey once predators are introduced depends on the *product of both* populations – the larger either are, the larger the negative effect. Similar relations act on the predators. The Volterra equations are complex compared to the Malthusian law, but they explain quite well the paradoxical fact that reduced fishing levels are actually *detrimental* to the food fish. There were actually *more* food fish with human predation acting on both food fish and sharks – it all depended on the balance of predator and prey. Similar paradoxical results have arisen with insecticides: application of insecticides in some cases has actually increased unwanted pest insects, because it had a relatively greater effect on the pest's natural predators, again in accordance with the Volterra equations[13].

Because of the intimate linkage between predator and prey, their populations can mutually oscillate, bobbing up and down in unison, but slightly out of phase. Figure 9-5 shows simulations of predator-prey cycles[14].

Oscillation is one common solution of the Volterra equation, and on reflection, it is easy to understand how it occurs. Turn loose a few predators in a habitat full of abundant prey. The predators feast on their prey, and their population correspondingly increases. Ultimately, however, the increasing number of predators causes the prey population to decline. With prey decreasing, there is no longer enough food for the burgeoning predators. The predators are now the ones in trouble: some must starve or emigrate, so their numbers now also fall. But with a much lower number of predators, pressure on the prey population eases. It can begin to rebound, and as prey species generally are more prolific than predators, they rebound quickly. That takes the populations back to their starting point of few predators and many prey, and the cycle starts again.

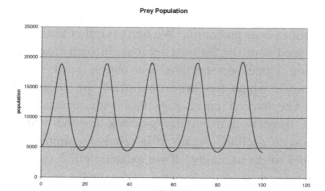

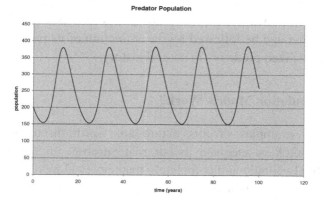

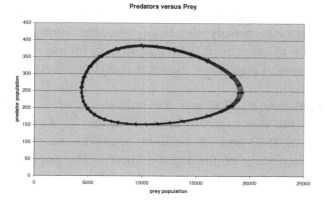

Figure 9-5. Predator - Prey Cycles.

Human beings are in a sense predators, but ones that can exercise an intelligent control over predation. We harvest rather than simply devour: we preserve seed corn for the next season. In such cases, studied from the population model perspective, we obtain what is known as a *harvesting curve*, which has been confirmed, for example, in fishing statistics[15]. The harvest curve says that with increasing effort, at a certain point there is a maximum payback beyond which the catch actually begins to decline. Again, it is relatively simple to understand why this model works in reality. If we make no effort (e.g., do not fish), we have no harvest at all. Likewise, if we make an unlimited effort, results will decline to zero, because we will kill off all the prey. So between these extremes there must be an optimum level of effort that produces maximum returns. (In reality, it is also possible for prey to become extinct and be followed by the extinction of its predator: the fate of most specialized predators in natural history.)

## Why do Population Models Work?

Many more examples of this nature are worth discussing, but the foregoing sketch is adequate to our real purpose: understanding why these relatively simple and completely mathematical models work at all. Consider a human population, for example, the population of the United States. One might suppose that the population of America could not be described by the equations, because of the unusual nature of that population growth: namely the large role that immigration played, and continues to play, in it. In actuality, it follows the logistic or S-curve equation of population growth remarkably closely, as Figure 9-6 shows.

The population in 1790 was 3.9 million. It grew rapidly in the 19th Century, but then began to level off in the 20th Century, reaching 248 million in 1990 and 281 million in 2000. As one can see, it follows the beginning of the logistic curve. The populations of the European countries, as well as Japan, have followed similar S curves to completion.

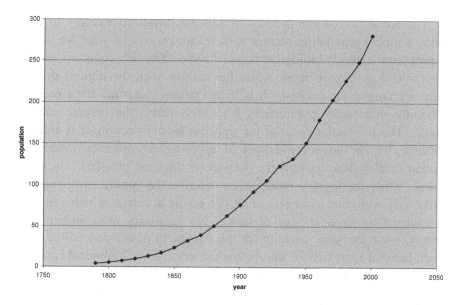

Figure 9-6. Population of the United States, 1790 - present.

Now comes a point worth pondering. A population ecologist viewing these curves would say that Europe was close to reaching its carrying capacity by the end of the 20th Century. The Europeans must have populated to the limit of their resources; the slowing of their growth rate must be due to some combination of starvation and emigration. The Europeans must once have been rich, with a vast continent and resources at their feet, but now they are impoverished. This view comes from approaching human population as if it were just like animal and plant populations.

But this is hardly the case, as we know. The leveling-off of the American population was not due to material factors at all. Indeed, Europeans are far richer today than in their days of maximum population growth rate. The leveling-off was due instead largely to cultural factors. People started having fewer children, although in purely material terms, they could afford to have more. In other words, Europe's carrying capacity has turned out to be psychological, not physical.

The same is true for the rest of the industrialized world.  In fact, today's global population picture is the exact *reverse* of what we would expect from a purely biological point of view.  The rich countries are the ones with low growth rates, while the nations with the highest growth rates are among the poorest.  It is by no means clear that for a modern economy that larger populations lead to poverty; the reverse can be true[16].  The population limit of present day Western countries is entirely *cultural*, which shows the danger of applying deterministic models to human affairs (leading into the subject of the next chapter).  In other words, while the logistic model does describe the American population amazingly well, that closeness of fit is a happy accident, which could be overturned by some change of taste.  No necessary laws underpin it. Surely, some carrying capacity for the American population will always exist, but that limit will lie well below the subsistence biological carrying capacity of the nation's resources.

Why, then, do population models work as well as they do?  First of all, they deal with living beings at the most abstract level possible: as distinct, identical, countable objects.  Whether young or old, male or female, the individual is treated as a countable unit that is born, can reproduce itself and move, and then dies.  In addition, these basic units always enter or leave the model *as units* – as whole individuals subject to birth, death, immigration, and emigration – not as fractions.  In other words, population is inherently the most quantitative view of biology. This is analogous to how physics at its most abstract level deals with all objects as mass-points in a four-dimensional space-time: an object orbiting the earth could be an astronaut or a satellite or a grand piano, but these particularities do not enter into the orbit calculation.  Likewise, the object of population biology is a point that can reproduce itself, endures for a certain time, depends on certain resources, and may be able to move in space.  Thus, it can be modeled with relative ease.

The constraints and forces acting on population are deterministic and quantitative.  We assume, for example, that if a being can reproduce itself, it will, and if it can obtain nutriment, it will.  If an animal is a herbivore, for example, we can measure the number of food plants available to it, and in turn measure the amount of nutrients, sunlight, and water available to the plants.  Similar quantitative relations can be obtained for competition between species, predation, and so on. They are what make dynamic population models and simulations possible.

Models are, as always, only as good as the match between their underlying assumptions and the realities they represent. Consider, for example, the related notions of population and distinct individual entities. They are based largely on the observation of animals, which are self-contained, moving, reproducing entities. But what about other organisms: do they necessarily fit this picture of population? In my sunroom I have an old cactus, a *Cereus Monstrosa*, which has branches and buds going off every which way. Each branch is almost its own cactus and is capable of being separated and growing on its own. So is it one cactus or many cacti? Even more radical examples may be found in the plant kingdom, like Banyan trees. Such organisms – consisting of repeated, but connected, entities – are termed modular[17]. Modular organisms grow by adding new modules. (Moreover, modular organisms are easily cloned, as in dividing plants.) Here the abstract model of population falters: what is the countable entity? Such are the problems inherent in any model. Once we stretch beyond the basic abstract assumptions in the model, the model breaks down.

## Social and Economic Analogies

Nonetheless, the real marvel is not that models of living systems break down, but that they work at all. It turns out those areas where models have been most successfully applied in human affairs are precisely ones that most closely resemble the biological models.

One such area is war. Modern operations research got its start as a military exercise, to improve the performance and use of weapons, the movements of troops and supplies, and to systematically examine possible strategies. War can be viewed as analogous to interspecific competition, except that it is the competition of nations and their armed forces, rather than the competition of different species. Yet both represent, on the abstract level, much the same thing: two populations struggling against each other to control the same patch of ground or the same set of resources. In both cases, the losers are either ejected or die: the competitive exclusion principle again.

Thus, it appears one could model war from a similar angle as interspecific competition. The model defines two populations (armies) of appropriate numbers, armed with their appropriate weapons – javelins and swords or tanks and jet fighters, depending on the technological level. Knowing the impact of the weaponry, the model can estimate the losses in men and materiel inflicted by combat. A simulation then brings the two armies together and predicts not only the victor, but also the casualties on both sides.

The first such model was built during the First World War by F. W. Lanchester[18]. He assumed the loss rate in one force over time was linearly proportional to the strength of the forces in the other force, and the effective superiority of the stronger force depended on the square of their strength. Withdrawals or reinforcements of troops on either side figured directly into the equation. In the 1950s, operations analysts tested Lanchester's model against the known force strengths over time for the battle of Iwo Jima. What they found was an astonishing agreement of model and reality. Despite its simplicity, the Lanchester law was widely used as a tool for military analysis during the Cold War and is still used today. Despite such successes, we are reluctant to think that war can be calculated. If it could, then warfare would merely be a matter of force strength and logistics, and the human elements, such as leadership and morale, could be disregarded.

Warfare models seem to have their greatest applicability in a war of attrition, such as Lanchester's western front in World War I. But in any other military situation, the human element, what is going on in the mind of one's enemy, or the asymmetric nature of guerilla warfare, can hardly be disregarded[19]. In the 1991 Gulf War, for example, computer models calculated that American forces would suffer thousands of casualties in a ground war. In fact, they suffered less than 200. The difference was made not by superior weaponry (although that certainly helped), but by superior strategy. In a like sense, any purely quantitative computer model of the American Civil War would have the Union defeating the Confederacy in the summer of 1862. But such a model can figure in neither the brilliance of Lee and Jackson on the southern side nor McClellan's inexplicable failure of nerve for the north. Nor can warfare models calculate the immeasurably important external factors of political leadership and national morale.

Most models of war are truly quantitative models only on the "micro" level of weaponry and terrain, while leaving the higher levels of simulation to human participants – hence, typically these are not war simulations, but war games. There is an entire industry of producing war games (whether of the traditional board variety or computer games) for armchair Napoleons, which attain a greater or lesser degree of reality in simulating weaponry. Simulations of weapons systems are an increasingly important part of military training – even personal computer flight simulators have proven valuable – but they are always "man in the loop." They are not about the calculation of war *per se.*

From the arts of war, then we turn to those of peace – or at least of peaceful activity. There are many economic facets are similar to the mathematical relations of biology — too many to list here, since the analogies run both ways. The Darwinian "survival of the fittest" was based on, as is well known, analogies to the competition of business enterprises. The competitive exclusion principle is at work all the time in the market economy.

Now, one reason for this success is that economics, like war, is the most emphatically quantifiable and "material" region of human affairs. Analogies to population models therefore can hold. For example, the basic notion of a "rate of production" is the same in both[20], and can be represented mathematically as:

$$Q = A \, L^a \, K^b$$

where, A, a, and b are empirically-determined constants. In economics, Q would be the rate of production, L the labor input, and K the input of capital services. In biology, L might be the number of regions or patches occupied by an inferior species, K the number of superior species, and Q the rate of conversion of inferior patches into superior ones. Such equations work in economics because they deal with similar phenomena; rates of production deal with quantifiable units, whose fabrication depends on the availability of labor and material resources, which also can be quantified. Consider a simple macroeconomic model[21]:

$$C(t) = b_0 + b_1 Y(t-1)$$
$$I(t) = nY(t-1) - nY(t-2)$$
$$Y(t) = C(t) + I(t) + G(t)$$

where Y is national income, C is consumption, I is investment, G is government expenditures, and $b_0$, $b_1$, and n are empirical rate constants. Given some reasonable numbers, the income growth is similar to production or population growth.

There are numerous other analogies between economic phenomena and the relations that govern life. One of these is the famous "pig cycle" and its interesting similarity to predator-prey cycles. The "pig cycle" is based on the fact that if farmers get high prices for pigs, they will raise many of them, while low prices lead to low supply. But demand – and hence prices – for pork responds quickly, while there is a time lag between when a farmer decides to raise a certain number of pigs and when those pigs actually get to market. So supply and demand get out of sync: at high prices, farmers raise many pigs, which when they get to market drive down prices, which in turn leads to fewer pigs being raised, which drives up prices, and so on[22].

To summarize, there are indeed regions of human life where models can be successfully applied. Such regions are inherently *quantitative* and are governed by *deterministic* or effectively deterministic laws (e.g., Americans could suddenly decide tomorrow to stop drinking Coca-Cola, but realistically there is no chance of this occurring). In such areas, models can be built and used with success. Analysis of business processes like inventory handling is a shining example. Whenever we encounter a system that consists of (or can be considered as) a collection of generic units or a flow rate, governed by consistent laws, it is a candidate for modeling. For example, however idiosyncratic the behavior of individual drivers, automotive traffic as a whole was discovered to behave like a compressible fluid, with well-defined characteristics[23]. As traffic density increases, its effective viscosity also increases, and slows the traffic down, ultimately bringing it to a standstill. These properties have allowed traffic engineers to build remarkably accurate models of traffic flow, and thus lead to better highway design.

On the other hand, as always in modeling, where the basic assumptions of the model paradigm do not apply, then no useful model can be built. And such are human affairs as a whole, as the next chapter will examine at length.

# Chapter 10

# From the Past into the Future: Is Historical Simulation Possible?

The last chapter showed it is possible to model at least some aspects of human affairs. An obvious prospect beckons: if we can model population, well, why not all of human history? Computer models reach one culmination by encompassing of all physical phenomena; a similar culmination for humanity would be a model of civilization and culture. We build a SimHistory program, plug in the initial conditions for, say, 5000 BC, then sit back and watch the pageant of world history unroll before us, leading us on a path from the pyramids to our own front doors. Needless to say, there are computer models and games out there purporting to do just that. The real question is: can these be something more than games? Could we, even in theory, simulate the course of human history? If so, we would have an awesomely powerful tool, since it could also predict the future from the present state of affairs.

Prediction is the problem. The model must be able to extrapolate from past and present states to future states, just like weather prediction, to simulate the course of history. But physical phenomena are one thing, and human affairs are quite another. Physical phenomena are governed by well-understood laws, reducible to mathematical relations. For civilization and culture, can we ever really be sure we have the right data, what is really important and significant? Even assuming that historical development is deterministic, how does one get a grip on a development for which only sparse data exists, data which moreover cannot be easily reduced to any "lawful" form? The previous chapter showed the limitations of modeling in economics and war, surely the two most deterministic areas of human action.

Yet typically we do not (and cannot, *a priori*) assume that the course of human history is deterministic. We approach history, politics, ethics, and so on *as if* there are free will, discovery, creativity, and chance – and that these are able to exert some meaningful influence with lasting effects. As Chapter Six explained, these essentially fall outside what can be modeled. Events resulting from them can be described and understood in retrospect, but they cannot be predicted.

The modeler also trespasses on well-trod ground here. It is an area squabbled over by generations of historians, philosophers, theologians, and sociologists. The question we must examine first is: what is history? Why must we (or why *should* we) approach human history differently than other processes?

## Through the Lens of the Modeling Paradigm

Suppo the above warning proviso, we look at historical development through the lens of the modeling paradigm. What comes to focus in the mind's eye?

The first step in the modeling process, to recall from Chapter 3, is to identify the system and disengage it from its background. For universal history, this is not a problem, since the Earth is a closed system as far as the student of human society and culture is concerned. The first relevant step in the modeling process is analysis of the system into parts: that is, the anatomy of human societies and cultures throughout history. History is not monist in character, despite what a Hegel, a Marx, or a Comte might think. To the contrary, it confronts us with a plenitude of different entities and levels. Some are of historical interest, others are not, but they are all linked in a hierarchical ladder, from the individual person up to nations and civilizations.

Indeed, "what" histories are about are social entities, whether we are writing a biography or an encyclopedic world history. Historically memorable events either occur "in" or "to" entities. Topical histories – e.g., of art or social structure or religion – also ultimately refer to actual entities, such as nations or individuals, to which the events of topical interest take place.

So the question is really what social or cultural entities it is proper to write histories about. Certainly, this is not the place to answer that question in full, but merely to recognize that the anatomical task of the historian, social scientist, and historical modeler demands an answer to it. Traditionally, historians have written national histories: that is, histories of political entities such as England, France, America, or the Roman Empire. The universal historian Arnold Toynbee in *A Study of History* questioned whether this was indeed the correct "intelligible field" for a historian to consider[1]. He pointed out that if we consider the history of England on a longer time scale, it is so intertwined with the histories of the other European nations that this larger cultural system of interactions – Western Civilization – is more important than the nation itself. England emerged from the matrix of the West and is inseparable from it. Toynbee offered instead the civilization, as a reasonably self-contained system, as the proper intelligible field for historians. He identified a whole set of civilizations: not just Western Civilization, but also the Hellenic Civilization of ancient Greece and Rome, as well as the civilizations of Egypt, Mesopotamia, India, China, and the Americas. Overarching the civilization, he identified the larger cultural (but not political) entities of the Universal Religions, such as Christianity, Islam, and Buddhism[2]. Regardless of the ultimate validity of his approach to universal history (his "metahistory," if you will), Toynbee clearly recognized the problem of systemic analysis. This was in distinction to national historians, who uncritically assumed the nation-state to be the only really important entity and politics as the supreme history-making activity. It also contrasted with the monist historical theorists like Hegel or Marx, who assumed history to be the unfolding of a single universal plan and a single meaning.

So far, human history places no irremovable roadblocks in the path of the historical modeler. For the historian must also perform socio-cultural analysis, or apply a metahistory, to locate social entities to write about.

Consider the following. The Second Punic War and the establishment of the Han Empire were more or less contemporary events. Unaided, linear historical narrative can grasp the meaning of each of these events. But it cannot tell us their relation. We know, of course, that they were independent: the Punic Wars in the Mediterranean and the

Han Empire in China had no relation to one another. But this knowledge is based on a causal reasoning which, however commonsense it is, does not belong to the isolated historical facts themselves. In other words, to write history on the universal scale, we *must* have recourse to some sort of model. The historian must reconstruct, on the basis of models and analogies, in order to write anything at all.

If narration and analogies drawn from direct personal experience are the only way of understanding the past, then history can be nothing more than a series of "portraits" or episodes. The larger unity of history is destroyed. Within the confines of the personal scale, one is limited to portrait-like histories such as those written by the Greeks and Romans. Biography, for example, exists purely on the personal scale. Greek and Roman histories were "biography-like." History in this case will be not a continuous motion, but a picture gallery.

National historians are also, even if unconsciously, relying on a socio-cultural or metahistorical model: the notion of the nation-state as a coherent "intelligible field" enduring in time and acting as the stage for historically significant events. So application of the modeling paradigm to human history is not only valid, but necessary. It brings out a whole spectrum of historical systems, from economic and political systems on one side to systems of cultural values and ideas on the other. The systems may overlap in space and in time, but that is not a hindrance, since they are humanly comprehensible and stand out as identifiable patterns.

## Historical Order as Natural Order?

The next step in the modeling process is to characterize the interactions both between and within the historical entities discovered in the first step. The most obvious way to do this is to treat social forces as analogous to physical forces. Such assumptions underlie much sociological modeling; for human population, it works very well.

We can go further and suppose the forces governing social and cultural changes *really are* reducible to natural forces. Historical order would be a natural order, and we would have a "social physics" capable of explaining and predicting any social state. Such was the intent of

Marx's economic theory of history, but one equally could start from technology, military force, natural resources, climate, genetics, or geography as the decisive material factor in the course of nations.

These views are hardly new of course[3]. The 19th Century witnessed a great profusion of naturalistic theories purporting to explain all historical development as the result of external, environmental factors: they reduced human history to natural history. The theory of biological evolution also had its influence here. The question is not whether material forces influence history – it would be impossible for them not to, since we are not free-floating spirits or Cartesian ghosts in machines. The real question is whether historical development can be explained *entirely* by natural forces, directly or indirectly, and if so, whether we can model these forces.

Human history begins with human acts and human perceptions. Undoubtedly, we seek natural ends. To the natural ends belong sheer physical limitation and necessity. We require air to breathe, water to drink, food to eat. We need to be sheltered and protected from the elements. Certain of these necessities, like air and often water, are so abundant and easily obtained that we give them no further thought. Others, like food or shelter, are scarce. Fulfilling our need for them requires work and effort. This quest can take up all of our time, leaving no time for anything else.

Certainly, the natural ends, as manifestations of natural forces, are that part of human affairs most amenable to modeling. They are characterized by deterministic laws, often well-defined entities, and quantifiable relations. And it is in precisely such areas, like economics, war, political administration, technological growth, or population, that models have met with the most success, as the previous chapter showed.

But the natural ends cannot be entirely explained by material conditions. Most of the supposedly "material conditions" of our lives far outstrip mere physical necessity. What are the two most ardently sought after "material" things in history, the objects of conquerors? Surely they are wealth and power. But these two things provide an ironic proof of the primacy of the psychological dimension of history. For while we can certainly invoke physical necessity to explain the search of the historical common man for his daily bread, how can necessity explain the drive toward immense wealth that vastly overfulfills all necessities? The desire for luxury is in the mental realm. (Such is true even if it is a matter of pleasure versus pain). In the case of power, the psychological dimension is even more evident. To exercise power and authority over others is a universal craving throughout history, but how can this "will to power" be construed as physical necessity? Here material factors appear mainly in the negative sense of limitations, not determining phenomena, but merely restricting their possibilities. External measures of the past — such as population, population density, degree of urbanization, wealth, distribution of wealth, national boundaries, language groups, technological level, and formalized social status — are at most the skeleton of history. They provide a framework and a starting point, but they are really indicators of historical impact, and not of historical meaning.

Historically speaking, there are no isolated or isolable material conditions — a "material condition" turns out to be something I need or desire[4]. Consider the case of economics. The order of economic life ultimately is rooted in human nature, desires, and choices. In the case of an ideal market economy, the order is provided by the choices of consumers. The market itself communicates this order to the whole array of producers. In other words, economic order is rooted in the order of values of consumers, and the ability to meet the ends pointed to by those values.

Nature by no means determines history. If it did, there would be no such thing as human history; there would only be a natural history moving on geologic time scales. Natural forces do represent both crucial limitations and enablers of human possibilities and thus have roles to play in history. In extreme cases, nature can almost completely determine the direction of a people or a culture. Toynbee offered the example of the Eskimos; living in the harsh conditions of polar climate, they are forced into a rigidly fixed mode of existence. But for precisely that reason, such societies are non-historical in the civilized sense of the term. Locked into a natural pattern, the potentialities of human nature never get a chance to express themselves. In such societies, life consists of sameness and order, except for chance natural disturbances, which are usually destructive and dangerous. In other words, in non-historic societies, human history gets reduced to "natural history"[5]. Of course, it is possible for non-historic peoples to break the bonds of blind fate and give birth to civilizations. Enslavement to nature always represents the dehumanization of man and his reduction to a natural object. Nature is a zone of limitation and scarcity: it is a *negative* factor in the historical process.

Thus, it is *not* possible to comprehend, model, or explain human history directly in terms of natural forces. Civilized society is not simply the product of the natural environment, as should be obvious. But what if, instead, we look at the human interaction with the material world and application of knowledge it. Animals adapt to their environments, but man actively adapts his environment to suit his own needs and whims. Thus, while we cannot explain history directly through natural factors, we still might be able to explain it *indirectly* in these terms, since tools and machines are still governed by natural laws.

Humanity both understands and controls the natural world through science and technology. All technology originates out of desire to control part of the natural world. (This is true even in the case of technique applied to a seemingly completely different end, the painter's control of a brush, for example. His end may be to produce a work of art, an aesthetic object. But to produce it he has to gain mastery over the physical media of his art.) Technology is always pragmatic in orientation, an instrument to some material end, an expansion of capabilities.

The most obvious expression of natural forces in history is what we might term the "iron triangle" of economic, technological, and military forces. Each of the three reinforces the other. Technology leads to economic growth and military superiority, both of which feed back into new technologies. Economic strength can be translated into military strength, while military strength acts to defend, and sometimes enhance, the economic sphere of a nation. When combined with population, this "iron triangle" defines the quantitative or extensive significance of events and institutions.

It is tempting to see history, then, as substantially a product of technology, economics, and military force, and in turn see these three as a product of natural forces. Our problem is solved: we model the "iron triangle" in our history simulator program and off goes the unstoppable march of Progress in a straight line from the Stone Age to the Space Age. But this is forgetting, once again, (above the starvation level) these forces are ultimately rooted in human nature.

Here is a simple example that shows how technological determinism can be misguided even for primary civilizations. Suppose we build our SimHistory based on analogies to the first civilizations of the Old World: the civilizations of Egypt, Mesopotamia, India, and China all arose in similar ways.  All four arose in relatively isolated river valleys, on a basis of agriculture, with some form of writing, and grew into populous empires.

Now, the civilizations of the New World, those of Mexico and Peru, are the *experimentum crucis* for any theory about cultural development. Having grown up in isolation from the early civilizations of the Old World (which all affected each other, however indirectly), we can tell whether civilizations are all flowers of the same species.  If so, they should sprout up and grow the same way. We should be able to take our SimHistory based on Egypt and Sumer and make a SimMexico and SimPeru.

But even on the purely technological level, our new models break down.  There is not a unique course of technological progress that all peoples are fated to tread.  The model would predict, for instance, agricultural civilization to appear in a desert river valley like that of the Rio Grande.  In fact, the cultivation of maize arose in the Mexican highlands and the first stirrings of Mesoamerican civilization occurred in the steamy jungle realm of the Olmecs — an environment very unlike the cradles of civilization in the Old World.  Going forward in time, we are treated to the spectacle of the Maya, a technically "stone age" people who nonetheless were highly literate, used the number zero, calculated the length of the solar year to incredible accuracy, and even had jars with screw-top lids.  In South America, we find something even stranger: civilization in Peru apparently originated along the Pacific coast, not on a basis of agriculture, but on fishing, its marine resources being among the richest in the world[6]. Intensive agriculture came later and on the basis of organization developed for fishing.  The ancient Peruvians, although in many ways more technologically advanced than Mexico (metallurgy appeared in the Andes at an early date, for example), were barely literate at all. They had no writing, only record-keeping using knotted strings. So our SimMexico and SimPeru models, operating by analogies to the ancient Near East, have failed to present an accurate picture of the development of the civilizations of ancient America.

Actually, the previous chapter demonstrated the breakdown of a naturalistic view of human history. The population of the United States was modeled quite accurately by the logistic law of population growth. Yet the apparent upper limit of the American population is not materially determined at all: it is *cultural*, based on changing values with regard to childbearing and immigration.

A naturalistic model of human history thus *cannot* be constructed. We cannot explain history on the basis of geography, or climate, or technological level, or economic station. While it is an indisputable fact that each of these factors has its influence on history, it is also indisputable that no single one can be considered *universally decisive*, determining every element of human affairs.

This conclusion has importance not only for the past but also for the future. Futurism is, in many ways, an offspring of the naturalistic attitude. It almost always extrapolates present trends, or the trends of the recent past, into the indefinite future: because the past ten or fifteen decades have been characterized by steady technological improvements and greater prosperity, therefore, the next ten centuries will be also. Because it usually concentrates on technological growth, futurology is really a continuation of the 19th Century vision of history. It posits the future as an endless upward progress of technological wonders. I call this the "Star Trek" vision of the future, and really there is a large overlap between science fiction and futurology. Indeed, it is sometimes hard to tell where the science fiction stops and the futurology begins.

Yet the predictive record of the futurists has not been good, or at best half-right. Many of the technological predictions of scientists (and writers of science fiction) have come to pass. On the other hand, their predictions of the social, cultural, and political future were not only wrong, but were often the exact opposite from what actually happened. Such are the dangers of naive extrapolation.

The whole model-building approach in fact conflicts with that of the historian on a number of important points. The modeler, whether in the guise of social scientist or philosopher of history, ultimately wants to *explain* history as one would explain any natural phenomenon. And on the basis of the model, it should then be possible to *predict* the future. But the end of the historian is quite different. The historian wants to the record the past precisely in all those particularities the theorist hopes to avoid, but more than that, to *understand* the past in human terms.

Every history is a record or narrative of certain past events; it is a representation of the past. But that fact, in and of itself, tells us nothing. The real question is: *what* facts, *what* events, and *what* persons should a history include? History is not just the past, but the *significant past*. There is a strong selectivity and ranking of events: history does not include everything that happened in the past, any more than a painting can include every detail of real landscape.

The criterion of what is important in history is human and subjective in a large number of cases, just as what we consider most memorable in our own personal lives might be unimportant to someone else. The historian must get sympathetically "inside" human facts in a way the scientist is precluded from doing with physical facts, always observing from without.

History really is mind-made in a dual sense. Authentic, fully historical existence requires conscious and rational actors. That which is *humanly* meaningful in history results from personal will or intention. A historical event is not merely an occurrence; it must have a "why" rooted in personal intention. Now, an act of will can only be interpreted by a human observer. To external, objective measures, it is unintelligible — the "why" of an action can never be objectively measured and quantified, only the "how" and "what." In the case of a natural process, one could, at least in theory, reconstruct its history without the aid of a human interpreter. This is absolutely precluded in the case of human history.

**Not Nature, but Culture**

The mind-madeness of human history leads us away from nature and towards culture.  On reflection, this shift of emphasis is required by the notion of civilization itself.  Civilization, of its very essence, means a certain liberation from natural determinism.  It means the replacement of the *natural* environment experienced by the animal with a *cultural* environment.  This cultural environment must, of course, work within the limitations presented by nature.  It is an *environment within an environment*.  Perhaps the best illustration of this principle is in shelter.  Houses construct an artificial and human environment within the natural environment, although governed by their own set of rules (expressed in engineering), they are nonetheless very much cultural, not natural, products, expressing a set of norms, usages, values, and symbols, as well as knowledge.  Architecture is the most visible expression of culture coordinating nature, of culture using nature and pushing against its limitations.

The progress of technique expands the zone of human freedom from nature[7].  It allows human nature expand its possibilities free of natural constraint.  Technical progress increasingly replaces the natural environment with a culturally-formed one.  The new, artificial environment brings its own constraints and limitations, which play an ever-larger role in history.  Indeed, civilization *is* just this:  the substitution of a synthetic environment for nature.

So the environment that matters for the would-be historical modeler is the *cultural* environment.  This is proven by the fact that two peoples inhabiting an identical natural location can have very different cultures.  The natural environment conditions the culture, of course, and often to a large degree.  But with the advance of technical civilization, the grip of nature on man becomes progressively less.  Historical processes appear more and more as the result of shared values as expressed in cultures and institutions.

To model any society and its development in time, a model must grasp that society's system of values, its culture, its knowledge, and its institutions.  The human forces of history are manifested in these, regardless of their ultimate origin. The ordering of values, the ethos of a people, is crystallized in a culture. The fact we have stable systems of cultural values and institutions constitutes the continuity of history. Without them, we would not even have stable and identifiable historical entities.

We are each born into some cultural field, and it forms the context of our lives. We can, of course, freely contribute to or change or resist some portion of it, but on the whole it is something outside our individual control, and most people simply "go with the flow," this being the path of least resistance for getting along with others. Thus, in this regard, the current of cultural symbols and institutions and knowledge has a life of its own, and can be modeled as something deterministic. Its rules are not natural rules, but the order of its own cultural norms, and ultimately, the order of its values.

A good example of "cultural environment" can be found in language. There are no people without a language, and none of us invents the language, except perhaps in some small detail. It is the vehicle of culture *par excellence*, and we are certainly free to use it as an instrument to express any idea we choose. Yet, at the same time, every language has rules, without which it could not function as a language at all. And the change of languages takes place on a time scale beyond that the individual can notice. Researchers have determined rules of linguistic drift and change. Language is a field with its own dynamic that can in some respects be modeled.

But the question is then: how can we possibly model cultures? This question looms large, since it is likely they fall outside the scope of the modeling paradigm. The key will be found in returning to the question of what is significant – that is to say, what is memorable – in history.

Historical significance naturally separates into two pieces. One assesses the *importance* or *impact* of a past occurrence, then one interprets its *meaning*. The assessment of importance or impact is a much more straightforward matter, and has a greater objectivity. Both are then weighed to find the significance. This can never be an exact science, of course. But it is clear that the historically most significant events and entities are those which are "big" and "original," while the least significant are "small" and "generic." (The representation of the "small" and "generic" events of everyday life may be interesting sociology, but it is not history. Such things are significant only if they shed light on larger occurrences.)

An event's significance changes with changing ratios of impact and meaning. For example, the opinions of a national leader obviously have greater historical significance than those of a randomly selected citizen. Why? Because his opinions, through the machinery of state, will affect many other people, even other nations. We all implicitly recognize this when we elect leaders — the responsibility of the position is generally proportional to its impact on society, and hence its historical significance. But the significant combination of meaning and impact is not necessarily an additive, linear one. Different meanings combined with the same impact will not only have different kinds of significance, they can also affect the impact itself. The opinions of a national leader on foreign policy will have a much greater impact than his opinions on higher mathematics. On the other hand, it is possible for a highly original meaning to have a much greater impact than an ordinary one.

There are two kinds of meaning that tend to have great historical significance. The first is a common meaning writ large because a large impact or force is attached to it. Such are the meanings of battles, political conflicts, technological and economic growth, and so on. They become historically significant only when they drive great entities like nations or great events like a world war. The second kind of significant meaning is a new, original meaning. This may be the meaning contained in an original idea, or system of ideas, or a new symbolic form. Such meanings are significant not because of the impact or force attached to them, but because of their originality. They represent entirely new directions in history. Every new meaning is a new purpose, a new historical form. Such are the meanings of religion, of philosophy, of art, of pure science. Historians are always dealing with, consciously or unconsciously, these two classes of historical significance. On the one hand, the histories of kings and battles. On the other hand, the histories of ideas and faiths.

There is a tendency, especially among ordinary people, to downplay the importance of ideas in history. In its extreme, this attitude degenerates into a materialist cynicism that sees all systems of ideas as pawns of material forces, as superstructures of the "real" material substrate.

Such cynicism misses the true source of the profound effect of ideas in history: they are an original, creative force. They introduce what is truly new into the stream of socio-cultural time. Even in the formally material areas of history, such as economics, the idea-element of progress is present. The economic progress of the past century and a half is almost entirely built upon technological progress. The two have reinforced each other, but the technological progress is the decisive factor. But the progress of technique rests upon the discoveries of impractical pure science. If the inventions and technology of the early industrial revolution went on more or less independently of science, those since 1850 have been integrally tied to it. The industrial steam engine without Newtonian physics is at least imaginable, but no science of electromagnetism, no electric motors or lights or telephones or radio; no quantum mechanics, no transistors or high-speed computers. The pure science of today has technical implications unknown to its developers. In turn however, the progress of modern science rests upon the mathematical, and even philosophical, achievements of the 16th and 17th Centuries. Is it an exaggeration to say that nearly all scientific progress of the past three centuries is little more than applied calculus? The economic progress of the past 150 years cannot be explained without reference to a more drawn-out development of ideas. It is new ideas that open the way not merely to new applications, but entirely new and hitherto unexpected fields of application.

The role of ideas in human society is growing. On reflection, this should not be surprising. In primitive life, and in the early civilizations, material scarcity forced man to spend life in a desperate struggle with nature. Human history barely floated above the surface of natural history; man was held down by a thousand natural chains. The progress of technology has given man control over nature and freedom from natural forces. Thus, what we think and believe attains much greater power in comparison to natural forces and constraints than previously. The power of ideas exceeds that of a few centuries ago, and vastly exceeds that of antiquity.

The central importance of ideas in history, it should be emphasized once more, is *originality*.   It is only through ideas that truly new principles are injected into human society.   It is this essentially creative element that sets ideas apart from other components of history.   Without this originality, there would be no meaningful "before" and "after" in history, only the recurrence of existing patterns or development within the scope of fixed laws towards some equilibrium, as in nature.   Each new idea, each novel crystallization of a value, is like one of the "seminal reasons" of the Stoics, waiting to germinate into new cultural orders.

While the drama of ideas is played out on a time scale of centuries, the creative events behind that drama are both personal and highly unpredictable.   Cultural history is full of sudden creative leaps, of fallow centuries interrupted by short golden ages.   These moments of change are when new religions, new philosophies, new world-systems, enter into history.   Even in science, the direction or possibilities of new discoveries cannot be anticipated, because foreknowledge of scientific progress implies foreknowledge of the science itself.   As Karl Popper has pointed out, that would imply knowing scientific discoveries and their import before they were discovered, which is clearly impossible[11].   The unpredictability of intellectual history is another reason why it is so important to human history.   But precisely for this reason, the future course of human affairs cannot be calculated like natural phenomena.

## Theory versus History: The Problem of the Indeterminate and the Singular

The foregoing points yield a set of important conclusions.   Despite some initial successes in the analysis of the societies and cultures of history, the modeling process reached a serious roadblock when it attempted to naively characterize the forces that order them.   There is good reason for this failure: as Chapter Six discussed, we are trying to push the modeling paradigm beyond its conceptual limits.   Of its essence, the model cannot ascend into the realm of freedom and intelligence.   To the degree history expresses these (albeit in an impure form), human history as a whole *cannot* be forced into the mold of a model.

In fact, this inability is a precondition for a meaningful notion of human history. Some degree of indeterminism, irreversibility, and uniqueness are needed for authentic historicity. That historians write about some entities and not others illustrates this fact. There are many histories of America and of England and of China, but none at all of lunar orbits, the motions of electrons, or the rotations of water molecules. The distinction here is between historical order and physical law: *the historical past is not reducible to complete order*. If something is absolutely systematized and predictable by necessary laws, if any state of the system may be derived exactly from any other state, then it has no history. It has no history because time is not really necessary to describe it. We can fully understand the system without reference to its past. A completely ordered or physical system is described by a theory, where the time element has been eliminated or reduced to spatial variables through formulas. Once we have found the correct theory, we can predict any future state of the system — Laplace's dream appears again.

There is thus a fundamental dichotomy between "theory" and "history," first enunciated by the scientist and philosopher Cournot. That which can be completely theorized is not historical, and the historical past will always escape the attempts of the theorist to confine it within the bounds of complete order. There is a theory of atomic orbitals, but there are no histories of atomic orbitals. On the other hand, while we can write a history of England, we do not devise theories of England. If past occurrences could be explained by a single law, if all historical changes could be predicted according to a mathematical model, then there would be no history. It might be "development" or "progress" or "evolution," but it would not be history.

All the problems in modeling complex systems discussed in Chapter Seven come into play in societies and cultures. Even if human relations could be modeled mathematically on the small scale, the complexity and non-linearity of systems would lead to chaotic and effectively indeterminate phenomena on the large scale. Only a few areas of social interaction (such as economic transactions) can really be reduced to a quantifiable form amenable to modeling, so the problem of a comprehensive model is even more difficult since the nature of the interactions are only qualitatively understood and are not invariant like natural laws. In addition, the existence of feedback in social phenomena means the historical world is partially organic. Perceptible causality gets lost among the branches and turbules of the historical current. There is no such thing as a completely isolated "socio-cultural atom." The historians' rule of thumb that, in general, a historical event cannot be ascribed to a single cause is based upon this.

History, in other words, depends on the flow of time in an authentic sense. It is an irreversible process, even if certain patterns are repeated from time to time. Each event is unique, and history is a sequence of unique events. This irreversibility is closely connected to the indeterminacy of human affairs, whether we are speaking of free activity or of chance. Introduce human freedom, and the modeling paradigm will not apply.

Another unpredictable factor in history is the crucial importance of the singular, and that ultimate singular, the individual person. Civilization not only insulates us from nature, it breaks the unity of total society. It means the emergence of free individuals from the lukewarm and brackish sea of the all-embracing community. The civilizational emergence of individuals has continued throughout history and is in fact a progression. The problem of individual life and of ethics has grown, however inconsistently or unevenly. Though far from being an absolute law, there is a grain of truth in Hegel's metahistorical formula of "one free — some free — all free." Said differently, history does narrate to us the story of liberty, as the philosopher Benedetto Croce would have it[12].

The problem of the singular person leads directly to the problem of "Great Men" in history – in other words, can individuals decisively affect the flow of human affairs or not? Consider the case of Alexander the Great, the very epitome of the Great Man. Was the empire of Alexander the Great the result of his brilliant heroics, or was he just lucky enough to be in the right place at the right time? Did he make history, or was he made by history? Really, it is a case of the key and the lock. Persia was decaying, vulnerable. But it took an Alexander to capture her. A different ruler of Macedon doubtless would not have. Inescapably, without Alexander, the histories of both Greece and the East would have run down different roads entirely. Therefore, he was a Great Man, who made history, and was not merely made by history. The Great Man acts as a catalyst — he strikes the decisive blow in an undecided situation.

We see then that human history – and thus also the human future – violates many of the rules laid down for models. It is obviously far-removed from the analytic, deterministic Laplacean universe that is the model's natural home. The appearance of crucial singular events, which cannot be characterized in terms of general laws and are not repeatable phenomenon, is one of the most serious problems a model can confront, while being essential to authentic historicity. The unique individual, as the ultimate singularity, makes clear the distinction between the theoretical and the historical. When we consider also that new ideas enter societies and cultures through individuals, the importance and difficulty is doubly obvious.

## Summary and a Modeling Thought-Experiment

I think the upshot of the foregoing discussion can be summarized in a few sentences. On the one hand, we will never be able to reduce human affairs to a unified, monolithic model — which is to say that we will never be able to reduce it to simplistic or deterministic laws. Such laws are contradicted by the course of history itself. Nor could we view the unpredictable element in history simply as random chance or fate, because truly new things have appeared in the course of history, which have fundamentally changed the structures of societies and cultures themselves, a change of substance and form, as it were, rather than simply a change of size or velocity. At the same time, we have seen that there are certain aspects of society that can be modeled. These aspects represent the influence of natural forces, such as economics or technology, or go beyond the conscious control of individuals, such as large-scale cultural patterns. And what the would-be constructor of SimHistory should pay attention to are cultural rather than material patterns.

Yet even the best model must fall short, due to the unpredictable element in history, especially on the level of ideas. As the role of ideas grows, civilization's predictability will diminish – at best, there will be certain tendencies possessed by different species of cultures. The pattern of ancient civilization was more predictable than modern civilization, because the former was closer to the earth and its iron rules. What can be modeled in history will necessarily be of a general nature, so both progress and cycles are not unreasonable models. For it is a fact, that while knowledge and technique have more or less accumulated over history, they have not done so evenly, nor all in the same place, and it is equally a fact that nations and empires have risen and fallen in the course of time, and presumably will do so in the future.

Socio-cultural models can at best anticipate the general direction of things and the general outlines of the future. They present multiple scenarios, of several alternate futures, towards which an entity is tending. A multiplicity of scenarios is inevitable and derives from the multiformed nature of the historical reality. They rank probabilities of possible futures. Each scenario is a thought-experiment.

Consider another thought-experiment about ancient America, based on a not unreasonable "what if." Suppose that, due to some calamity like a Mongol invasion, the Europeans never discovered America. The civilizations of Mexico and Peru would have continued to develop without outside disruption. We proceed to examine this question using a comprehensive computer model; the model would represent the Americas as a grid of cells modeling the topography, climate, resources, rivers, and so on, of the Western Hemisphere. It would, as its initial conditions, populate those cells with the societies known to exist in 1492. The model would then be stepped forward in time based on rules drawn from both the ancient American past and analogous societies of the Old World, such as the civilizations of the ancient Near East, China, India, and Europe. It would also apply everything we know about economics, the diffusion of technology, and so on.

So could a computer model reliably extrapolate from 1492 to predict the future – really an alternate present – of the Americas? On the qualitative level, many things seem reasonable to predict: that civilized life would steadily spread from Mexico northward into North America, taking root in the Southwest and in the Mississippi River valley, as it already was beginning to do so. By analogy, Mexico was to ancient

North America what Egypt and Mesopotamia were to ancient Europe. We would also suppose the expansion of trade and technology, the emergence of substantial contacts between Mexico and Peru (bringing metallurgy and beasts of burden to Mexico, as well as more advanced forms of writing and intellectual life to Peru). Societies throughout the Americas would become both more populous and more complex. Our model would fill in many of the details of where and how and when these changes would take place.

Driving the analogy further, can we espy the "Greeks and Romans" of America somewhere in the broad fields of North America? Here our model begins breaks down. We don't know how it will turn out, since we are asking questions about singular events. We can anticipate more advanced civilization in North America, but not its details. Would there have been a "Socrates of Taos" or a "Caesar of Cahokia"? This is exactly the sort of singular thing the model cannot predict. What it does predict is an entirely reasonable alternate present, but that is merely one alternate present out of many.

In a physical model – such as a climate model – we could at least theoretically escape most of these limitations by using a more detailed grid, by obtaining better data about the phenomena in question, and so on. But for human affairs – because of decisive singular events, rules that are both variable and non-quantifiable, and complexity – this approach is ruled out. So the computer model can never reach its second destination of a comprehensive explanation of human affairs – or can do so only a vague way.

# Chapter 11

# Virtual Reality ... and Reality

We have explored the possibilities of rendering the physical world with a palette of Boolean ones and zeros. We have also seen the more limited and problematic potential for modeling human affairs — the second dimension of the modeling universe. Now we turn to the third and perhaps most intriguing goal of the modeling enterprise: the model *as* reality. The ordinary term, virtual reality (VR for short), does not do the concept full justice. Virtual signifies "not real", like a virtual image in a mirrored globe. Yet are not images in some sense real? They are not, after all, always fictional, but representations of some reality.

Chapter One gave a thumbnail definition of virtual reality. It is an expanded imagination, an imaginary world, a synthetic world with different structures and rules. This definition was provisional, but accurate enough. The question remains, however, as to what qualifies as a virtual reality and what such realities must possess. Although this may seem a somewhat trivial technological question, it in fact raises important questions about reality itself. Virtual reality has attracted attention as a topic worthy of serious philosophical contemplation[1].

Probably the best examples of rudimentary virtual realities are games, especially those games that set up a world in which the players must interact through rules, whether different or similar to those of everyday life. To command pawns, rooks, bishops, and knights on the chessboard is to be inserted into imaginary world with its own laws. Many games have appeared in recent decades whose goal is precisely to simulate a reality, whether historical (e.g., war games) or fantastical (e.g., Dungeons and Dragons). Many virtual realities are, in fact, just extensions of role-playing games. They allow one to become, for an hour or two, a general, a tycoon, a king, or an imaginary hero from a bygone era.

Still, no one will mistake a chessboard for reality. The old-fashioned game is an assemblage of paper, plastic, metal, wood, and cardboard, and however brightly painted, it is seen only as that. The game, rather like a novel, requires the active imagination of the players to give it life. It does not live on its own.

Authentic, full-fledged virtual reality awaited a technological leap to make autonomous action possible. Along with the vital roots of virtual reality — the desire to create imaginary worlds — there are equally important technological preconditions. Virtual reality has to seem real, not just act out the real.

Such technology was not available until the middle of the 20th Century. One obvious technology necessary to virtual reality is a way to make things *appear* real to a human observer, and that means a way of making and displaying images. Such appearance is what the motion picture and television were able to provide. Television, having a sensory immediacy which print lacks, drove out the feebler medium. In the process, it weakened literacy and imagination, but exercised sensation and brought a floodtide of superficial images. It did so because it seemed to bring us into closer contact with reality.

Another technical precondition for virtual realities was a means of generating a detailed enough artificial world to truly to make it seem real. Moreover, there has to be a way to allow participants into that virtual world, to make it interactive. That required the computer -- but not until the 1970s did computer hardware have enough muscle and sophisticated software to make virtual realities possible. The computer acts as the container or substrate of a virtual universe, enduring and maintaining the reality even as the virtual entities in that universe come, go, and change. The software is the lawgiver, defining the rules of the game governing the entities in the virtual world.

Once the preconditions were in place, virtual realities emerged in attempts to solve practical problems or tap into an entertainment market. The first true virtual realities were aircraft simulators. The reason was quite simple. Modern aircraft — whether civilian or military — are expensive both to build and to operate. A major mistake in their operation can easily be catastrophic. Thus, there was a strong motivation to build a virtual airplane to use in training. The flight simulator allows new pilots of an aircraft to become familiar with it cheaply and safely. And if a virtual accident occurs, nothing is lost and experience needed to avoid future mishaps is gained. Now, for an aircraft simulator to be of any use, it has to be as realistic as possible. It has to truly simulate reality and present it to the pilot. On the user interface level, this is achieved simply by providing the pilot with an exact replica of the aircraft's cockpit and its controls. But the display of the world outside the virtual airplane and its performance characteristics required major innovations, making the aircraft simulator the most proximate root of virtual realities.

A second source of virtual realities was computer or video games. Games have always stood for imaginary worlds with their own structure and objects. What they lacked was the sensory immediacy of reality. The video game supplied that missing piece. The lowly Pong of the 1970s begat the Asteroids, Pac-Man, and Missile Command of the 1980s. Soon, specialized video games of the Nintendo sort followed, providing ever higher levels of action and sensory realism. Now the industry has attained the photorealism of Playstation-3 and Xbox. With the computer game and networked internet role-playing games, virtual reality became something as near as most people's desktops.

Virtual reality is something still emerging today. It will improve dramatically in the years ahead with increasing computer speeds, more vivid displays, better controls, and expanding communications bandwidth. Today's popular image of virtual reality is quite naturally heavily conditioned by video games. It is viewed as little more than an extension of these, with greater roles for players and more realistic displays. These are authentic examples of virtual reality. But they will likely not be the most important expression of it in the longer term. The popular image of virtual reality is likely to change a great deal in the years ahead. In a decade or two, when one thinks of VR, it will not be of video games, but of participatory educational software, simulated visits to ancient Egypt, a vastly expanded Internet telepresence and teleconferencing capability, and a means of cultural dispersion.

## The Interactive Image

Let us return to the chapter's central question: what constitutes virtual reality? Virtual reality as expanded imagination — as an imaginary world that nonetheless has the authentic ring of reality — implies many things. But the essential features can be, I think, condensed down to this: *virtual reality is a set of interactive sensory images*, with rules for getting from one image to another. Each part of this definition is important. The virtual reality, to warrant the name, must have *images* that appear real enough to us. Without images, just with words, we would have the information, but not the immediacy of reality. Every image is a projection of what is real or what can be real. Images are thus essential to virtual reality — and images mean not only *visual* images (the normal use of the term), but also images appropriate to the other sensory modes: of sounds and textures, smells and tastes.

Virtual reality must also be *interactive*. Without a means of acting on the world, however small, the virtual world is just a separate universe. It is not fully real *for me*. Without the possibility of participation, the simulated world will simply develop along the deterministic lines its internal rules dictate (or vary randomly).

Finally, there must be a set of *rules* for getting from one set of images to another. This could be as simple as allowing a participant to select arbitrarily which path to pursue in the virtual world, or as complex as trying to simulate the behavior of objects according to scientific laws. But without for rules linking images, a virtual reality is just a photo album.

The above definitions also clarify what virtual reality is *not*. Movies and television do not constitute virtual realities, because they have no interactivity. One's experience of a motion picture is purely passive — much more passive than either a book (which requires the reader's imagination) or a true virtual reality (which demands action by the participant). Thus, while television constitutes a crucially important technical foundation for virtual reality, it is not itself a virtual reality. Moreover, the movie is a fixed and invariable reality, always moving along a predetermined path. No matter how many times I rerun a movie, the same sequence of frames always appears.

Computer models of phenomena, all by themselves, are a component of virtual reality, but not the entire story. They calculate the behavior of objects on the computer according to rules, and then validate predictions against empirical data. But computer simulations — again like television — lack interactivity. They also generally lack images (although this is changing with improved computer graphics capability). Very often, the result of a computer model is a table of numbers.

Virtual reality is not simply an instrument for something else, as in robotics. Take, for example, the robot rovers recently sent to Mars. The Mars rover, in how it is controlled and how it operates, has many aspects similar to virtual realities. In fact, virtual reality techniques were used to control the rover: the rover's software or a human operator is presented with a three-dimensional visual Marscape in order to plan what places the rover should visit next. Yet the rover is not virtual reality. The reality it investigates is quite solid, objective, and material. It is really an extension of the robot arm, operating in a hazardous environment, manipulated from another room by a human technician. A virtual reality, on the other hand, is an imaginary world in the literal sense of being *a world of images.*

Virtual reality is the modeling process put in reverse and turned inside out. Instead of starting from empirical data to build an accurate representation of that data, the virtual reality starts from a model (which may be built with the solid foundation of scientific laws or may be completely imaginary) and translates it into an image, synthetic data. The image is then viewed by a participant as if it were reality. This is important: the shimmering surface of the model, beamed out in images, takes the place of "real" reality.

Virtual realities *must* have active players or agents somewhere in their imaginary world. This is another difference with the model. Such participation could be as simple as a single observer that clicks a mouse on various parts of a picture to proceed to other pictures or as elaborate as a cast of thousands. The virtual reality, being composed of images that are acted upon, requires actors and observers. It need not be universal or multi-actor. It could be accessible only to one person — perhaps a highly personal and idiosyncratic "cybermonad". Moreover, the virtual worlds are called into existence in response to the needs and desires of their creators.   There is no program without a programmer. Virtual realities, like art, are meant to viewed and acted upon. Without that, they lose their meaning.

They also must have a display system to bring its images to its human actors.  Not just images, but images that seem "real enough" to a human observer.  To be "real enough", the images presented must engage the observer's senses to effectively become real for that observer — real in a sensory way, not an intellectual way.  So there is a subjective element here.  The necessary image quality will vary from subject to subject. The image need not be photorealistic or three-dimensional to achieve the desired effect.  Often the grainy image on a television screen is enough to make us react and feel *as if* we are dealing with reality, even if the events are fictional or were long in the past.   Once again, by "image" is meant not simply the visual image, but also presentations to the other senses. Vision is the most important human sense by far, but hearing is essential for communication and experience of the human world, while the ability to reach out and touch solid, weighty objects is an equally essential component of our experience of physical reality.  Taste and smell, while auxiliary senses in human beings (they are far less important to us than to most animals) nonetheless can be particularly relevant to certain experiences and memories.  Further, they are closely associated with food, and thus with the fulfillment of an essential human need.  And, unlike our other senses, they often have an implied value judgment associated with them: some things, like perfume, freshly baked bread, or a newly opened can of coffee, naturally smell good to us. Others, like skunks and anything rotten, are repulsive.  Similarly with taste.  This actually provides the key to what is real enough for virtual reality.  The image is real enough when it presents not only realistic appearing objects -- this requirement by itself would mean that virtual reality must always attain the photorealistic limit.  It need only present a world that involves us, draws us in, and engages our potential actions.

Because it is interactive, virtual realities must have a way for the participants to affect the reality.  There must be controls of some sort that allow the human actors to drive the reality.  They must be able to act and get results in the virtual reality, just as in ordinary reality. Further, the actions must be conveyed not only to the information system that holds the reality, but also between participants in the virtual reality. The sort of controls used by a virtual reality system can vary widely. They can be various keys or buttons to be pressed, a mouse or trackball that moves a cursor, up to the sophistication of active controls that trace the motion of the human eye, head, or hands, or recognize voice commands. Once again, the question is what controls are real enough for virtual reality. An aircraft simulator, for example, to be of any use, must present the user with a suite of controls like those on the real aircraft, and these controls must have the same effects as the real controls. At the same time, the controls of the aircraft simulator need be only that. There is no need to provide any special conformal controls such as gloves, helmets, etc. The controls on many video games are often simply up, down, and sideways buttons, but that is enough for the purposes of the game and its players.

Last, but far from least, there must be an information system that holds the virtual reality. In other words, there must be a real substrate to the virtual world. Information system may be taken as synonymous with electronic computer. The computer contains the virtual reality in its memory and governs its development in time according to the rules defined for objects in the virtual world and the actions of its participants. It must be powerful enough to present a virtual world that has enough continuity in space and time, and detailed enough objects. The actors in the virtual world must be able to manipulate the objects, while at the same time the objects seem to have natures and behaviors of their own. The computer must be able to react promptly to the actions and commands of participants, while also quickly presenting an up-to-date picture of the virtual world. These are highly demanding requirements that need a great deal of computing speed and memory. It meant that virtual realities could be built at first only on very expensive supercomputers. Only in the past decade have advances in personal computers put that kind of power on everyone's desktops.

## Fictions, Simulations, and Cyberspace

Within the scope of virtual reality, one can discern three broad categories: fictional reality, simulated reality, and cyberspace. Each area fulfills a different need, but all three are interrelated, and each in its own way must be considered as virtual reality.

*Fictional reality* means virtual reality in the narrow sense, like a video game. Fictional reality is, in fact, the stereotype of virtual reality. The aim of any fictional reality is to transport the viewer to "another world" and to entertain. In other words, the fictional reality is much like the motion picture or theater, on the one hand, and like a game, on the other. Really, they are the fusing of games and movies, which is obvious at the high end of video/computer game sophistication.

Fictional reality also offers the possibility of stories whose plot and characters can be controlled or influenced by the viewer at certain points in time: an interactive movie where the viewer becomes a participant. Fictional realities will doubtless grow as a source of entertainment in the years ahead and become a regular part of show business. Once broadband Internet connectivity becomes as ubiquitous as the television, there will be an almost limitless market for fictional realities. Fictional realities could in fact absorb the motion picture altogether, if audiences really do enjoy changing the flow of events with the click of a remote control button.

*Simulated reality*, in contrast, attempts to present the viewer with as realistic and interactive a model of ordinary reality as possible. If the best example of fictional reality is the video game, the prototype of simulated reality is the aircraft simulator. And if the aim of fictional reality is overwhelmingly one of entertainment, the aim of simulated reality is education and training. Simulated reality is something closer to the modeling paradigm, precisely because its aim is to produce a replica of reality. Built by extraction of data from images, it replicates those same images. Indeed, it is possible for a simulated reality to simply be a collection of images bound together by links. Perhaps the most striking commonly available simulated reality at present is Google Earth. Fusing satellite imagery with topographical data, it makes possible such simulated reality feats as flying through the Grand Canyon from the safety of home. A fusion of Google Earth with web camera technology would get close to the Mirror World ideal, at least for the sight-seer.

That *cyberspace* – the linked world of the Internet—can be considered a virtual reality seems at first invalid: the Internet, rather like a telephone or television, only puts us in contact with what is far away. It changes the *structure* of spatial reality for us, turning our normal three dimensions into a web of hyperlinks. It brings a vast world just an arm's length away. But what a web page brings us is not necessarily reality. It presents a series of interconnected images. Of course, television is often like this, too (a microscope through which we view some carefully selected slice of reality — or unreality), but cyberspace is even to a greater degree a hall of mirrors.

But the most important reason why cyberspace falls into the category of virtual reality is its interactivity. The Internet, unlike television, is interactive. It is a world with participants. It is a world that obeys rules of its own, determined by each page that the user reaches. As television and the Internet gradually merge over the next decade or two, this will become even more apparent. Cyberspace is not so much one world, with a single uniform structure, as a collection of worlds, each with its own particular laws[2].

### Seeing is Believing?

Perhaps the key point of the virtual reality problem is this: at what point does seeing become believing? What is real enough? It is the key because the structure of virtual reality is the *reverse* of the ordinary modeling problem. The model starts from the real world, as given in images or data, and attempts to replicate it to the best degree possible. The virtual reality, on the other hand, starts with a model and then generates images from it. It can, as for simulated realities, aim at the best degree of fidelity to the real world. But fictional realities mean the generation of entirely imaginary worlds, which could be completely unlike our own except that they are extended in space, endure in time, have sensory presentations, and are susceptible to our actions.

Any virtual reality is a model that tries to set itself in the place of normal reality, to function *as a reality for us* either in part or in whole. As explained previously, it provides images we can sense, and also controls that we can act on. (Virtual reality can not go directly to the mind, at least not yet.) To do this means the virtual reality is not just a model. It must have a set of image producers, or *actuators*, that match our senses the way that normal reality does. It must also have a set of controls or *sensors* that match our bodies and allow us to act on the virtual reality as if it were physical reality. The displays and controls can be something as simple as a video screen and a keyboard, or as complex as display helmets and sensor systems that locate all surfaces of the body, but the principle is the same. It is just a question of the quality of the "window" into the virtual world.

A short digression into the nature of sensors, actuators, and their role in both the virtual reality and ordinary reality might be of help here[3]. Let us first compare the system of participant and world for the two kinds of reality.

The "ordinary" world produces an unbidden stream of sensations, which we receive through our natural sensors: the five classical senses of sight, hearing, touch, smell, and taste, as well as internal senses like proprioception. Our senses are our points of contact with the world; without them, we would know nothing directly about the world, nor could we act in a purposeful or rational fashion in it. We process this information and respond to it in ways that serve our various purposes. We then act on the world through our set of bodily actuators: hands and arms, feet and legs, tongues and jaws. Other animals have different sensors and different actuators than we possess — occasionally radically different, like echolocation in bats or electrical shocks generated by certain fishes — but the basic principle is the same. To live, we need both a means of sensing the world and a means of acting on it[4]. As Aristotle pointed out long ago, there is an essential link between sensing and acting.

Sensors and actuators (in a simplest approximation, the bodily surface) are our interfaces to the world. This is precisely what makes virtual reality possible.

The virtual reality, like the real world, produces a stream of sensations. It also provides a way to act *as if* it were the real world.

The keys to virtual reality are the *limited* capabilities of the human senses. Two systems very different in the inner structure can *appear* to have the same sensory qualities: a rose and a neon sign can appear to us as an identical shade of red, even though the physical processes producing the stimuli of our experience of red are quite different in each case. Or, put another way, the real is not exhausted by human sense qualities — *esse* is not *percepi*[5]. Behind the same appearance can be different things. Virtual reality relies on the same principle that many animals do: it is a camouflage reality, a mimicry that deceives. Something can appear real to us without much difficulty, because our senses do not provide us with an immediate grasp of the natures of things. The sensible world is for us, in essence, an interactive image. The virtual reality substitutes its own interactive image for that of the world.

Along these lines, the limitations of human sense are also responsible for sensory illusions[6]. We can't perceive something from all aspects, with all sensory modes, at the same time. But the illusion, the camouflage, is never absolute: as I have argued elsewhere, there are no general sensory illusions. They are relative to the limitations of the sensors involved. Likewise with virtual realities: we can ultimately smash the video screen and prove we are not in an airplane or a subterranean dungeon. Suppose, for example, we could build a sensor system that sensed in every possible sensory mode — not just sight, for example, but every frequency of electromagnetic radiation from radio waves to gamma rays. And imagine that it could sense with perfect reliability and complete detail in each one of these modes. This is what I call the Argus Sensor — it is the theoretical upper limit of sensing capabilities. The Argus Sensor truly has no illusions, and neither would virtual reality be possible for it: for an image to seem real enough, the virtual reality would have to pass over into reality itself.

This points us in the direction of what VR is "real enough" for human participants. The effectiveness of the virtual reality depends in part on the participants involved: a virtual reality for pit vipers, for example, would be quite different than for people.

For every mode of sensation, there can be a corresponding mode of actuation. But not all modes can be simulated equally well. It is relatively easy nowadays to present virtual realities for sight and sound. Since these are the primary human senses, this means virtual reality can present a world that is almost real. But touch, taste, smell, and sense of balance are another matter. We can simulate flying a fighter jet, but imagine how difficult it would be to build a virtual reality of a Thanksgiving dinner! It would be most difficult to present virtual food, that smelled, tasted, and (perhaps most difficult of all) chewed like the real thing. I can walk through virtual buildings, but can I touch their walls? Could I feel the texture of the virtual curtains in the virtual living room? I can drive a virtual race car, but do I feel the centrifugal force in turns? Do I feel the rush of air on my face? Here virtual reality butts up against almost intractable technological problems. It is no accident that virtual realities have been most successful in cases where the sensory feedback to the participants is almost entirely of a sight and sound nature, and that the user's control over the virtual reality is through a control panel of some sort, rather than by direct contact.

Thus, the main limitation on virtual realities is not the model of the phenomena behind them, it is the technology that displays the images to and receives actions from its human participants. The virtual reality is an interactive viewscreen or porthole into an imaginary world. The main limitation on the model's side is providing enough detail and being able to provide it quickly enough. When I act on something in the physical world, it responds to my action immediately. In virtual reality, this may not be the case.

## Virtual Bodies

I am present in the world through my body, which exists in both space and time, and is the point where I receive sensations and exert actions. I am "in" the world through my body, while this is not the case with images. My body does not take me into the image. Either the image is in me or in front of me. Sometimes images affect us as if we are in them, but once the momentary spell is broken, we immediately realize this is not the case.

But virtual reality is not simply an image: it has a model behind it. Reality is interactive, but so is virtual reality, because provides a way for us to act on it and responds in ways to our actions. Reality is independent of me, but so is virtual reality. Objects in virtual reality can have laws and behaviors of their own. They can resist my actions, and they can exist independently of me, in a universe of their own, as long as the virtual reality is in operation. Can I be "in" a virtual reality, the same way I am "in" the world? This is mostly a question of the limitations of the displays and controls that available, so it is perhaps the one point where virtual reality most clearly falls short of full reality. Nonetheless, even the simplest virtual reality has at least some approximation of the quality of "being there" that the most impressive motion picture lacks. And that is because it is interactive. The most vivid movie will always follow the same sequence of events, regardless of how many times it is replayed or how many fast or slow I run the film. But the virtual reality, even early computer games like Pong, responds to my actions. The displays and controls of the virtual reality have, in effect, given me a body—a virtual body—in the virtual world. And in many role-playing computer games, these virtual bodies can be vivid in themselves. So the present lack of completely effective sensors and actuators does not rule out being "in" the virtual reality, any more than it does for someone who has some sensory privation like blindness in the "ordinary" world. The key point is that I am in some respect in it because I am part of its system; I am "in the loop".

Since many computer games and virtual realities try to represent ordinary reality, a virtual body is often roughly similar to the normal body. But one can imagine situations that are radically different. Consider a virtual reality whose spatial structure is not that of the three dimensions of ordinary space, but instead is a network: a land of connections and pipes, in bewildering complexity. At each node of the network, there are little worlds in which we can sense and act. Now this is, of course, just what the Internet is like. We don't imagine ourselves having virtual bodies when we hyperlink from one web page to another, but we do nonetheless, even if we cannot see it. It is a very strange sort of body, a complex of eyes, hands, key presses, mouse clicks, and digital impulses on wires. It takes up a certain volume on the network, its own sliver of bandwidth, as it darts at high speed from one point to another. Nearness and farness in the ordinary sense mean nothing in this world, and the structure of the virtual body reflects that fact: its spatiality is more or less meaningless. It is a body like a visual finger, a telescope, a remote-controlled robot arm.

If there is one major shortcoming of virtual realities, it is in the feedback between action and touch. As was pointed out, there is a close relation between action and touch. Touch is the only mode of *active sensation* possessed by humans[7]. An active sense is one where the subject generates a stimulus to interact with its object and then senses its response. The best example for artificial sensors is radar: it beams out radio waves that bounce off objects, which are then received back by the radar antenna. In addition, the active sensor can choose or tune the nature of the stimulus to bring out desired information. When we reach out and touch something, this is just what we are doing: it is acting in order to sense rather than sensing in order to act. Sensing and acting can be seamlessly joined, as in working with hand tools or playing a musical instrument.

There is a close relation between our perception that something is "really real" and the fact we can touch it. If we can both see and touch something, we will assent to its reality. Our everyday idea of matter is closely wrapped up in such experiences. So the sensible real, on the macroscopic level, must be tangible. (In an absolute sense, of course, this is false: radio waves, sound waves, and light are real, but we cannot feel them. But this is more due to the levels of energy involved. Intense light or sound waves exert a pressure, too.) The "tangibility test" is due to the fact that real things resist our actions on them. This is possible because touch is an active sense. There is a feedback between ourselves and the object touched, a feedback which is missing for the other human senses.

## The Real and the Objective

Virtual reality can have the properties of interactivity, independence, and even corporeality we have enumerated as essential aspects of reality.

That fact raises the question again: are virtual realities real? Is not the distinction between "virtual" and "true" reality illegitimate if taken absolutely — is it not more a difference of degree rather than difference of kind?

The problem calls for a finer distinction. Under normal circumstances, we identify the *real* with the *objective*. The real world around us is governed by objective laws. The real is that which coheres, which exists, having a continuity in time or "substance", and has its existence in some respect independent of my own. If something is real, it is not a product of personal whim, to vanish the instant I no longer imagine it. The unreal, in contrast, is incoherent, nonexistent, a dream, a vapor rising from the imagination; perhaps it is an inconceivable chaos. It has no continuity in time; it flies apart or is a random agglomeration.

The objective is true for everyone. It is universal, necessarily true; it is an *a priori* law. It does not depend on my perspective or opinions or inclinations. That would be the opposite of objective: namely, subjective -- the subjective being what is by definition *not* universal, but particular and individual.

It is our experience of the world and the impress of natural science that leads us to link the real and the objective so strongly. The natural world is governed by natural laws, presumably objective and universal, governing natural phenomena everywhere in the universe the same way with a necessary and unbreakable rule, the same as billions of years ago and the same into the indefinite future. The closer we get to the iron laws of the physical world, the more the real and the objective seem interchangeable.

But *are* they interchangeable? Are they *necessarily* one and the same? Consider an ideal mathematical circle. Is it objective? Certainly: the rules that govern it are absolute and invariant, necessary and the same for everyone. And so for any mathematical object or relation you wish to name: triangles, squares, $2 + 2 = 4$ — all objective, not governed by the individual, inner world of my subjectivity, nor anyone else's. A being in an entirely different kind of universe would regard circles just the same as I do. So the circle is without doubt objective. But is it *real*? Here we waver. Certainly, the circle is not some sort of dream, to evaporate in the next instant. But neither can it be said to exist in the normal sense of the word. We only see imperfect approximations to circles in this world: each with a thickness and wavering. No ideal circles come rolling down our street. The circle is static and does not exist in time at all. It is not a physical object, but an ideal prototype, a Platonic form. It has an essence, but no existence. At best, we see the perfect circle subsisting in the imperfect phenomena of our world (or the imperfect things of the world "participating" in the perfect circle). And the ideal circle is not entirely separate from me. It is not subjective, but it is only given to me in my subjective experience, in images, and the order of images: an infinitely thin line turned upon itself.

So mathematical objects are an instance where the linkage between the real and the objective breaks down. The circle is objective, but it is *not real* — not real in the way we ordinarily use the term. It is ideal. Mathematical laws, of course, have proven their immense usefulness in understanding the physical world. But this does not change the fact that mathematicians do not build proofs of mathematical laws from empirical data or physical objects, but on the basis of logic and intuition.

Let us consider the reverse possibility. Just as mathematical objects are objective, but not real, suppose there was a class of things that were real, but not objective. In other words, there could be things that, while having existence, coherence, continuity in time, and independence of me, were nonetheless governed by their own laws unlike any those of any other system. Each would be a subjective world with its own tongue, a realm of being that is its own nation. Perhaps its rules can change as its objects and participants go along. It could be a pliable reality, where the rules do not necessarily apply the same everywhere or for all instants of time. Different persons might experience such a non-objective reality in an entirely different way. It is an individual, particularized kind of reality. Now, this is exactly what a virtual reality is: it is a *private reality*.

Virtual reality *is* thus a kind of reality — as real in its own way as the world at your door — but *it is not universal and objective*. Each is subjective in its way, too. Whatever objectivity it possesses pertains only to the boundaries of its looking glass world. Some virtual realities, as we have seen, attempt to replicate the world of ordinary experience, and hence its laws. Others may try to devise fictional worlds where dragons stalk the land and magic shoots from your fingertips like lightning. Cyberspace reconnects the world into a strange universe of marquees and text, like an endless shopping mall. But in all cases, these are non-objective or private realities. I can make up one set of rules, and you can make up another.

That is why virtual reality — while being a reality — is nonetheless virtual. Its virtual nature comes from the fact of its non-objectivity, as well as the practical limitations of technology. The interactive images, all tied together by a model, are a kind of reality, a new kind of reality whose existence was never recognized until now. Virtual realities are not simply a collection of images; they are images we can act upon according to rule within the model. They are existences, however, without universal essences. The laws within on virtual reality may or may not correspond with the laws in another virtual reality.

We can, of course, drive the distinction of real and objective too far. While distinct, they are both in some degree present in all experience. The mathematical object, although not physically real, is given to us within our experience of the real. The virtual reality, although not universal and objective at all levels, must nonetheless conform to the conditions of human sensation and action. It must exist in space and time, present us with objects, and so on. On the human level, at least, we cannot completely separate the real from the objective. The fact we can distinguish them at all is the important thing.

We see also that reality has degrees. The "real world" outside us has a larger degree of reality than any present virtual reality, because it is richer, more self-subsistent, more engaging of our capabilities. Virtual realities have a lesser degree of reality, because they are sparser, more relative, less full, experience.

### Summary: The Mixed Success of VR

We are now ready to assess if computer models have, or ever can, reach their last destination of fully realistic virtual realities: the computer model as a reality in itself. The foregoing investigation leads to a mixed verdict. For the long-range human senses of vision and hearing, virtual reality is already effective, and promises to only improve in the years ahead. Since we receive by far the most information about the world through sense and hearing, the computer model has in this respect successfully reached its destination. In contrast, present virtual realities fall far short for the other human senses: smell, taste, and especially touch. Given that the combination of seeing and touching is so important to our judgment of reality, this lack is serious. Moreover, there seems no easy way (save bypassing the entire human sensory system) of remedying this shortcoming. Virtual realities are a long way from the "feelies" imagined by Aldous Huxley.

Current abilities to act on virtual realities are also fairly limited, but one can suppose that many improvements can be made. Again, however, the principal limitation of such actuators is the lack of touch and its role as an active mode of sense. What computer virtual reality lacks is ironically what the old-fashioned, non-interactive physical model has: tangibility, heft.

Yet these shortcomings of sensory presentations and of controls are not the fault of the model. In fact, there is no reason why the model cannot simulate properties that result in sensations of smell, taste, or touch. It is really the limitation of our interface into the computer and the software model it holds.

In still other ways, virtual realities are less limited than other kinds of models. They can represent not only what is (the model as simulated reality), but also what could or should be. The virtual reality model as fictional reality can be not merely fantasy but also an idealization – a more perfect reality. At this point, virtual reality intersects with art.

We have come full circle, then, to our point of departure, the jade mountain. For the jade mountain was mean to represent a perfected nature. On the one hand, it is a small replica of a mountain — a model of a mountain. Most of the real mountain is left out: it is a montane form imposed on a block of semiprecious green rock. On the other hand, it is the mountain in concentrated form. It is a *perfected* mountain — another kind of model: the model of what the mountain *should* be. So the jade mountain, drawn from the world, also goes beyond the world, to point out possible other worlds.

# Notes and References

## Chapter One

[1] David Gelernter, *Mirror Worlds, or the Day Software Puts the Universe in a Shoebox ... How It Will Happen and What Will It Mean* (New York: Oxford University Press, 1991), pp. 3, 30.

[2] ibid., p. 2.

[3] Clifford Stoll, *Silicon Snake Oil: Second Thoughts on the Information Highway* (New York: Doubleday, 1995), pp. 151-153.

[4] ibid., p. 149.

[5] See, for example, Stillman Drake (translator and editor) *Discoveries and Opinions of Galileo* (Garden City: Doubleday, 1957); Raymond J. Seeger, *Galileo Galilei, his life and his works,* (Oxford: Pergamon Press, 1966).

## Chapter Two

[1] David Guralnik, editor, *Webster's New World Dictionary of the American Language,* (Cleveland: World Publishing Company, 1972).

[2] Francis Neelamkavil *Computer Simulation and Modeling* (New York: Wiley, 1987), p. xv.

[3] Harold Chestnut, *Systems Engineering Tools,* (New York: Wiley, 1965), p. 107f.

[4] J. M. Haile, *Molecular Dynamics Simulation,* (New York: Wiley, 1992), p. 5.

[5] Neelamkavil, pp. 6, 29-30.

[6] A. K. Dewdney, *The Armchair Universe: An Exploration of Computer Worlds* (New York: W.H. Freeman, 1988), p. 29.

[7] P. Atherton, P. Borne, editors, *Concise Encyclopedia of Modeling and Simulation* (New York: Pergamon Press, 1992), p. 257.

[8] Stephen McMenamin, John F. Palmer, *Essential Systems Analysis* (New York: Yourdon Press, 1984), p. 5.

[9] M. Gitterman and V. Halpern, *Qualitative Analysis of Physical Problems* (New York: Academic Press, 1981), p. 2.

[10] W. R. Franta, *The Process View of Simulation* (New York: North-Holland, 1977), p. 2.

[11] Neelamkavil, p. 1.

[12] ibid., p. 20.

[13] ibid., p. 7.

[14] Chestnut, p. 125.

[15] Neelamkavil, pp. 3, 12; Franta, p. 1.

[16] Jack P. C. Kleijnen and Willem van Groenenthal, *Simulation: A Statistical Perspective* (New York: Wiley, 1992), p. 168.

[17] Chestnut, p. 107; Haile, p. 5.

[18] Neelamkavil, p. 11.

[19] ibid., p. 135.

[20] Franta, p. 17.

## Chapter Three

[1] W. R. Franta, The Process View of Simulation, p. 1.

[2] ibid., p.10; Neelamkavil, pp. 9-10.

[3] Neelamkavil, p. 1; Franta, p. 1.

[4] Neelamkavil, pp. 17-18.

[5] McMenamin, p. 3, 22.

[6] ibid., p. 23.

[7] ibid., p. 25.

[8] Stephen McMenamin, *Essential Systems Analysis*, p.10.

[9] ibid., pp. 12-13.

[10] Bernard Zeigler, *Theory of Modeling and Simulation* (New York: Wiley Interscience, 1976), p. 28.

[11] Grady Booch, *Object-Oriented Analysis and Design* (Reading: Addison-Wesley, 1994), p. 12.

[12] Henry Margenau, *The Nature of Physical Reality: a Philosophy of Modern Physics* (New York: McGraw-Hill, 1950), p. 178.

[13]  Booch, p. 82-84.

[14]  Neelamkavil, p. 23, 38.

[15]  Foster Morrison, *The Art of Modeling Dynamic Systems: Forecasting for Chaos, Randomness, and Determinism* (New York: Wiley-Interscience, 1991), p. 87.

[16]  Bruce Hannon and Matthias Ruth, *Modeling Dynamic Biological Systems* (New York: Springer-Verlag, 1997), p. 10.

[17]  Kleijnen, *Simulation: A Statistical Perspective*, p. 78.

[18]  Morrison, p. 3, 316.

[19]  ibid., pp. 146-148.

[20]  See, for example, Charles A. Whitney, *Random Processes in Physical Systems: An Introduction to Probability-Based Computer Simulations*, (New York: Wiley-Interscience, 1990), p. 61, 73.

[21]  Kleijnen, p. 95, 129; Neelamkavil, pp. 136 - 157.

[22]  Neelamkavil, p. 76.

[23]  Kleijnen, p. 210 - 212; Neelamkavil, p. 11.

[24]  Zeigler, *Theory of Modeling and Simulation*, p. 5.

[25]  Neelamkavil, p. 76.

[26]  Kleijnen, p. 210 - 212.

[27]  Morrison, p. 168.

## Chapter Four

[1]  Kleijnen, p. 128.

[2]  Neelamkavil, p. 161, 199.

[3]  ibid., pp. 207-208, 251 - 278.

[4]  P. Atherton, P. Borne, editors, *Concise Encyclopedia of Modeling and Simulation*, p. 309.

[5]  Franta, p. 29, 62.

[6]  Booch, p. 90.

[7]  Bjarne Stroustrup, *The C++ Programming Language*, (Reading: Addison-Wesley, 1991), Section 1.4.

[8]  There are now many works available on UML. A couple of summaries are Sinan Si Alhir, *UML in a Nutshell* (Sebastopol: O'Reilly, 1998) and Martin Fowler, Kendall Scott, *UML Distilled: Applying the Standard Object Modeling Language*, (Reading: Addison-Wesley, 1997).

[9] See, for example, Bertrand Meyer, *Object-Oriented Software Construction* (Upper Saddle River: Prentice-Hall, 1997). For further similarities to systems analysis methods, see also Grady Booch, *Object-Oriented Analysis and Design*, pp. 12 – 25.

[10] As reported from June 15, 1999 Defense Science and Technology Organization Lecture Series, Australia.

[11] Dewdney, *The Armchair Universe*, p. 229ff.

[12] Erich Gamma, Richard Helm, Ralph Johnson, and John Vlissides, *Design Patterns: Elements of Reusable Object-Oriented Software* (Reading: Addison-Wesley, 1995), often nicknamed the "Gang of Four book." See especially pages 1 – 31 for the pattern idea in general. See also Martin Fowler, *Analysis Patterns: Reusable Object Models* (Reading: Addison-Wesley, 1997). Some applications of patterns to scientific computing are given in C. L. Blilie, "Patterns in Scientific Software: An Introduction", *Computing in Science and Engineering* **4**, 48, (May/June 2002).

[13] See, for example, R. W. Hockney and J. W. Eastwood, *Computer Simulation Using Particles* (Philadelphia: Adam Hilger, 1998).

[14] Tommaso Toffoli, *Cellular Automata Machines: A New Environment for Modeling* (Cambridge: MIT Press, 1987), p. 8.

[15] Dewdney, p. 135.

[16] Toffoli, p. 3.

[17] Stephen Wolfram, *Theory and Applications of Cellular Automata* (Singapore: World Scientific, 1986). p.1.

[18] Toffoli, p. 8.

[19] Dewdney, p. 137; Figures 4-3 and 4-4 were generated using the free cellular automata Java program available from http://www.mirekw.com/ca/mjcell/mjcell.html

[20] Dewdney, p. 142.

**Chapter Five**

[1] Margenau, *The Nature of Physical Reality*, p. 28.

[2] J. Haile, *Molecular Dynamics Simulation*, p. 7.

[3] Robert Eisberg and Robert Resnick, *Quantum Physics* (New York: Wiley, 1974), p. 95.

[4] Alfred North Whitehead, *Science and the Modern World* (London: Free Association Books, 1985, orig. 1926), p. 30.

[5] Technically, induction is a variety of reduction, where a multitude of particulars get reduced to some more general relation. See, for example, J. M. Bochenski, *The Methods of Contemporary Thought* (New York: Harper and Row, 1968) p. 92.

[6] On the close relation of induction to statistical summarization of data, see Jagjit Singh, *Great Ideas of Operations Research* (New York: Dover, 1972), p. 22, 67.

[7] One must also not forget the degree to which, in Platonic and Aristotelian thought, that the "cement" between theory and the world was provided by teleology -- the notion that everything has a purpose or the theory of final causes. Probably the most important theoretical break that modern science made with Aristotle was the denial (or at least denial of relevance) of final causes.

[8] In Bacon's view, the flaw of previous reflection on the order of nature had been its hasty generalizations, a tendency to jump to certain very general axioms and then deduce consequences. This he considered false induction. Instead, the success of science was based on a *true* induction of proceeding from empirical data to laws governing only that data (the best line through the data points), and then gradually to more general axioms. Hypotheses are formed directly on the basis of the facts and tested by making predictions of future observations. Bacon downplayed the role of mathematics and theory in both science and induction. He thought that induction itself could be carried out mechanically -- in modern terms, that scientific laws could be ground out by a computer fed tables of data.

[9] Butterfield, *The Origins of Modern Science*, p. 137.

[10] F. Copleston, *A History of Philosophy, Volume VIII*, (New York: Doubleday, 1994), p. 53ff.

[11] John Stuart Mill, *Logic*, I, p. 355.

[12] Michael Polanyi, *Personal Knowledge: Towards a Post-Critical Philosophy* (Chicago: University of Chicago Press, 1962) p. 11

[13] Whitehead, p. 4.

[14] David Hume, *An Enquiry Concerning Human Understanding*, IV.1.

[15] Polanyi, p. 168.

[16] Hume himself readily admitted this: no one could actually live as a pure skeptic -- induction remains necessary for living on the practical, commonsense, everyday level.

[17] Margenau, p. 229, 248.

[18] See, for example, the discussion in John Cowperthwaite Graves, *The Conceptual Foundations of Contemporary Relativity Theory* (Cambridge: MIT Press, 1971), p. 43.

[19] ibid., p. 44.

[20] ibid., p. 4, 53-55.

[21] ibid., pp. 48-49, 109-110.

[22] Margenau, pp. 117 - 120. There are, in fact, two sets of convergence that go on. Margenau calls these internal and external convergence. *Internal convergence* is the improvement of the same data with more and more measurements -- as more data is collected on a given phenomenon, the errors inherent in measurement steadily shrink (technically, we attain a more accurate mean data value, a stochastic limit). Internal convergence is best seen in measurements of constants like the speed of light or the charge of the electron. *External convergence* is the agreement of different sets of measurements, made by different means of measurement -- like measuring the length of your living room with a measuring tape and then remeasuring it with a laser rangefinder. Margenau points out that external convergence -- the comparison of different sets of measurements -- fails for the Heisenberg uncertainty principle.

## Chapter Six

[1] One exception to the closed system assumption is the appearance of comets from the regions just beyond the solar system (the "Oort cloud"), but this has essentially no effect on the dynamics of the planets.

[2] Ptolemy (Claudius Ptolemaeus), *The Almagest* in *Volume 16 of Great Books of the Western World: Ptolemy, Copernicus, Kepler* (Chicago: Encyclopedia Britannica, 1948); from the introduction by R Catesby Taliferro, p. 1.

[3] Nicolaus Copernicus, *On the Revolutions of the Heavenly Spheres* in *Volume 16 of Great Books of the Western World: Ptolemy, Copernicus, Kepler* (Chicago: Encyclopedia Britannica, 1948); from the introduction by Charles Glenn Wallis, p. 481.

[4] As emphasized, for example, by Pierre Duhem, *To Save the Phenomena* (Chicago: University of Chicago Press, 1969), p.3. Harmony, optics, and Archimedean statics were other examples, but they did not become fully and rigorously mathematical like astronomy until the birth of mathematical physics.

[5]   Ptolemy, pp. 7-8.

[6]   Ptolemy, pp.86-87; also Taliferro's introduction, p.2.

[7]   Taliaferro, p.1.

[8]   Since the planets and stars were self-moving, they were for Aristotle intelligences of a sort.

[9]   Just as, later on in Western Christendom, the infinity of God was felt to demand an infinite cosmic space – a idea that appears in the thought of Henry More and is still felt strongly by Newton.

[10]  Taliaferro, p. 3.

[11]  Ptolemy, p. 270.

[12]  Taliferro, p. 291n1.

[13]  Herbert Butterfield, *The Origins of Modern Science, 1300 - 1800*, p. 41.

[14]  Copernicus, introduction by Charles Glenn Wallis, p. 483.

[15]  ibid., p. 484.

[16]  Copernicus, p. 521, 526.

[17]  Appendix B of Ptolemy, op. cit., p 470: "The passage from Ptolemy to Copernicus depends on the interpretation of certain fundamental numbers resulting from observation and from the Ptolemaic system.    And furthermore certain laws of Kepler come from a scrutiny of these same numbers and a certain correlation of them.    The great revolutions in astronomical theory have not depended as much as one might think on more accurate observations or on better instruments, but rather on the reinterpretation of the symbols presented by the appearances and of the numbers immediately symbolizing these symbols."

[18]  See, for example, H. C. King, *Exploration of the Universe: The Story of Astronomy* (London: Secker and Warburg, 1964), p.109.

[19]  Elske Smith and Kenneth Jacobs, *Introductory Astronomy and Astrophysics* (Philadelphia: Saunders, 1973), p. 63ff.

[20]  Kepler, pp. 897-898, 934-935.

[21]  Actually Kepler was aware of some of Galileo's discoveries, such as the phases of Venus.  But Kepler did not use the data from Jupiter's moons as a key confirmation of his celestial mechanics.

[22]  It is worth keeping in mind, however, that Aristotle's "biomorphic" physics was considerably broader in scope that post-Galilean mathematical physics – it was a theory of change in general.  Modern physics treats only one particular kind of change (locomotion in Aristotelian terms).

[23]  King, p. 164.

[24]  ibid., pp. 172-173.

[25] Nicholas J. Giordano, *Computational Physics* (Upper Saddle River: Prentice Hall, 1997), p 94.

[26] See, for example, J. B. Marion, *Classical Dynamics of Particles and Systems* (New York: Academic Press, 197), pp. 266-267, and J.M.A. Danby, *The Fundamentals of Celestial Mechanics*, (Richmond: Willmann-Bell, 1992), p. 67-68.

[27] King, p.176.

[28] For a (very) technical discussion of the precession of Mercury's perihelion in general relativity, see Steven Weinberg, *Gravitation and Cosmology: Principles and Applications of the General Theory of Relativity* (New York: Wiley, 1972), p. 14 and p. 195ff. The measured value of precession for the earth is 5.0 +/- 1.2 seconds of arc per century – a difficult-to-measure quantity.

**Chapter Seven**

[1] P. Laplace, as quoted in Margenau, p. 397.

[2] J. Haile, *Molecular Dynamics Simulation*, pp.1-2.

[3] It is worth noting that in this reductionist view, that physics bears the heavy burden of showing that everything in the world is reducible to mathematical/mechanical laws. More than that, it must show not only that everything that exists is mathematical, but also everything that could *possibly* exist is also mathematical. Such an assertion represents the transformation of theoretical physics into metaphysics.

[4] We may identify strong and weak versions of reductionism. The strong reductionist would make everything collapse to mathematical physics -- all properties and aspects of reality can be explained directly by fundamental laws. The weak reductionist, in contrast, thinks that the "derivative" sciences such as chemistry or biology may deal with properties or categories not strictly reducible to physical law, but that these categories or properties are working assumptions that will later be shown to be derived from fundamental laws. Both the strong and the weak reductionists agree, however, that everything is ultimately founded on laws that are strictly mechanical.

[5] McMenamin, p. 29.

[6] Margenau, p. 399.

[7]   This points to one capability the mind has that computers do not:  the ability to grasp continuity, which forms the basis, for instance, of both differential and integral calculus.

[8]   For a technical discussion of the Courant criterion see, for example, William Press, Brian Flannery, Saul Teukolsky, William Vertterling, *Numerical Recipes: The Art of Scientific Computing* (Cambridge: Cambridge University Press, 1986), p. 627.

[9]   Foster Morrison, p. 81.

[10]  ibid., p. 308, 344.

[11]  Margenau, p. 416.

[12]  Haile, p. 2.

[13]  See, for example, Raymond Aron, *Introduction to the Philosophy of History*,(Boston: Beacon Press, 1961), p.16; Aron was arguing for the distinction of historical phenomena from general laws; Chapter 10 will pursue this further in the context of modeling.

[14]  Meyerson, p. 147, 253.

[15]  Morrison, p 168.

[16]  ibid., pp.177, 213, 214, 219.

[17]  One should hasten to add, however, only the *possibility* of indeterminacy - - it remains unproven one way or another, and it could happen that the seeming randomness of quantum phenomena will someday be understood in terms of some deterministic higher perspective (different from local hidden variables theories, however).

[18]  Werner Heisenberg, *Physics and Philosophy: The Revolution in Modern Science* (New York: Harper and Row, 1958), p. 42.

[19]  Giordano, *Computational Physics*, pp. 157-158.

[20]  Margenau viewed the Pauli exclusion principle as an example of saturation of forces in physics (p.444-445): "In the process of constructing a crystal from its atomic parts, new properties are seen to emerge, and these properties have no meaning with reference to the individual parts:  among others, ferromagnetism, optical anisotropy, electrical conductivity appear, all 'cooperative phenomena' ( the term is actually used in the theory of crystals) which owe their origin directly or indirectly to exclusion principle."

[21]  Giordano, pp 303-305.

[22]  *Encyclopedia of Modeling*, p. 42ff.

[23]  Giordano, p. 60ff; Morrison, p. 11.

[24] Morrison, pp. 270 - 271. Along the same lines of the "butterfly effect", one thinks of the famous short story by Ray Bradbury where time travelers to the age of the dinosaurs step on a butterfly and change all history.

[25] See, for example, Benoit Mandelbrot, *The Fractal Geometry of Nature* (New York: Freeman, 1983).

[26] Giordano, p 42ff, 67ff.

[27] Ivars Peterson, *Newton's Clock: Chaos in the Solar System* (New York: Freeman, 1993), p. 14, 189, 142, 251.

[28] ibid., p. 160, 169.

[29] Morrison, p 342.

## Chapter Eight

[1] Naturally, this is bad for science – when ill-informed politicians, journalists, and lawyers get hold of a topic, we can be sure that any serious concern for truth has flown out the window. In their defense, politicians, lawyers, journalists, and advertisers all belong to a world where perceptions (and emotional reaction to those perceptions) are what matter most. After all, that is how elections are won, juries swayed, Nielsen ratings get racked up, and cars are sold.

[2] See, for example, Glenn Trewartha, *An Introduction to Climate* (New York: McGraw-Hill, 1980).

[3] Jose P. Peixoto and Abraham H. Oort, *Physics of Climate* (New York: American Institute of Physics, 1992), p. 14.

[4] ibid., p. 37.

[5] On longer, geological and astronomical time scales, the climate system is not entirely closed: it gains mass from volcanism as well as the cosmic infall of meteors and comets, while losing mass through the slow escape of air from the top the atmosphere into space. Most of the Earth's primordial atmosphere, consisting predominantly of hydrogen and helium, was lost in this way.

[6] Important changes in solar intensity have definitely occurred in the history of the Earth; whether more recent fluctuations have affected the climate is still undetermined. But the climate modeler can regard the solar influx as constant for the sake of reproducing the present climate.

[7] Again, on a longer time scale, one must consider the precession of the earth's axis, any wobbling (nutation) about the precession, and slightly elliptical nature of the earth's orbit about the sun, resulting in what are

called Milankovitch cycles. These can be ignored in an ordinary climate model, but do contribute to long-term climate changes, such as the alternation of glacial and warmer interglacial periods of the most recent Ice Age.

[8] Peixoto and Oort, p. 14.

[9] Richard P. Wayne, *Chemistry of Atmospheres: An Introduction to the Chemistry of the Atmospheres of Earth, the Planets, and their Satellites* (New York: Oxford University Press, 1991), pp. 10-11, 116.

[10] ibid., p. 5.

[11] ibid., p. 5.

[12] Peixoto and Oort, pp. 29, 207.

[13] Wayne, pp. 398-399.

[14] ibid., p. 6.

[15] Stephen H. Schneider and Randi Londer, *The Coevolution of Climate and Life* (San Francisco: Sierra Club Books, 1984).

[16] Peixoto and Oort, p. 30.

[17] Wayne, p. 29.

[18] Peixoto and Oort, p. 30, 114.

[19] This is in contrast to, for example, the planet Mars, where a portion of its atmosphere can condense out into dry ice in the winter.

[20] See, for example, J.M. Wallace, "A Historical Introduction", in *The General Circulation: Theory, Modeling, and Observations* (National Center for Atmospheric Research, 1978), pp. 1-14.

[21] Peixoto and Oort, p. 465.

[22] ibid., p. 456.

[23] ibid., p. 458.

[24] ibid., p. 451.

[25] ibid., p. 466.

[26] See, for example, Wayne, p. 402, 415. The atmosphere as we know it was manufactured by life (and some would say, for life), from an initial atmosphere that would be poisonous to the complex organisms that now dwell on this planet. (This was apparently a long process: it took something like 2 billion years for oxygen levels to rise high enough even for cells with nuclei to be viable.) And despite the sun having brightened by over 25% over the earth's history, global temperatures have apparently remained amazingly constant.

[26] ibid., p. 415.

[27] See the discussion of the Permian Ice Age in L. Frakes, J. Francis, J. Syktus, *Climate Modes of the Phanerozoic: The History of the Earth's Climate over the Past 600 Million Years* (Cambridge: Cambridge University Press, 1992), pp. 190 - 192. Apparently, there is a cycle of warm and cool modes in the Earth's climate with a duration of about 300 million years. We are currently the midst of the coolest global climate since the Permian – ironically, a human-induced global warming would have the effect of restoring a more "normal" global climate, from a long term point of view.

[28] Thomas J. Crowley, Gerald R. North, *Paleoclimatology* (New York: Oxford University Press, 1991), p. 252f. The warmth of the Cretaceous era was, of course, entirely natural in origin and was probably caused by volcanic activity.

[29] Frakes argues for the following causes of Ice Ages: (1) a large amount of land at polar latitudes, providing a base on which ice can accumulate (which then sets up a positive feedback to cool the climate still further), and (2) weakening of the greenhouse effect due to the removal of atmospheric carbon dioxide, especially in the marine biosphere. (Frakes, p. 191). Even less understood, however, are why Ice Ages have typically come to abrupt ends.

[30] On the rapid climate changes at the end of the most recent Ice Age, Crowley, p. 85f.

[31] Peixoto and Oort, p. 433.

[32] ibid., p. 434; Wayne, p. 409.

[33] Wayne, p. 241.

[34] ibid., p. 21-22.

[35] Peixoto and Oort, p. 437.

[36] Wayne, p. 413.

[37] Peixoto and Oort, p. 436.

[38] No more than 10% of recent global temperature changes can be attributed to changes in the solar influx. However, even small changes in solar output can have large affects on global temperature – the "Little Ice Age" was apparently due to solar variability, and a 1% increase in solar output would raise the global temperature comparable to a doubling of atmospheric carbon dioxide. See Crowley, pp. 88, 256.

[39] Peixoto and Oort, p. 413; the article "Climate of the Future" from the National Center for Atmospheric Research web site, www.ucar.edu/reasearch/climate/future.shmtl.

[40] Crowley, p. 87.

[41] from the document "For a better understanding of the Global Warming Issues by using the Earth Simulator", available on the Earth Simulator web site, www.es.jamstec.jp.

[42] Bertram Schwarzschild, "Turbulent Liquid-Sodium Flow Induces Magnetic Dipole in a Laboratory Analogue of the Geodynamo," *Physics Today*, February 2006, p. 13.

[43] Diagram as published on the NOAA Climate Prediction Center web site at http://www.cpc.ncep.noaa.gov/products/fcst_eval/html/skill.shtml

[44] Based on data published on NOAA Paleoclimatology web site at http://www.ncdc.noaa.gov/paleo/pubs/jones2004/jones2004.html; originally appeared in P.D. Jones and M.E. Mann, "Climate Over Past Millennia," *Reviews of Geophysics,* Vol. 42, No. 2, RG2002, 6 May 2004.

[45] Based on data in Petit, J.R., et al., 2001, "Vostok Ice Core Data for 420,000 Years", *IGBP PAGES/World Data Center for Paleoclimatology Data Contribution Series* #2001-076. NOAA/NGDC Paleoclimatology Program, Boulder CO, USA.

## Chapter Nine

[1] Gelernter, *Mirror Worlds*, p. 99, 210.

[2] Michael Begon and Martin Mortimer, *Population Ecology: A Unified Study of Animals and Plants* (Sunderland: Sinauer Associates, 1986), p. 3.

[3] ibid., p. 4.

[4] The mathematics of the Malthusian law of population growth are discussed at length in M. Braun, *Differential Equations and Their Application* (New York: Springer-Verlag, 1979), p. 27ff.

[5] ibid., p. 29.

[6] Begon, p. 22.

[7] ibid., p. 42.

[8] For a model of vole populations with seasonality, see Hannon, *Modeling Dynamic Biological Systems*, p. 159ff.

[9] Begon, p. 49.; Hannon, p.44.

[10] Begon, p.155ff.

[11] ibid., p. 63, 78.

[12] Braun, p. 413ff., also Hannon, p. v.

[13] Braun, p. 418.

[14] A more sophisticated predator-prey model simulation is given in Hannon, p. 290ff.

[15] Begon, p. 147.

[16] The classic statement of that large populations are beneficial is that of Julian Simon, arguing against the "population bomb" thesis of P. Ehrlich. Simon may be correct that a world with a population of (say) 100 billion could be more prosperous than the world of today – however, most of us would find such a crowded world exceedingly unpleasant to live in.

[17] Begon, pp 18-19.

[18] Braun, p. 381f.

[19] See the recent survey of the effectiveness of Lanchester's equations in C. A. Fowler, "Asymmetric Warfare: A Primer", *IEEE Spectrum Online*, March 2006.

[20] Kleijnen and Groenenthal, *Simulation: A Statistical Perspective*, p. 60; Hannon, p. 8.

[21] Kleijnen, p. 1

[22] ibid., p. 67. Some other analogies include the similarity between the Keynesian Phillips curve (unemployment decreases with increasing inflation) as similar to population growth, while the Laffer Curve of the supply side economics is essentially a harvest curve: there are diminishing returns in taxation, just as in predation.

[23] *Encyclopedia of Modeling*, p. 471f.

## Chapter Ten

[1] Arnold J.Toynbee, *A Study of History (abridged)*, Volume 1 (London: Oxford University Press, 1946), Chapter 1, on "The Unit of Historical Study".

[2] Toynbee, *A Study of History (abridged)*, Volume 2, (London: Oxford University Press, 1957), p. 76ff.

[3] See, for example, the discussion in F. A. Hayek, *The Counter-Revolution of Science*, (Glencoe: The Free Press, 1952), pp. 17-165.

[4] John Lukacs, *Historical Consciousness*,(New York: Harper and Row, 1968), p. 138.

[5] Historic here is meant in the sense of significant unique events, not in the sense of recorded in documents and monuments. This should not be taken to imply that everything we "civilized moderns" do is "historic". In fact, only a small part of what we do is of historical relevance, even for

ourselves, because so little of what we do is meaningfully unique. Sleeping, eating, working – these things are not historical unless they have historical effects and historical memorability.

[6] See, for example, Michael E. Mosely, *The Incas and Their Ancestors: The Archaeology of Peru*, (New York: Thames and Hudson, 1992), p. 102. For a discussion of the surprisingly varied origins of civilization, see Steven Mithen, *After the Ice: A Global Human History, 20,000 - 5000 BC* (Cambridge: Harvard University Press, 2004), p. 505.

[7] Technical progress, of course, should never be confused with ethical progress, because it represents greater freedom and power to do both good *and* evil. Technology is a two-edged sword.

[8] Karl Popper, *The Poverty of Historicism*, (Boston: Beacon Press, 1957)

[9] Benedetto Croce, *History as the Story of Liberty*, (New York: Norton, 1941)

## Chapter Eleven

[1] See, for example, Michael Heim, *The Metaphysics of Virtual Reality* (New York: Oxford University Press, 1993).

[2] This means, in a sense, that we must split virtual realities into two spatial layers, that of near and far. The near layer is that of each separate virtual world, as on-line games or travel walkthroughs are. The far layer is the network that ties all the smaller worlds together, the least common denominator, the *lingua franca*, the trading organization, of all those smaller worlds. The smaller virtual realities are those that correspond most closely to the modeling paradigm: they replicate or create a world for us.

[3] This section is a summary of my arguments in C.L. Blilie, *The Image as Information: A General Theory of Sensors and Sense-Data* (Nova Scientific, 1997).

[4] One is tempted to say, what about plants?, but plants do have both sensation and actuation, as phototropism and carnivorous plants show.

[5] Blilie, *Image as Information*, p. 143f.

[6] ibid., p. 113f.

[7] ibid., p. 91f.

# Index